MANAGING MIGRATION

This study has been prepared with the support of the International Organization for Migration. The opinions expressed herein are those of the authors and do not necessarily reflect the views of IOM or its member states, or the Project on New International Regime for Orderly Movements of People (NIROMP).

Managing Migration

Time for a New International Regime?

edited by

BIMAL GHOSH

OXFORD

UNIVERSITY PRESS

OXFORD
UNIVERSITY PRESS

Great Clarendon Street, Oxford ox2 6dp

Oxford University Press is a department of the University of Oxford.
It furthers the University's objective of excellence in research, scholarship,
and education by publishing worldwide in

Oxford New York

Athens Auckland Bangkok Bogotá Buenos Aires Calcutta
Cape Town Chennai Dar es Salaam Delhi Florence Hong Kong Istanbul
Karachi Kuala Lumpur Madrid Melbourne Mexico City Mumbai
Nairobi Paris São Paulo Singapore Taipei Tokyo Toronto Warsaw

with associated companies in Berlin Ibadan

Oxford is a registered trade mark of Oxford University Press
in the UK and in certain other countries

Published in the United States
by Oxford University Press Inc., New York

© Bimal Ghosh 2000

The moral rights of the author have been asserted
Database right Oxford University Press (maker)

First published 2000

British Library Cataloguing in Publication Data

Data available

Library of Congress Cataloging-in-Publication Data

Managing migration: time for a new international regime?/edited by Bimal Ghosh.
Includes bibliographical references and index.
1. Emigration and immigration—Government policy.   2. Emigration and
immigration—International cooperation.   3. Globalization.   I. Ghosh, Bimal.
JV6038.M35 2000   325—dc21   00–025533

ISBN 0–19–829764–5

1 3 5 7 9 10 8 6 4 2

Typeset in Minion by
Cambrian Typesetters, Frimley, Surrey

Printed in Great Britain
on acid-free paper by
Biddles Ltd
Guildford and King's Lynn

ACKNOWLEDGEMENTS

The editor of this volume and director of the project New International Regime for Orderly Movements of People (NIROMP) is deeply grateful to the United Nations Population Fund (UNFPA) and the Swedish government for their generous financial support of the NIROMP project. But for their support it would not have been possible to bring out the volume. Acknowledgement is also due to the International Organization for Migration, which acted as the executing agency of the NIROMP project and provided valuable administrative and other support to this venture.

A special word of thanks to all the contributors who, while adhering to the rigours of their respective fields of specialization, made a particular effort to develop their analyses and arguments within a common framework and willingly responded to a host of requests from the editor. This cohesive teamwork entailed, among other things, two days' intensive and stimulating consultation among the contributors before they finalized their respective texts. The consultation was held at the Arrábida monastery, near Lisbon, which was hosted by the Fundação Oriente and was partly supported by a contribution from Fundação Serra Henriques. The assistance of the two foundations and the interest of Carlos Monjardino and Rita Pinto Coelho are gratefully acknowledged.

The editor is also thankful for the special efforts made by Oxford University Press (OUP), and especially by Dominic Byatt and Amanda Watkins, in bringing out the volume on time and for the most efficient way they managed the publication process.

Sincere thanks are also due to Sarita Sehgal, who so efficiently and cheerfully assisted the editor throughout the whole venture, including checking the texts, organizing the Arrábida meeting, monitoring the work progress, and meeting the publisher's deadline.

CONTENTS

NOTES ON CONTRIBUTORS

BIMAL GHOSH is Senior Consultant to the International Organization for Migration and the Director of the international project on migration management: 'New International Regime for Orderly Movements of People (NIROMP)'. A former senior director in the United Nations system and an academic, he led several inter-agency missions on migration, refugees, and development-related issues in different regions. Ghosh is the author of numerous reports and publications on international economic, political, and human rights issues with a focus on migration, development, and economic globalization. Recent publications include *Huddled Masses and Uncertain Shores: Insights into Irregular Migration* (1998) and *Gains from Global Linkages: Trade in Services and Movements of Persons* (1997).

GUY S. GOODWIN-GILL is Professor of International Refugee Law and Rubin Director of Research at the Institute of European Studies, University of Oxford, and a Fellow of Wolfson College. Editor-in-Chief of the *International Journal of Refugee Law (IJRL)*, Goodwin-Gill is also President of the Refugee Legal Centre and he continues as Co-Rapporteur of the International Law Association's Committee on Refugee Procedures. Recent Publications include *The Refugee in International Law* (1996).

JAMES HOLLIFIELD is Arnold Professor of International Political Economy and Director of International Studies at Southern Methodist University in Dallas, Texas. He has also worked as a consultant for the US government and several organizations including the United Nations and the OECD. His recent publications include *The State and Public Policy* (1998), *Immigration et l'état nation* (1997), and *Controlling Immigration: A Global Perspective* (1995).

GILBURT LOESCHER is Professor of International Relations at the University of Notre Dame in Indiana, USA. Previously he served as a consultant to the United Nations High Commissioner for Refugees and for several years he chaired the Academic Advisory Committee of the UNHCR's report, *State of the World Refugees*. Recent publications include *Beyond Charity: International Cooperation and the Global Refugee Problem*.

B. LINDSAY LOWELL is Director of Research at the Institute for the Study of International Migration at Georgetown University. Previously he was Director of Research at the US Commission on Immigration Reform and Assistant National Coordinator of the Mexico/US Binational Study of Migration. He recently published the edited volume *Temporary Workers in America: Policies for Benefiting the U.S. Economy.*

PHILIP MARTIN is Professor of Agricultural and Resource Economics at the University of California, Davis, and Chair of the University of California's sixty-member Comparative Immigration and Integration Program. Martin has published extensively on labour migration, economic development, and immigration policy issues and he is on the editorial boards of the journals *International Migration Review* and *International Migration.*

MARK MILLER is Professor of Political Science at the University of Delaware. He is also an Assistant Editor for the journal *International Migration Review* and a member of the Center for Strategic and International Studies Steering Group on population and US foreign policy. Recent publications include 'International Migration and Security: Towards Transatlantic Convergence?', in Lydio F. Tomasi (ed.), *In Defense of the Alien* (1995), and *The Age of Migration* (1993).

HENK OVERBEEK teaches International Relations and European Politics at the Free University in Amsterdam. His research in global political economy concerns the impact of globalization on international governance, especially in the areas of labour market regulation and migration and refugee policies. He is co-editor of the RIPE Series in Global Political Economy (Routledge) and recent publications include 'Towards a New International Migration Regime: Globalization, Migration and the Internationalization of the State' in R. Miles and D. Thränhardt (ed.), *Migration and European Integration* (1995).

THOMAS STRAUBHAAR is Professor of Economics and Director of the Institute for Economic Policy Research at the University of the Bundeswehr Hamburg. Since 1998 he has also been the Director of the Institute for Integration Research at the Europa-Kolleg in Hamburg. His recent publications include 'Does Migration Policy Matter?' in *New Community*, 23 (1997) and *Migration and Economic Integration in the Nordic Common Labour Market* (1996).

EDWARD TAYLOR is Professor of Agriculture and Resource Economics at the University of California, Davis. He is also co-editor of the on-line quarterly *Rural Migration News*. His recent publications include *Poverty Amid Prosperity: Immigration and the Changing Face of Rural California* (1997) and *Development Strategy, Employment and Migration: Insights from Models* (1996).

LIST OF FIGURES

LIST OF TABLES

ABBREVIATIONS

APEC	Asia Pacific Economic Cooperation
ASEAN	Association of South-East Asian Nations
CBI	Caribbean Basin Initiatives
CIS	Commonwealth of Independent States
EC/EU	European Community/European Union
ECOSOC	Economic and Social Council (United Nations)
ECSC	European Coal and Steel Community
ETS	European Treaty Series
FDI	Foreign Direct Investment
FTAA	Free Trade Area of Americas
GAMP	General Agreement on Movement of People
GATT	General Agreement on Tariffs and Trade
GATS	General Agreement on Trade in Services
ICFTU	International Confederation of Free Trade Unions
ICMPD	International Centre for Migration Policy Development
IGC	Intergovernmental Consultations on Asylum, Refugee and Migration Policy in Europe
ILO	International Labour Organization
IMF	International Monetary Fund
IIRIRA	Illegal Immigration Reform and Immigrant Responsibility Act (US)
INS	Immigration and Naturalization Service (US)
IOM	International Organization for Migration
IRCA	Immigration Reform and Control Act (US)
LDCs	Least Developed Countries
MFN	most favoured nation
NAFTA	North American Free Trade Agreement
NICs	Newly Industrializing Countries
NIROMP	new international regime for orderly movements of people
OAP	offshore assembly processing
OAU	Organization of African Unity
OECD	Organization for Economic Cooperation and Development
OSCE	Organization for Security and Cooperation in Europe
RCA	Revealed Comparative Advantage
SAVE	Systematic Alien Verification for Entitlement (US)
STEP	Special Targeted Enforcement Programme (US)
TNC	transnational corporation
UN	United Nations

UNCHR	UN Commissioner for Human Rights
UNCTAD	United Nations Conference on Trade and Development
UNDP	United Nations Development Programme
UNEP	UN Environment Programme
UNFPA	UN Population Fund
UNHCR	UN High Commissioner for Refugees
Unicef	UN Children's Fund
UNTS	UN Treaty Series
WFP	World Food Programme
WHO	World Health Organization
World Bank	International Bank for Reconstruction and Development including International Finance Corporation and International Development Association
WTO	World Trade Organization

Introduction

Bimal Ghosh

In 1993, responding to a request from the Commission on Global Governance, which was co-chaired by Mr Ingvar Carlsson, then Prime Minister of Sweden, and Sir Sridaht Ramphal, former Secretary-General of the Commonwealth Secretariat, I presented a paper entitled *Movements of People: The Search for a New International Regime* to facilitate the Commission's discussion on emerging global migration issues.[1] The paper outlined some of the inadequacies of existing arrangements for managing global migratory flows, highlighted the problems and pitfalls inherent in the present policies and practices, and argued for a comprehensive, coherent, and internationally harmonized regime. Such a regime would ensure greater orderliness and predictability in movements of people—serving and balancing the interests of the sending and receiving countries and the migrants alike.

The Commission's wide terms of reference, and inevitable time constraints, prevented it from undertaking an in-depth examination of the various issues involved, but it recognized the critical importance of developing 'more comprehensive institutionalized cooperation for international migration management', and pleaded for freer movements of persons as part of a GATT/WTO regime on trade in services.[2] In fact, the paper submitted to the Commission already foresaw such an arrangement for trade-related mobility as an integral part of the proposed, overall migration regime.

Around the time of the Commission's discussion on the subject, there were signs of growing interest in a comprehensive, multilateral approach to the management of international migration—and of greater awareness of the inadequacies of a unilateral, reactive, and essentially restrictive migration policy, in the face of the gathering pace of economic globalization and greater interdependence of nations.

A report issued by the Trilateral Commission in 1993, *International*

---

[1] Included in Commission on Global Governance (1995), *Issues in Global Governance*, London: Kluwer Law International, 405–24.

[2] Commission on Global Governance (1995), *Our Global Neighbourhood: The Report of the Commission on Global Governance*, Oxford: Oxford University Press, 208, 224.

Migration Challenges in a New Era, saw a clear and compelling need for evolv-ing a comprehensive migration regime to 'provide a viable international framework within which to manage migration pressures effectively'.[3] In the following year, Fred Bergsten, Director of the Washington-based Institute for International Economics, echoed the feeling by arguing that the world 'needs to seriously consider creating an international migration regime'.[4]

James Purcell Jr., then Director-General of the International Organization for Migration (IOM), also called for a new migration order to better manage population movements,[5] while economists such as Thomas Straubhaar and Klaus Zimmermann were urging nations to adopt a General Agreement on Migration Policy (GAMP), on grounds of greater efficiency in the world econ-omy and the benefits they could derive from it.[6]

The humanitarian crises in Iraq, the former Yugoslavia, the Horn of Africa, and elsewhere contributed to the growing recognition of the deficiencies of the existing international arrangements to deal with several new types of refugee or refugee-like flows and situations. In a speech at the University of California, Berkeley, in April 1992, Sadako Ogata, UN High Commissioner for Refugees, voiced the urgent need for wider and more effective multilateral responses to these new humanitarian challenges, which remained inadequately covered under existing international arrangements and mandates.[7] In the same year, an international meeting held in Bellagio, Italy, went further and listed several groups of internally and externally displaced persons who needed additional support either under existing international law or through new arrangements.[8]

Meanwhile, the success of the Uruguay Round of multilateral trade negoti-ation and particularly the adoption (Marrakesh, 1994) of the General Agreement on Trade in Services (GATS)—which included, for the first time, trade-related movement of persons—provided a new impetus to the search for a concerted multilateral approach to international migration.

At the national level, new policy initiatives were being taken in several countries such as Sweden and the Netherlands, which sought to manage

---

[3] D. M. Meissner et al. (1993), *International Migration Challenges in a New Era,* the New York: Trilateral Commission, 92.

[4] C. F. Bergsten (1994), 'Managing the World Economy of the Future', in Peter B. Kenen (ed.), *Managing the World Economy,* Washington, DC: Institute for International Economics.

[5] See, for example, James N. Purcell, Jr. 'The World Needs a Policy for Orderly Migration', *International Herald Tribune,* 8 July 1993.

[6] T. Straubhaar (1993), 'Migration Pressures', *International Migration,* 31/1: 5–41; K. F. Zimmermann (1994), 'The Labour Market Impact of Migration', in *Immigration as an Economic Asset, London:* IPPR/Trentham Books, London, 39–64.

[7] S. Ogata, (1992), 'Refugees: A Multilateral Response to Humanitarian Crises', Institute of International Studies, University of California, Berkeley, Apr. 1992.

[8] 'Belagio Statement on Humanitarian Action in the Post Cold War Era', Meeting spon-sored by the Refugee Policy Group and the Pew Charitable Trust, Bellagio, Italy, May 1992.

migration through a more comprehensive approach, linking migration policies to those concerning trade, aid, investment, and human rights, and laying greater emphasis on cooperation with the sending countries.[9]

These developments prompted us to give some further thought on how best to carry forward the work started in the Commission on Global Governance and develop a new, multilateral approach to the management of the movement of people. Despite the sensitive nature of the subject, it was felt that launching a global project to promote wider recognition of the need for a harmonized multilateral approach to the issue was a worthwhile undertaking—and could perhaps be a first step to the eventual establishment of a global regime for movements of people.

As this idea was gaining ground, the UN General Assembly adopted Resolution 48/113 in 1993, calling for the holding of a world conference on migration and development—a call echoed in various other fora.

Many of us, both within and outside the United Nations, however, felt strongly that, to be meaningful, such a global conference needed careful planning and preparation: without setting out the key objectives of the conference, and building at least a measure of consensus around them, the whole initiative might backfire.

We also believed that the establishment of a new multilateral migration regime—with its implications for promoting world development and for stemming the flows of irregular migrants—was an ambitious, yet attainable goal for this conference. But doing so would require a strong consensus through dialogue and debate at both regional and global levels as well as a solid foundation of underlying analytical research and studies—activities to which our project could substantially contribute.

Meanwhile, after extensive discussion and debate, the UN General Assembly decided that the immediate follow-up to the original resolution should take the form of a series of consultations on the relevant issues. This was an interesting coincidence vindicating our project approach; since it was clear that the project activities could provide timely and useful inputs into the process of consultations envisaged in the UN decision, and indeed lend a specific focus to it.

Late in 1996 the Swedish government made a financial contribution to help initiate the project to be known as the New International Regime for Orderly Movements of People (NIROMP).[10] I was designated the director of the

---

[9] See, in this connection, Swedish Ministry of Labour (1990), *A Comprehensive Refugee and Immigration Policy*, Stockholm; *Swedish Refugee Policy in a Global Perspective* (1995), Stockholm; also, *Migration and Development* (1997), Netherlands Development Assistance (NEDA), The Hague, Feb. 1997.

[10] See in this connection 'Background, Objectives and Methodology of the Project' and the 'Meeting Report' from the Informal Meeting on NIROMP, 26–7 Sept. 1997, IOM, Geneva.

project. It was decided at the same time that the project activities should be
executed through the IOM, in close collaboration with other international
and regional organizations concerned. The project became operational in
March 1997. Since then it has received valuable support, including financial
contributions, from UNFPA (United Nations Population Fund) and several
governments including those of the Netherlands and Switzerland. Consistent
with its objectives it has devoted special attention to policy dialogue and
consensus building through a range of activities such as meetings and discussions, field visits and networking with the civil society, including in particular
professional institutions and migrant-serving associations.

The present study is undertaken as part of the NIROMP's activities to
sensitize the policy-makers, practitioners, and the general public on the issues
and prospects of a multilateral response to the challenge of movements of
people in the twenty-first century. However, despite its links with the wider
project, it was considered useful to plan the study from the outset as a self-
contained and independent exercise, making it possible for an eminent group
of specialists to look at the wide range of complex issues involved and express
their own views about them freely, without any external constraints imposed
on them.

International migration is essentially a multidimensional phenomenon—
the main reason why it defies a unisectoral approach. Recent experience has
also shown that despite their distinctive features, different migratory flows
often interact with one another, both in their root causes and their subsequent
behaviour as reflected for example in 'category jumping', from asylum seeking
to movements through irregular channels. For policy formulation purposes
this makes it difficult to deal with them in isolation. The study therefore seeks
to combine critical appraisals of the issues and prospects of a multilateral
regime from different perspectives—political, economic, and juridical, just as
it embraces all types of migratory flows, including refugee movements, within
its scope.

As is to be expected, the perception and the methods of analysis of the various contributors to the volume vary, as each of them brings his own considerable knowledge and expertise as well as conceptual acumen to bear upon the
endeavour. Some contributions are more policy-oriented, others less so; some
are more normative, others tend to be more analytical and empirical. But they
all address—painstakingly and with great professional rigour—issues, including prospects and constraints, related to the development of a coherent,
multilateral regime to manage migration. This serves as the central theme and
the common focus, binding the various pieces together within a single framework.

The first and last chapters, which are more closely attuned to the overall
objectives of the NIROMP project, seek to further enhance the thrust and
cohesiveness of the study as a whole. In arguing for a multilateral migration

regime Chapter 1 deliberately uses a policy-oriented normative approach, while the last chapter moves the discussion further by providing an indication of the configuration of a new migration regime and delineating some of its main contours and salient features.

This joint study is aimed at policy makers, academics, and the general public alike. The contributors to the study, including the editor, will consider their team work and individual efforts more than compensated if it succeeds, even in small measure, in generating an awareness across nations of the need for a new multilateral approach to cooperative management of international migration as the world moves into the next millennium.

1

Towards a New International Regime for Orderly Movements of People

Bimal Ghosh

The world migration system is under strain

The present international migration system is clearly under strain. There are visible signs that the system is finding it increasingly hard to cope with the new challenges that movements of people now entail or to exploit the opportunities they present. Why is this so? In analysing the reasons for the situation this chapter highlights some of the inadequacies of existing migration policies and practices, and argues for a more comprehensive, balanced, and transparent multilateral regime to manage migration. What will such a regime look like? And why should nations opt for such a regime? These and other related questions are taken up in the concluding chapter which also revisits some of the key points raised in the intervening parts of the volume.

Rising levels of migration

The reasons why nations are finding it increasingly difficult to manage migration are many and varied, but rising levels of migration are no doubt an important part of the problem. True, despite some year-to-year variations, the stock of migrants as a ratio of the world population has changed little over the past few decades. In 1990 it represented 2.3 per cent of the world population, almost exactly as it had done in 1965 (Table 1.1). However, the picture could be misleading if important regional variations are ignored. In several regions of the world the ratio in fact has seen a sharp upward swing. This is particularly true in Western Europe where it almost doubled in five years, rising from 3.6 per cent in 1985 to 6.1 per cent in the 1990s.

In the context of migration management what is of immediate significance is the absolute numbers involved. Measured in these terms, it is clear that there has been a spectacular increase in the world stock of migrants in recent years—jumping from 75 million in 1965 to 120 million in 1990. Although

TABLE 1.1. Migrant stock by region, as percentage of the total population and growth rate of the migrant stock by region, 1965, 1975, 1985, and 1990

Region	Estimated foreign-born population (thousands)				As percentage of total population				Annual rate of change				Percentage distribution by region			
	1965	1975	1985	1990	1965	1975	1985	1990	1965–75	1975–85	1985–90	1965–90	1965	1975	1985	1990
World total	75,214	84,494	105,194	119,761	2.3	2.1	2.2	2.3	1.2	2.2	2.6	1.9	100.0	100.0	100.0	100.0
Developed countries	30,401	38,317	47,991	54,231	3.1	3.5	4.1	4.5	2.3	2.3	2.4	2.3	40.4	45.3	45.6	45.3
Developing countries	44,813	46,177	57,203	65,530	1.9	1.6	1.6	1.6	0.3	2.1	2.7	1.5	59.6	54.7	54.4	54.7
Africa	7,952	11,178	12,527	15,631	2.5	2.7	2.3	2.5	3.4	1.1	4.4	2.7	10.6	13.2	11.9	13.1
Northern Africa	1,016	1,080	2,219	1,982	1.4	1.1	1.8	1.4	0.6	7.2	-2.3	2.7	1.4	1.3	2.1	1.7
Sub-Saharan Africa	6,936	10,099	10,308	13,649	2.9	3.2	2.5	2.8	3.8	0.2	5.6	2.7	9.2	12.0	9.8	11.4
Asia	31,429	29,662	38,731	43,018	1.7	1.3	1.4	1.4	-0.6	2.7	2.1	1.3	41.8	35.1	36.8	35.9
Eastern and South-Eastern Asia	8,136	7,723	7,678	7,931	0.7	0.5	0.5	0.4	-0.5	-0.1	0.6	-0.1	10.8	9.1	7.3	6.6
China	266	305	331	346	0.0	0.0	0.0	0.0	1.4	0.8	0.9	1.0	0.4	0.4	0.3	0.3
Other Eastern and South-Eastern Asia	7,870	7,419	7,347	7,586	1.9	1.5	1.2	1.2	-0.6	-0.1	0.6	-0.1	10.5	8.8	7.0	6.3
South Central Asia	18,610	15,565	19,243	20,782	2.8	1.9	1.8	1.8	-1.8	2.1	1.5	0.4	24.7	18.4	18.3	17.4
Western Asia	4,683	6,374	11,810	14,304	7.4	7.6	10.4	10.9	3.1	6.2	3.8	4.5	6.2	7.5	11.2	11.9
Latin America and Caribbean	5,907	5,788	6,410	7,475	2.4	1.8	1.6	1.7	-0.2	1.0	3.1	0.9	7.9	6.8	6.1	6.2
Caribbean	532	665	832	959	2.4	2.5	2.7	2.9	2.2	2.2	2.8	2.4	0.7	0.8	0.8	0.8
Central America	445	427	948	2,047	0.8	0.6	1.0	1.8	-0.4	8.0	15.4	6.1	0.6	0.5	0.9	1.7
South America	4,930	4,695	4,629	4,469	3.0	2.2	1.8	1.5	-0.5	-0.1	-0.7	-0.4	6.6	5.6	4.4	3.7
Northern America	12,695	15,042	20,460	23,895	6.0	6.3	7.8	8.6	1.7	3.1	3.1	2.5	16.9	17.8	19.5	20.0
Europe and USSR (former)	14,728	19,504	22,959	25,068	2.2	2.7	3.0	3.2	2.8	1.6	1.8	2.1	19.6	23.1	21.8	20.9
Transition Economies	2,835	2,394	2,213	2,055	2.4	1.9	1.6	1.7	-1.7	-0.8	-1.5	-1.3	3.8	2.8	2.1	1.7
USSR (former)	140	148	156	159	0.1	0.1	0.1	0.1	0.6	0.5	0.5	0.5	0.2	0.2	0.1	0.1
Other Europe	11,753	16,961	20,590	22,853	3.6	4.9	5.8	6.1	3.7	1.9	2.1	2.7	15.6	20.1	19.6	19.1
Oceania	2,502	3,319	4,106	4,675	14.4	15.6	16.9	17.8	2.8	2.1	2.6	2.5	3.3	3.9	3.9	3.9

Source: United Nations (1998), World Population Monitoring, 1997, New York: United Nations.

more recent official figures are yet to be available, from all indications it may now have well exceeded the 130 million mark. The annual flows, too, have been rising fast, with both North America and Western Europe receiving around 1 million new migrants every year. At a global level, when all movements—including those that occur through trafficking and other irregular channels and are not necessarily reflected in official statistics—are taken into account, total annual migration may well be hovering above the level of 5 million. If so, it would imply that every minute some nine or more new migrants are crossing borders around the world—not counting the much larger numbers of other short-term or non-migrant visitors, including tourists.

Changing configuration of contemporary migration

But absolute numbers do not tell the full story; they notably fail to capture the increasing complexity and changing configuration of contemporary migration. Clearly, managing the movements has now become more difficult due, for instance, to unpredictability and periodically high intensity of many of the massive flows—whether they are driven by political, ethno-political, environmental, or economic factors, or a combination of them. In Europe, the 1989–90 east–west movement of 1.3 million people following the seemingly sudden collapse of the communist regimes took most of the western governments by surprise (Ardittis 1994). This did not turn out to be a harbinger of even larger outflows from the eastern region—'Russians didn't come'—as many in the west had apprehended. Instead, however, the ethno-political conflicts in Bosnia and more recently Kosovo generated large flows of internally and externally displaced people running into millions.[1]

Similar conflicts elsewhere, such as in Rwanda, Liberia, Sierra Leone, and the Horn of Africa, were often exacerbated by economic discrimination and gross violation of basic human rights and produced massive human displacements, both internal and external. In Rwanda and Liberia, for example, the displacement affected as many as one-fourth of the entire population of the country.

Such massive, largely unpredictable, and painfully poignant human flows have not been confined to Eastern Europe or Africa alone. In Central America, bitter internal conflicts and large-scale violence in El Salvador and Guatemala, and political upheavals, including the 'contra' movements in Nicaragua often

---

[1] It was estimated that out of the 2.6 million people dislocated by the conflict in Bosnia, some 600,000 were externally displaced. In Kosovo, at the height of the crisis, 0.9 million persons were displaced, most of them having moved into Albania and Macedonia.

interacted with economic and ethnic factors to produce massive movements involving more than 2 million refugees and internally displaced persons.[2] Although the whole process spanned a good part of the last two decades, the movements were sporadic, haphazard, and often non-predictable. The 1991 hostilities in the Gulf countries witnessed the exodus of some 1.9 million labour migrants and their dependants within a matter of weeks, just as the Asian financial crisis in 1998 suddenly led to considerable return flows to the countries of origin.

The enormous human hardships for the migrant workers and their families caused by such unexpected flows were often accompanied by economic and social difficulties. This was especially true in ill-prepared source countries where the return of migrants caused fiscal dislocations and put a heavy strain on the administrative structure. In some cases, as in south-central Africa, Central America, and South-East Asia the outflows/inflows have also ruffled inter-state relations and sharpened resentment and tensions between groups and communities within them.

A striking feature, common to almost all these situations, is the non-predictability of the movements, coupled with, as will be further discussed below, the lack of an adequate policy and a sound operational framework to deal with most of them.

Diversity of the source countries

Another source of complexity in managing migration stems from the ever-widening number of source countries. Geographical contiguity, historical ties, or cultural affinity, though still important, are no longer the only factors that shape the pattern or determine the direction of international migration. Dramatic progress in communication, a sharp fall in transport costs, wider expansion of social networking, and multi-country operations of migrant traffickers have combined with powerful push and pull factors to make international migration a veritable global process. Changes in the established direction and traditional composition of the flows are presenting new challenges to integration policies and institutions of the receiving countries.[3]

For most industrial receiving countries, diversity in the immigration flows—in terms of religion, culture, ethnicity, or education and skills—is not

[2] Recent estimates of uprooted Central Americans vary between 2 and 3 million. In this connection see Ferris 1993.

[3] As more and more countries are becoming involved in sending (and receiving) migrants, the traditional distinction between source and receiving countries is itself becoming blurred. See ILO/IOM/UNHCR 1994. The selection of 98 countries and territories is based on a set of criteria involving stocks of migrants and flows of remittances. The figures possibly are underestimates because of the lack of complete data for emigration and immigration in a number of cases.

entirely new, but in the past, historical, mostly colonial and trade-related links had already brought them in contact with the sending countries. Thus, they were more or less familiar with the immigrants, their cultural traits, and their general ways of life. This has now changed considerably. At the same time, the gathering political clout of immigrants in the receiving country and their alliances with political parties in the host society have endowed them with a new sense of assertiveness not seen before. The political emergence of the former colonies in a politically multi-polar world and the fast growing recognition of the human rights of migrants have lent additional strength to this newly found assertiveness of certain immigrant communities.

For the immigration policies and systems in the receiving states, especially in the industrial world, it has not always been easy to adapt to the new situation. In many cases, the process has been extremely stressful, adding to the tension in the migration system as a whole.

The build-up of emigration pressure

But, for most receiving states no other source of tension and anxiety has been more powerful than the fear, both real and perceived, of huge waves of future emigration from poor and weak states in the years and decades to come. Since 1991 the Group of seven most industrial countries (G7) and the EEC/EU have repeatedly expressed concerns over the rising immigration pressure at their summit meetings. While much of this fear is exaggerated, it cannot be lightly dismissed.

In most developing regions the emigration pressure is clearly mounting, driven by a number of interrelated factors: widespread poverty and unemployment; the feeling of relative deprivation; growing inter-country disparities in income and job opportunities; infringement of human rights; increasingly violent civil wars; and rapid environmental degradation. High, and often haphazard, rural-urban migration contributes to the process. For example, in China the large numbers of internal migrants (both rural-urban and across regions), estimated at 100 million in 1994, and widespread rural unemployment affecting another 100 million were causing serious concern in neighbouring countries (BBC 1994; *Migration News,* June 1994).

Behind all these push factors the still continuing demographic explosion looms large. In sub-Saharan Africa the fertility rate is still 5.5 children per woman. More than 95 per cent of the world population is located in developing countries, with 700 million young people poised to enter the labour market between now and 2010—more than the entire labour force of the developed world in 1990 (UNFPA 1998, 1999).

Statistics abound showing deteriorating trends in poverty and income distribution.[4] World consumption has jumped sixteen times since 1900. But in more than a hundred countries income per head has declined in the past fifteen years. The absolute number of Latin America's poor today is twice what it was forty years ago. In the CIS (former Soviet Union) countries, the number of poor people has grown more than tenfold in the past decade. In East Asia it is anticipated to double in the next two years. Worldwide, but concentrated mostly in poor countries, as many as 1.4 million people are struggling to survive on less than one dollar a day.

The build-up of this seemingly huge migration potential may not all translate into actual movements, but even if a part of it does, the impact could obviously be overwhelming. It is important to underline that poor and deprived people also move. The myth that those who are extremely poor do not travel has finally been exploded. Recent migration trends have demonstrated that under extreme economic hardship and despair even the poor move or at least try to move—not so much as a matter of choice as under compulsion. In the past, such movements have generally been confined to the neighbouring states, and have mostly remained invisible in official statistics. Today, however, they often move far beyond, helped by the increasing and surprisingly agile activities of migrant traffickers who operate through multi-country networks and often change their destinations at short notice.

If unable to pay the trafficker in cash, the potential migrant need only sign a bond to repay the debt owed to the traffickers. Sadly, as so many recent cases have revealed, for large numbers of migrants this could become a bond for long-term, even lifelong, servitude. Recent events in places as different as North Korea (where some 2–3 million were reported to have starved to death since the mid-1990s) and Kosovo have shown that conditions of forced migration could open up an attractive potential market for human traffickers.

Admittedly, however, there are situations when these people, however desperate, do not or cannot move across borders. In cases such as these, a real risk remains that poverty and deprivation may sharpen political tension and internal conflicts, often generating large-scale violence, and eventually leading to internal and external displacements of people. The situation becomes worse when the displaced people, as in many parts of sub-Saharan Africa or Eastern Europe,[5] belong to ethnic communities that cut across borders of the neighbouring states. This holds the potential of creating a spiral of disruptive migration within an entire region or subregion.

It is not just the push factors in the source countries that account for the

---

[4] Most of the figures used in this paragraph are based on World Bank and UNDP sources.

[5] For a succinct discussion of the ethnic composition of the population in Eastern European countries and their migration implications see Ghosh 1991.

build-up of migration potential; the pull of relative affluence and better economic opportunities, and the attraction of political freedom and stability in the destination countries also play a powerful role. The image of *el Dorado*—the land of gold—at the end of the journey is often illusory. This is particularly (but not exclusively) the case in those source countries which have suffered from information asymmetry due to political isolation and the absence of a free media for decades, for instance in the former communist countries of Eastern Europe, notably Albania. The illusion tends to endure due to false publicity and propaganda of traffickers, lopsided media stories and images, and inflated reports of success about those who have already migrated.

But this does not mean that the attraction of the destination countries is not at all real. In the industrial world, for example, even in those economies which are currently suffering from a difficult employment situation—such as Japan and several in Western Europe—there is considerable unmet labour demand. It is not just limited to dirty, difficult, and dangerous (the 3D) jobs, but extends to several other categories of occupations and sectors including construction, hotels and tourism, and distributive services. These apart, there is a pressing demand for highly skilled workers, especially in sectors such as computer and information technology, and most OECD member countries are scrambling for them.

But a very distorted and persistent source of demand for labour lies elsewhere—in the fast expanding informal sector or the black economy of many of these countries (Figure 1.1). An increasing number of less competitive firms and sunset industries seek to survive in this sector by using cheap, docile, and mostly irregular migrant labour while evading taxes. The black economy now accounts for 16 per cent of the European Union's GDP, compared to 5 per cent in 1970. Between 10 and 20 million jobs, corresponding to between 7 per cent and 19 per cent of declared employment, are located in the informal sector, and a high proportion of them are occupied by irregular migrants (European Commission 1998: *Financial Times*, 8 April 1998). In countries like Belgium, Italy, and Spain the expansion of the underground economy has reinforced the segmentation of the labour market while both investment capital and entrepreneurial skills have tended to shift to the informal sector draining the rest of the economy (Weiss 1987: 38, 216–33; Contini 1982: 199–208). In addition, public revenue suffers—Sweden, for example, may be losing between $2.6 and $5.2 billion a year. A most disturbing trend is that, driven at least in part by high fiscal burdens including social charges, and rigidities in the labour market—many reputable firms in the organized sector are also seeking to lower their production costs by taking advantage of the black economy through subcontracting arrangements. This further swells the demand for irregular foreign labour.

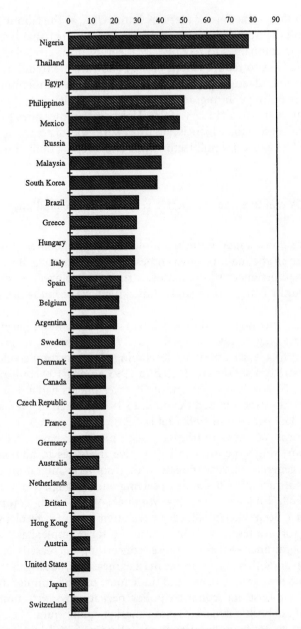

Note: Developed economies 1998, estimated using the currency-demand approach. Emerging economies various years 1990–9 estimated using the physical-input method. Data for japan is from 1993.
Source: *The Economist*, based on Friedrich Schneider.

FIG. 1.1. Economic penumbra: shadow economy as percentage of official GDP

Although the problem is less serious in the USA, as the labour market has tightened and the wages for regular workers gone up, there has been a noticeable trend for companies to rely on 'sweat shops' using irregular immigrant labour in the USA to reduce labour costs. Following the trend, in California, even regular manufacturing companies are using legal immigrants and traffickers to recruit irregular migrants from Mexico in order to profit from cheap labour (*Migration News*, January 1998). Unless recent measures to curb these practices are successful, which is far from sure, the distorted demand will continue to be a powerful pull factor while encouraging human trafficking.

A reactive and restrictive response to the challenge

The policy response so far to this manifold challenge of contemporary migration has been in the main reactive and essentially restrictive. Border control, internal law enforcement through more stringent employer and carrier sanctions, and punitive measures against trafficking have been the principal focus of attention.

While this anti-immigration sentiment has been more pronounced in industrial receiving countries, notably in Western Europe, it has also been shared, albeit to a lesser extent, in developing and transition economy countries. To illustrate, a survey conducted in 1993 among 190 countries showed that while in 1976 only 6.4 per cent of all governments had a policy to lower immigration, the ratio jumped threefold to 19.4 per cent in 1986 and almost six times to 35.3 per cent in 1993 (Table 1.2*a*).

The majority of these restrictive policy measures have been devoid of support from complementary and proactive measures to address the root causes that generate or fuel pressures for disorderly migration in sending countries or attract migrants to the receiving ones through irregular channels (Goodwin-Gill, Chapter 7 in this volume). When such complementary measures have been taken at all, they have often remained feeble, vacillating, and perfunctory. In few destination countries, for example, has a clear set of specific programmes—such as those concerning increased labour force participation and other active labour market measures, appropriate structural and technological adjustment, and judicious use of immigration—been woven into a robust and balanced policy package to satisfy unmet labour demand and establish a dynamic labour market equilibrium.

Political pressure from employers and other powerful lobbies have led a number of OECD countries to allow the admission of temporary foreign workers to meet industry-specific short-term needs (OECD 1998 and Papademetriou 1996), but these programmes are not necessarily linked to the enhancement of future human capital development as part of a long-term

TABLE 1.2. *Government's policy towards the level of immigration, 1976–1995* (percentage of countries)

(a)

Year	Raise	Maintain or no intervention	Lower	Total	Number of countries
1976	7	87	6	100	156
1978	6	84	10	100	158
1989	6	79	15	100	165
1983	5	78	17	100	168
1986	4	77	19	100	170
1989	5	64	32	100	170
1993	4	61	35	100	190
1995	5	61	35	100	190

(b)

Year	Raise	Maintain or no intervention	Lower	Total	Number of countries
1976	4	83	13	100	156
1978	4	80	16	100	158
1989	4	81	16	100	165
1983	5	75	20	100	168
1986	5	74	22	100	170
1989	3	72	25	100	170
1993	3	77	20	100	190
1995	4	76	20	100	158

Source: The Population Division Policy Data Bank maintained by the Population Division of the department for Economic and Social Information and Policy Analysis of the United Nations Secretariat.

policy.[6] Some countries such as Japan and the Republic of Korea have allowed limited labour immigration, but through the side or back door in the form of trainee or fellowship programmes for foreign nationals. In practice, however, they were often used as low or unskilled labour in small companies.

Such half-hearted or distorted practices to meet labour shortages tend to actually encourage irregular migration, rather than alleviate it. In the Republic of Korea, for example, nearly one-third of the trainees—there were 70,000 of them in 1996—were reported to have left their original job and become irregular workers because of the attraction of higher wages (Kang 1996). In a number of countries, despite declared official policies against irregular immi-

[6] For a discussion of the recent situation in the USA see, Papademetriou and Yale-Loeh 1996.

gration, the latter has been allowed to continue as part of the government response to a tight labour market situation in specific sectors. And, most strikingly, little progress has been made in curbing or transforming the black economy as a source of employment for cheap and docile irregular immigrant workers.

As already noted, inadequacy is also reflected in the receiving countries' response to sudden movements generated by humanitarian emergencies. Several groups of internally and externally displaced persons needing assistance and protection have remained inadequately covered under existing international mandates and national practices. To illustrate, even with their long humanitarian tradition and strong commitment to refugee protection, individual Western European countries were hard put to come up with a quick, effective, and coordinated response to the human emergency caused by the conflicts in Bosnia. In the absence of a harmonized set of norms and principles, each government had to gauge the public feeling and assess the political mood of the electorate before moving cautiously towards a policy stand. In most cases the process of adjustment and readjustment was slow, wavering, and painful and the decision has remained fragile. The political costs and administrative strain implicit in such improvised and uncoordinated action, as well as its inhibitive effect on operational efficiency, are becoming clear and widely recognized. Not surprisingly, despite the many delicate and still unresolved issues, the EU member states are now striving hard to agree on a common approach to the issue of temporary protection.[7]

Meanwhile, uncertainties have been increasing in connection with the application of the 1951 UN Convention on the Status of Refugees. This is not only because foreign policy considerations have quite frequently been allowed to intercede (as in the case of Salvadoran refugees), but also because of the exclusion of cases of persecution perpetrated by non-state agents and the gradual emergence of a whole new doctrine of 'imposed return' in UNHCR.[8] In the wake of large-scale flows and even larger fears of refugees from North Africa and the Balkans, the Dublin Convention served as Western Europe's defensive response to a perceived external threat of mass arrivals (Newland and Papademetriou 1998–9).

The response of the developing and transition economy countries, too, has remained weak and unstable, although for different reasons. Some of these regions—such as Africa and Latin America—have developed normative frameworks which are sufficiently wide and flexible to provide temporary protection in situations of human emergency.[9] But a major problem common

---

[7] This includes a most recent proposal to be put forward by the Finnish presidency of the EU to establish a common fund to facilitate burden sharing among the member states.

[8] For a discussion of these issues see Ghosh 1999*b*:17–20.

[9] In 1969, the Organization of African Unity (OAU) adopted a Convention Governing

to countries in these groups—which taken together already host the majority of world's refugees—is that of resource constraints. Also, the highly diversified ethnic composition of the national population in many of these countries makes them potentially more vulnerable to ethno-political conflicts. Even the temporary influx of large numbers of refugees could disturb the delicate inter-ethnic balance and easily sharpen internal tension, as has long been the case in Central Africa and was recently witnessed in Macedonia during the Kosovo crisis. Or, the country itself may be thrown into a civil war while hosting refugees as was the case when Ethiopian refugees were temporarily sheltered in Somalia.

What about the policies addressing the supply-push or emigration pressure in the source countries? Here again it would be misleading to suggest that the response so far has been any more effective or convincing. Despite the public announcements by policy-makers in numerous regional and international fora for a concerted use of aid, trade, and foreign investment to reduce emigration pressure in labour-abundant countries, there is little evidence that the strategy is being consistently applied or that it is making a real impact at the global level. A few countries, notably the Netherlands and Sweden, are more firmly committed to such a comprehensive policy as an instrument of migration management. But even in these cases concrete results are yet to be seen.

Meanwhile, despite the declared policies of some developing country governments to reduce emigration pressure, the general attitude of many source countries has remained one of relative indifference or benign neglect. Some of them continue to actively encourage migration (except for a few specified categories of persons) both as a political safety valve and as a valu-able source of foreign exchange earnings through remittances. In general, little substantial progress has been made in enabling and encouraging the source countries to reduce pressure for disorderly migration through appropriate macroeconomic, sectoral, and regional policies, which would affect employ-ment, income distribution, and demographic trends and thus migratory movements. Equally important, although the concern for human and minor-ity rights is now more widely shared than probably ever before, the infringe-ment of those rights nonetheless seems to continue unabated, East Timor being now added to the long list of ghastly events in recent years.

the Specific Aspects of Refugee Problems in Africa, which expanded the UN definition of a refugee. It included those persons who are outside their countries 'owing to external aggres-sion, occupation, foreign domination or events seriously disturbing public order'. The Declaration of Cartagena, adopted by Latin American governments in 1984 as a non-bind-ing statement of policy, went even beyond the OAU definition. It included not only those individuals who met the UN criteria, but also those 'who have fled their country because their lives, safety, or freedom have been threatened by generalized violence, foreign aggres-sion, internal conflicts, massive violation of human rights or other circumstances which have seriously disturbed public order'.

Co-management of international migration has become a favourite theme of public announcements and policy statements. However, from all indications, some of the critical elements for a genuine commitment of both sending and receiving states to a meaningful cooperative endeavour are still missing.

Movements in defiance of established laws: is migration getting out of control?

A most striking example of the inadequacies of the present migration system lies in the magnitude of the movements that take place in defiance of the established laws and administrative mechanisms. Out of a total world migrant stock of some 130 million, as many as 30 million—or about one-fifth—may well be in an irregular situation. Even more disquieting is the rate at which the irregular movements have continued to take place despite the stepped-up efforts and markedly increased allocation of budgetary resources to curb these flows (Ghosh 1998).

The irregular flows of migrants are now estimated at between 250,000 and 300,000 (roughly one-quarter of the total yearly intakes) in the United States and between 300,000 and 500,000 (about one-third of the total yearly flow) in Western Europe. Thus, at least one in every three or four migrants entering these regions uses the irregular channel. These are hardly shining examples of the effectiveness of existing restrictive policies or a convincing proof of the long-term viability of the system as a whole.

Indeed, indications abound of the inadequacy of a narrowly focused restrictive approach, regardless of attention to the interplay of the various causal factors involved. In the early 1990s the main industrial countries (excluding Japan) faced a dramatic rise in asylum applications (the number reached a peak of 841,000 in 1992). Stringent measures and restrictive interpretation of the asylum laws enabled the countries to drastically reduce the number of applications (a substantial proportion of which was clearly non-bona fide cases) over a number of years, reaching a much lower level (389,000) in 1997. But the pressure for migration into Western Europe continued; and, significantly enough, a sharp rise in irregular immigration coincided with the drop in asylum seeking.

As I have argued elsewhere, when there is high emigration pressure in sending countries and powerful pull factors in destination countries, and especially when the two converge, regulatory restrictions alone cannot arrest the movements; they are simply diverted to irregular channels. The greater the interpenetration of markets and economies, the higher the risk. In such circumstances a direct trade-off can be envisaged between legal exclusion and illegal migration (Ghosh 1998: 35, 146).

An important negative fallout of the persistent trends towards high irregular migration, including in particular trafficking in migrants, is the growing feeling that migration is getting out of control. As this fear takes hold, formulation of proactive and forward-looking policies becomes even more difficult. In a climate of crisis management quick and short-term responses take precedence, and the longer-term perspective is often forgotten or ignored. A vicious circle thus sets in (Ghosh 1994).

The impact of economic globalization

While restrictive immigration policies are thus revealing their limits, they are also being challenged by other, opposing or conflicting, forces, embedded in the current globalization process. Economic globalization, though not entirely new, is now being driven by a set of powerful and largely interrelated forces, including rapid technological change.[10] It has narrowed the distance of time and space and is propelling national economies and people to come closer and interact with each other. World trade has now crossed the $6.3 trillion mark; the ratio of trade to world GDP has been rising three times faster than in the preceding decade; and direct investments across borders has now reached a level never seen before (Ghosh 1999*a*; Overbeek, Chapter 3 in this volume).

All these fast-evolving developments have important implications for movements of people. In some ways they reduce the need for people to cross borders, while in many other ways they create for them both new exigencies and opportunities to move. Clearly, certain types of movements—for example, short-term movements linked to trade and investment—have become a concomitant feature of interpenetration of markets and economies and a structural aspect of interdependence of nations. It is not just a coincidence that in 1994, despite the continuing restrictive migration climate, trading nations in the GATT/WTO recognized the need for liberalizing temporary movements of natural persons as service providers and consumers. This was a clear signal that the restriction of temporary movements of persons impedes the expansion of world trade in services. Although under the General Agreement on Trade in Services (GATS) the commitments made by individual governments in the form 'national schedules' have so far remained confined (with some exceptions) to movements of high-level personnel as intra-company transfers, what is of special significance is that the principle of liberalization applies to all natural persons as service providers and consumers (Ghosh 1997).

---

[10] For a recent discussion of the salient features of the current phase of economic globalization and its implications for migration see Ghosh 1999*a*.

In summing up the lessons drawn from the 'great depression' of the 1930s Mark Miller observes in this volume (Chapter 2): 'All states are interdependent. Autarchy is not an option. Globalization of markets and economies is irreversible.' A somewhat different view is however taken by James Hollifeld when he argues in Chapter 4 that the process of economic globalization is not irreversible. True, depending on how it is managed, there can be popular protests against some of its disruptive and exclusionary effects.[11] For example, unfettered competition among unequal actors may generate resentment and conflicts within and between nations and excessive financial volatility and its contagion effects may unleash a powerful backlash.

Conceivably, this could drive nations to pull back from the globalization process, and drive them to seek safety by closing borders against foreigners and erecting high walls of trade protection, as they did in the 1930s. But this could endanger the world prosperity tenuously built over the past half-decade and seriously weaken the whole liberal democratic system underpinning it. One of the biggest challenges of the 21st century is precisely to avoid that and harness the forces of globalization, including movements of people, within a fair, transparent, and durable world system.

In search of a new policy approach

The above analysis reveals the need for a more comprehensive, updated, and transparent approach, with a new set of rules and principles, to manage international migration. But how to determine a common policy approach which can serve as a meeting ground for the wide range of conflicting and converging forces and interests that impinge on the world migration system? Can any lessons be drawn from recent history of policy development affecting movements of people?

Lessons from policy development since the Second World War

In the period immediately following the Second World War when there was an acute labour shortage in the industrial states, notably in Western Europe, there were calls for liberalizing movement of workers. These were echoed in the formal declarations of a series of international organizations including the

[11] At the time of writing, a coalition of 1,100 public interest groups in 87 countries was launching a protest movement against trade liberalization ahead of the WTO ministerial meeting in Seattle in Nov. 1999. Separate demonstrations in 15 countries were being planned by Public Citizen, a consumer activist group and Friends of the Earth organization. Earlier public protests against economic globalization were held, *inter alia,* in Lyon in 1996, in Cologne in 1999 during the G7/8 meeting, and in Geneva on the occasion of the 50th anniversary of the GATT/WTO in 1998.

ILO in 1949, OEEC (now OECD) in 1953, and the EEC in 1957.[12] Immigration was an actively pursued goal. With the onset of the Cold War a new political concern coincided with the economic need of the industrial states: resettlement of Eastern European refugees who also served as a valuable source of labour in western host countries was actively encouraged. Although at the insistence of the Soviet Union the then newly established International Refugee Organization (IRO) had formally adopted voluntary repatriation to countries of origin as a lasting solution of the refugee problem, resettlement in the host country was the preferred option of western industrial countries.[13]

But, in the early 1970s, under the impact of the first oil crisis, recessionary trends and rising unemployment, labour shortage was no longer a problem in industrial countries. The attitude towards migration as a factor of world development changed. Labour migration was virtually banned, and at the global level migration ceased to be a desirable objective. International organizations joined in to highlight losses in economic growth and social welfare associated with migration. In 1976 the ILO called for a new international division of labour in trade in order to create employment in migrant-sending countries and replace or reduce the need for workers to emigrate.

However, by the late 1970s world trade and the economic environment had sharply deteriorated. The Tokyo Round of multilateral trade negotiation had only a limited success. Not surprisingly, the new policy approach to international migration failed to make much headway. Meanwhile, irregular migration was increasing, alongside a rising stream of asylum seeking in industrial Europe. By the mid-1980s there was again a change in the international migration policy. Reducing the need for migration was still the main objective, but emphasis had shifted from international division of labour to wider economic cooperation between sending and receiving countries as means to achieve the goal.

As regards refugee flows, the preference turned towards voluntary repatriation; and, in 1985, notwithstanding some hesitation on the part of the office of the UN High Commissioner for Refugees, the UNHCR Executive Committee clearly expressed itself in favour of it (Chimni 1999; Ghosh 1999*b*).

The current phase of policy development, marked by a growing fear of

---

[12] See in this connection the ILO Migration for Employment Recommendation (Revised), 1949, No. 86: 'It should be the general policy of Members . . . to facilitate the international distribution of manpower and in particular the movement of manpower to those countries that have a deficiency.' The 1953 OEEC decision C (53) 251 provided that 'applications by employers to employ foreign workers who were nationals of signatory countries should be granted virtually automatically if national workers were not immediately available' (ILO 1974).

[13] During its lifetime the IRO repatriated some 72,340 refugees, only a meagre 5% of the total number of displaced persons registered with IRO. See in this connection Stossinger 1963: 111.

migration, started at the beginning of the 1990s. Policy-making was largely influenced by several new massive migratory flows; including the 1989–90 east–west movements in Europe and the influx of Haitians to the USA; and the EEC/EU's efforts to strengthen external borders in order to allow free movement within the Community. In Western Europe there was also heightened concern over high levels of unemployment and sharply rising flows of irregular migration. The latter included human trafficking, human rights abuses, and other associated crimes. Increasingly stringent restrictive and punitive measures (as discussed in the previous section), reinforced by new initiatives to encourage return and readmission of migrants, shaped the policy approach. At the same time, some renewed attention was being given to more effective migrant integration, but more as a balancing act.

The global refugee policy followed a similar trend. The year 1991 was declared by UNHCR as the Year of Return. In a restrictive political climate, worsened by resource constraints, the concepts of safe return and even 'imposed return' seemed to be gaining ground and legitimacy at the expense of voluntary return, which was strenuously upheld in the past (Chimni, 1999; Ghosh 1999*b*).

Three broad conclusions can be usefully drawn from the above for policy formulation purposes. First, the policy approach to international migration cannot be easily isolated from the wider political and economic context. Second, a wide convergence of the policies and perceptions of powerful states about these issues at a given time invariably have a direct impact on the nature of global arrangements for managing migration. Third, to be sustainable, any new policy framework to manage migration must be sensitive to such changing global realities and flexible enough to effectively address them.

Two main doctrines: the fortress and the open gates

The alternation of liberal and restrictive approaches to international migration as has been seen in the past few decades is of course nothing new. Since the emergence of the nation state migration policies have all too often been shaped by clashes and compromises between two extreme approaches based, respectively, on the liberal doctrine and the restrictive, 'statist' (or 'realist') principles. The primacy of the one or the other has depended largely on the contextual political, economic, demographic, and other circumstances, and their interaction with the prevailing global situation. What kind of guidance or inspiration can we derive from these alternative doctrines?

Undeniably, as the above discussion shows, in recent years it is the restrictive approach that has assumed a dominant role in influencing migration policies at both national and global levels. The discussion has also demonstrated that policies and systems relying primarily on restrictive principles are ill-equipped to grapple with the new issues and emerging challenges of migration. The direct and indirect costs, in financial, political, and ethical terms, of the approach are becoming too heavy. A further point that needs to be underlined here is that the exclusionary overtones of the policy are creating tension and impeding confidence building between nations, thus undermining an essential prerequisite for cooperative management of international migration.

Open gates and free movement: the liberal doctrine

If the restrictive principles are failing to deliver, does it imply that the world society would be better off by opting for the liberal doctrine of an open door policy? The liberal doctrine[14] envisions an open world society based on free exchange of goods, services, and capital, just as it insists on free flow of information and free movement of people. The political ideology of the liberal tends to consider free movements, whether within or between countries, as one of the basic freedoms upholding liberal democracy.[15] Economists belonging to the liberal school marshal forceful arguments in favour of free movements of people. They can, for example, point to the great gains that liberalization of population movements can bring to both sending and receiving countries and the world economy as a whole (this is further discussed in the final chapter of this volume).

Historical experiences lend considerable support to the liberal doctrine favouring free movement of persons. Examples abound of nations that have developed their economies and built their prosperity through the dynamism, knowledge, and innovativeness brought by immigrants over the decades. European nations have derived immense benefits both from emigration and immigration flows in different periods of their history. It is widely agreed that this could not have been achieved under a restrictive migration regime.

The argument of enhanced allocative efficiency for the world economy through liberalized migration can be reinforced by ethical considerations involving distributive justice between nations. In urging greater liberalization of labour migration, the 1992 UNDP Human Development Report underscored the point that in the absence of immigration restrictions in industrial countries, the yearly emigration of only 2 per cent of the labour force from developing countries could yield a total annual income of at least $220 billion. Of this amount between $40 and $50 billion would be sent home per year thus implying a total incremental income of between $200 billion and $250 billion over a five-year period (UNDP 1992: 58).

---

[14] This is very different from neoliberalism, which is reticent to allow free movement of labour as distinct from goods, services, and capital (see Hollifield and Overbeek in this volume).

[15] The liberal doctrine seems less explicit on how free movements and free choice of domicile across borders are to be reconciled with state sovereignty. See, for example, Hoffmann-Nowotny 1997: 104–5.

Of no less importance is the support given on cultural grounds to the free movement of persons. The liberal doctrine upholds such free movement as part of the free flow of information and ideas, serving as a source of flourishing cultures. It is seen as a powerful vehicle for advancement of knowledge and scientific progress, leading to cultural enrichment of the world society.

These are certainly powerful arguments. However, one main weakness in the liberal doctrine is that while it highlights the benefits that individual nations and the world society may derive from free movement of persons, it ignores, or at least says little about the potential costs or negative externalities involved (see Straubhaar, Chapter 5 in this volume). For the receiving countries the costs, real or perceived, concern: the loss of sovereignty; threat to security (including fears of increase in crime and violence); economic dislocation; strain on existing social services and facilities; social instability resulting from sudden and massive migratory movements; and erosion of cultural homogeneity and cohesiveness—especially when the immigrants are of a markedly different cultural background.

The sending countries, especially those with a weak human resources base, are concerned about 'brain drain' and are fearful that the depletion of human capital can have a negative multiplier effect not only on current output but also on future human capital development. Since human skills often act as a complement to capital and technology, skill migration not only lowers the average incomes of the non-migrant population, but also tends to depress wages of unskilled workers, thus aggravating poverty. It is also argued that when several types of labour outflows take place at the same time, causing production bottlenecks, economic dislocation, and worsening of safety conditions, it can have adverse consequences on output, employment, and labour welfare.

Evidence over time and across countries seems to suggest, however, that except in extreme cases of disorderly and massive movements, most of the costs of migration, whether for the sending or the receiving country, are probably less obvious or real than some people might think and would like others to believe. Preconceived notions and prejudices, often fuelled by political propaganda that reflects narrow, sectional interests, often play their part in projecting a one-sided, negative image of migration.

Even so, the stark reality is that as of now the liberal doctrine is not making much impact on the formulation of migration policies; nor is it likely to do so in the near future. With receiving countries erecting, as a recent United Nations report put it (United Nations 1997), 'an ever increasing number of barriers to all types of migratory movements', the prospects for an undisputed acceptance of the liberal doctrine seem extremely meagre. In fact, as already noted, from all indications, more and more nations are becoming less and less enthusiastic about migration, especially of longer duration. This applies to policies relating not only to immigration but also to emigration, as confirmed by the recent UN survey cited earlier in this chapter. The ratio of countries seeking to lower emigration nearly doubled—from 13 per cent to 25 per cent—between 1976 and 1989, followed by a slight decline to 20 per cent in 1993 (Table 1.2*b*).

These trends cannot be ignored. Clearly, the general mood of the nations around the world is hardly favourable to a system that permits or encourages free and unfettered movements of people as envisioned in the liberal doctrine.

Regulated openness as a guiding principle

The discussion above suffices to bring out the inadequacies of both the liberal doctrine and the restrictive principles as a basis for modelling a viable, widely acceptable, and cost-effective migration regime. If lessons are to be drawn from the past, and realism to prevail, the regime should follow a pragmatic approach focusing on what is politically achievable and operationally viable. More specifically, it should be based on the principle of *regulated openness*[16]— a principle which shuns the doctrine of *exclusion*, but does not advocate free and unfettered movements across sovereign states

What then should be the configuration and main features of such a regime? And what exactly will individual nations and the world society gain from the adoption of such a regime?

These are important questions which must be adequately addressed (this is attempted in the concluding chapter). But in order not to run ahead of ourselves we first need to know more about the wide range of issues involved and be fully aware not just of the prospects but also of the pitfalls and constraints that may have to be faced and tackled on the way. The incisive and thoughtful discussions in the following seven chapters, and the diversity of the disciplines they cover, precisely serve this purpose.

REFERENCES

Ardittis, S. (ed.) (1994), *The Politics of East-West Migration*, London: Macmillan Press.
BBC (1994), summary of World Brodcasts, 25 Apr.
Chimni, B. S. (1999), 'From Settlement to Involuntary Repatriation: Towards a Critical History of Durable Solutions to Refugeee Problem', Working paper No. 2, Centre for Documentation and Research, UNHCR, Geneva.

[16] The expression 'regulated openness' was also used in a speech by Mrs Catherine Lalumiere, then Secretary-General of the Council of Europe at the Conference of Ministers on the movement of persons from Central and Eastern European countries, Vienna, Jan. 1991.

Contini, Bruno (1982), 'The Second Economy in Italy', in V. Tanzi (ed.), *The Underground Economy in the United States and Abroad*, Boston: D. C. Heath & Co.

Ferris, E. G. (1993), *Beyond Borders*, Geneva: WCC Publications, 203.

Ghosh, B. (1991), *East-West Migration: The European Perspective*, Geneva: IOM.

—— (1994), 'The Future of East West Migration', in Ardittis 1994.

—— (1997), *Gains from Global Linkages: Trade in Services and Movement of Persons*, London: Macmillan Press.

—— (1998), *Huddled Masses and Uncertain Shores: Insights into Irregular Migration*, The Hague: Kluwer International.

—— (1999*a*), 'Challenges and Opportunities of Economic Globalisation: Some Implications for Labour, Industry and Nation-States', paper prepared for the Bündesanstalt für Arbeit Workshop: 'Internationalisierung der Arbeitsmärkte', Apr. 1999, Frankfurt am Main, Germany.

—— (1999*b*), 'The Promise and Pitfalls of Return Migration', paper presented to the Conference on International Migration, Development, and Integration, held in Stockholm by the Ministry for Foreign Affairs in Sept. 1999.

Hoffmann-Nowotny, H. J. (1997), 'World Society and the Future of International Migration: A Theoretical Perspective', in E. Ucarer and D. Puchala (eds.), *Immigration into Western Societies*, London: Pinter, 104–5.

ILO (1949), Migration for Employment Recommendation (Revised), No. 86.

—— (1974), 'Some Growing Unemployment Problems in Europe', Report II, Second European Regional Conference, Geneva.

ILO/IOM/UNHCR (1994), *Migrants, Refugees and International Cooperation*, Geneva.

Kang, S. D. (1996), 'Globalization of the Labour Market also in South Korea?', paper presented to the International Conference on the Dynamics of Labour Migration in Asia, Nihon University Tokyo, Mar. 1996 (mimeo).

Newland, K., and Papademetriou, D. (1998–9), 'Managing International Migration: Tracking the Emergence of a New International Regime', *UCLA Journal of International Law and Foreign Affairs*, 3/2.

OECD (1998), 'Report on the Temporary Employment of Foreign Workers in Several OECD countries', in OECD, *Trends in International Migration*, Paris: OECD.

Papademetriou, D. G., and Yale-Loeh, S. (1996), *Balancing Interests: Rethinking US Selection of Skilled Immigrants*, Washington, DC: Carnegie Endowment for International Peace.

Stossinger, G. (1963), *The Refugee and the World Community*, Minneapolis: University of Minnesota Press.

UN (1998), *World Population Monitoring*, New York: United Nations.

UNDP (1992), *Human Development Report*, New York: Oxford University Press.

UNFPA (1998, 1999), *The State of World Population*, New York: UNFPA.

Weiss, L. (1987), 'Explaining the Underground Economy: State and Social Structure', *British Journal of Sociology*, 38.

2

International Migration in Post-Cold War International Relations

Mark J. Miller

Introduction

The dramatic upheavals that have roiled global politics in the late twentieth century have inspired scholarly inquiry germane to the question of prospects for cooperative management of international migration in the future. This literature is extensive, inconclusive, and rarely deals directly with international migration, thereby prolonging a puzzling tradition of neglect of the subject matter by students of international relations and world politics. Nevertheless, this literature sheds important light on phenomena and issues that will shape future cooperative management of international migration.

The study of international relations comprises a vast field of inquiry. There are contending approaches to understanding it and there is neither scholarly consensus in scope of inquiry nor methodology. Nevertheless, unless radical postmodernist tenets concerning ontology are embraced, it is possible and meaningful to inquire into the effects of international migration upon international relations.

Of necessity, any such inquiry cannot be comprehensive—or richly descriptive. At the most, one can hope to identify important questions, patterns, and variations and to shed some light upon them. Limitations arise from the sheer scope and complexity of the subject matter. International migration alone constitutes an enormous and incompletely understood subject matter. Seeking to understand its place and role in the broader scheme of international relations is daunting but imperative.

International migration has significantly affected international relations from time immemorial, but its saliency has increased in the post-Cold War

The author acknowledges with appreciation the valuable contribution made to this chapter by Daniel Green, Professor of Comparative Politics and International Relations at University of Delaware.

period. At the twilight of the twentieth century, international migration centrally affects questions of peace and war, security, prosperity or poverty, and democratic or authoritarian rule. On the whole, students of international relations have been remiss for not taking international migration seriously enough. By the same token, students of international migration have been remiss for insufficiently delving into the geo-strategic and political consequences of their subject matter. Conceptual and ideological blinders have long impeded comprehension of international migration and therefore of a major dynamic in international relations. The post-Cold War period, however, has witnessed enormous strides in theorizing about international relations and this has allowed for a richer appreciation of the significance of international migration. It entails a two-way process. The better international relations are understood, the deeper the understanding of the significance of international migration to states and societies. The more completely international migration is understood, the deeper the appreciation of its import upon international relations.

From the 1880s to the 1950s: reflections on past cooperation on international migration

Most scholars trace the contemporary migratory epoch back to the third quarter of the nineteenth century when the industrial democracies of the transatlantic area began to regulate international migration. Migration for employment is viewed as the defining feature of the contemporary period. Events like the adoption of the Chinese Exclusion Act of 1882 in the United States and the breaching of the Berlin Wall and the subsequent collapse of European communist governments demarcate the period. The final decade of the twentieth century was marked by a widespread conviction that the international system was undergoing transformation and that a new world order, or disorder, was replacing the Cold War order that had prevailed from 1947 to 1990. The last ten years have been witness to dizzying changes which prompted serious questioning of the sovereign state system which had structured global politics since at least the seventeenth century.

That sovereign state system, of course, had been questioned since its inception (Hinsley 1963). In late nineteenth-century Europe, which then dominated the world, socialist and other movements yearned to transcend the sovereign state system viewed as an instrument of capitalist and imperialist oppression as well as the permissive condition for war. Yet the independent states in the transatlantic area would continue to accrue powers, in no small part due to their national security dilemmas, and one feature of this was regulation of entry by international migrants. Particularly in Europe, population was viewed as a vital element of national security. Frictions over access to migrant labour actually would exacerbate those tensions which eventually erupted into the First World War (Olsson 1996).

As international migration for employment intensified and spread, it affected bilateral and regional relations. Then as now, immigrants frequently became targets of violence. Killings of Italian migrants in the United States and France adversely affected bilateral Franco–Italian and US–Italy relations. Imperial Germany attempted to reduce frictions arising from widespread employment of seasonal foreign workers in agriculture by crafting bilateral agreements to regulate the recruitment, admission, and repatriation of foreign workers. A significant problem arose from seasonal workers violating the terms of their entry by taking up employment at nearby farms which offered better pay or working conditions. The concept of punishing employers who illegally employ aliens appears to have arisen in this context. To the burgeoning German labour movement, expulsion of the foreign workers who violated their contracts exculpated employers. By the inter-war period, the labour law of the German successor state would specifically punish employers who hired aliens illegally.

Despite the lack of interest shown by students of international relations for the subject of international migration, it is important to recall that migration figured prominently in the domestic politics and international relations of many industrial states. The international socialist movement debated what was the proper stance to adopt vis-à-vis foreign labour. Anti-immigrant sentiment not infrequently sparked violence. By 1885 in the United States, a law was adopted prohibiting entry by foreign contract workers to prevent them from being used as strike breakers or to otherwise undercut organized labour. At the same time, immigrant workers frequently were in the forefront of militant worker strikes and demonstrations. The contract labour prohibition was largely thwarted in practice (Calavita 1984: 39–71).

The First World War constituted a watershed event for international migration too. First, it sounded the death knell of European colonial empires. The Second World War would largely complete the process although the sequels would last into the 1960s, as in the Franco–Algerian case, and, as the Israeli historian Avi Schlaim has argued, the Middle East region may remain under imperial domination as the twenty-first century nears (Schlaim 1995). The significance of the decline of colonialism for international migration arose from the unfettering of people long subjugated to restrictions upon their residential and labour market mobility by European masters. Colonial powers, of course, had authorized huge population movements, some of which, as in the inter-war case of Palestine, would be largely viewed as illegitimate by the indigenous population and lead to conflict and huge further dislocation of populations in the future engendering, in turn, more extensive conflict. The decades-long demise of colonialism and emergence of post-colonial independent states diffused the sovereign state system born of Europe to the rest of the world. International migration has been a feature of world politics from time immemorial. It has always been a global phenomenon. But the situation in the late twentieth century differed significantly from that in the late nineteenth century because colonialism had ebbed. For better or worse, many successor states would attempt to regulate international migration on the model of transatlantic industrial democracies. Problems of illegal entry and illegal employment of foreign workers became global phenomena by the 1970s and 1980s as a result.

A second lasting effect of the First World War was its setting into motion of migratory flows that continue today. In the south-west of the United States, the exclusion of Asian labour in some instances prompted employer recourse to Mexican labour. In 1917, a wartime labour shortage emergency was declared, and bilaterally organized recruitment of temporary Mexican workers for employment primarily in US agriculture was authorized. In wartime France, tens of thousands of Muslims from Algeria were authorized to journey to metropolitan France to serve in the military and work. Deliberate recruitment of colonial workers and workers from subordinate but independent peripheral areas would set into motion complex processes which continue to structure international migration in the late twentieth century.

It is important to note that these flows, even when voluntary in nature, usually arose in a context of domination and subordination. With the eventual eclipse of colonialism, migratory flows arising from deeply enrooted patterns of subordination and domination would come to be regulated by nominally equal sovereign states. Two of the key questions attending the future of international migration are: (1) to what extent will international migration reflect underlying patterns of domination and subordination in the international system and (2) how will this affect cooperative management of international migration? The First World War resulted in the demise of three great empires—Czarist, Austro-Hungarian, and Ottoman. It is fitting to recall at this juncture that massive labour migration was only the defining feature of a new migratory epoch. There also were huge flows of involuntary migrants. In the several centuries preceding the final collapse of the Ottoman Empire, some 5–7 million Muslims were displaced by Russian expansion and the emergence of independent Balkan states (Karpat 1996). These massive population movements associated with the decline of the Ottoman Empire have much more to do with nationalism and ethno-religious enmity than they do with employment and they clearly will affect questions of peace and war in the twenty-first century. The dispersed and then deported Chechens are a harbinger as are the largely Christian Armenians.

The ethnic cleansings and forcible population movements that attended the collapse of the three European empires warn against an oversimplification of international migration complexity. Cooperative management of international migration in the twenty-first century will involve much more than matching foreign worker qualifications in one country to unfilled job vacancies in another. History and collective memories often will intrude and complicate matters. Forces like nationalism were discounted in a brief post-1989 period of worldwide amnesia and euphoria but they came back to haunt international relations at the close of the twentieth century (Hutchinson and Smith 1994).

The inter-war period in Europe and elsewhere generally witnessed declining international migration. States and societies drew inward as hopes for a transformed world order faded. International migration to major receiving states gave way to mass deportations by the mid-1930s, most notably in France and the United States. Individual states could contemplate autarchial solutions. Barriers to international trade increased as did mass unemployment and immigration restrictions. For many students of international political economy, there was a singular failure to apprehend global socio-economic interdependency through trade and the result was disastrous. The lessons drawn from the 1930s shape thinking about the future of the world economy. They can be summarized as follows. All states are interdependent. Autarchy is not an option. Globalization of markets and economies is irreversible. State structures suited to modern capitalism are becoming anachronisms in a globalized economy and will give way to new forms of governance in the perhaps not so distant future. Nationalism itself is obsolete. France was a particularly noteworthy case during the inter-war period because, for a while, it became the world's premier country of immigration. Its devastating losses during the First World War dictated mass immigration for both demographic and labour market purposes. While recruitment was organized by employer cartels, many foreign workers arrived spontaneously without going through established procedures (Cross 1983: 45–70). Nevertheless, immigration was regulated by a series of bilateral treaties (Ministère du Travail 1931).

By the late 1930s, a move was afoot to draft an international instrument which would serve as a model for bilateral agreements regulating international labour movements and which would protect the interests of all involved—foreign workers, employers, and the respective governments affected. The Second World War would intervene. Widely perceived mistreatment of foreign labour during the inter-war period and during the long dark night of the Holocaust would profoundly affect the initial post-Second World War period. In post-war Europe, cooperative management of international migration was thought possible and desirable. It was widely believed that organized international migration could foster better bilateral relations and international comity.

Three pillars of an embryonic international regime pertaining to international migration had begun to take shape during the inter-war period and particularly during the later stages of the Second World War and its immediate aftermath. By 1949, the International Labour Organization adopted its first convention pertaining to recruitment and employment of migrant workers. The Intergovernmental Committee for European Migration (ICEM), the predecessor to today's International Organization for Migration, had also come into existence and played a huge role in organizing mass population movements worldwide. In 1951, the Geneva Convention on refugees created the United Nations High Commissioner for Refugees. Palestinian refugees were excluded from the UNHCR's mandate because of the United Nations' unique responsibility for the circumstances engendering their flight. A special United Nations agency for them was created—UNRWA, the United Nations Relief and Works Agency for Palestine Refugees in the Near East. One should also note the creation of the predecessor to today's OECD, the Organization for Economic Cooperation and Development, which came into existence in the context of the Marshall Plan. The OECD viewed international migration for employment between member states as conducive to development and as mutually beneficial to all involved. It adopted guidelines for member states to ensure such an outcome.

Hence, efforts to foster international cooperation in regulation of international migration were not *sui generis* to the post-Cold War period. By and large, however, students of international relations did not attach much significance to population movements between states. There was a disjuncture between their actual and perceived significance which arose in large part from the prevalent way that international relations were studied.

The post-Cold War unchaining of inquiry into international relations

Writing and teaching about international relations was long dominated by realism and its variant neo-realism. As an approach to understanding international relations, realism assumes that sovereign states shape international relations. The key questions to understand are those pertaining to peace and war. Only states are presumed to importantly affect those questions. States are unitary, purposive, and rational. They pursue interests which can be apprehended although miscalculations are frequent and conflicts sometimes ensue. The simplicity and abstractness of realism enabled comprehensive analysis of international relations in the sense that all state entities and their interactions could be assessed through time and across the world. But international migration could only marginally affect international relations because it did not bear centrally upon questions of peace and war.

Realism and neo-realism comprised the dominant approach to the study of international relations in the United States and in many other industrial democracies in the twentieth century, particularly after the Second World War. The major focus was upon national security, which was understood in terms of conventional military and nuclear capabilities. In the 1960s, an important critique of realism emerged which was most centrally concerned with transnational relations. This alternative approach focused more on socio-economic relations between societies and assumed that such relations could importantly affect international relations. What came to be known as the transnational or low politics approach to international relations was sometimes viewed as complementary to the realist or high politics approach (Keohane and Nye 1977). In the former, unlike the latter, international migration could and did importantly affect security, but the dominance of realist ideology rendered the transnational approach suspect and hindered study of international migration as a factor in international relations. The result was a paucity of inquiry into the political and foreign policy effects of international migration, a level of understanding incommensurate with the real world significance of the phenomenon. It would take the momentous events that defined the end of the Cold War period to open the way to a fuller appreciation of international migration in international relations. Several events and processes were involved.

Perhaps most importantly, the demise of most communist systems and elimination of Cold War-related international tensions allowed for reconceptualization of national security. As evidenced particularly by the transnational school of analysis, this had been in the making for some time. Suddenly, however, the realist preoccupation with conventional and nuclear war potentials and arrangements seemed less important. Security could be understood more broadly and became inclusive of societal security—the ability to maintain dominant patterns of culture and behaviour within a society (Waever et al. 1993). An influential conceptualization of the post-Cold War world divided it into a dominant sphere of peace and stability centred in the transatlantic area, with war and conflict delimited to peripheral areas (Goldgeier and McFaul 1992). Theorists foresaw expansion of the realm of democratic states through democratization and predicted that the post-Cold War liberal moment would be more durable than those following the First and Second World Wars (Green 1997).

These developments affected perceptions and conceptualizations of security. Where international migration once appeared marginal, save perhaps for its connection to international terrorism, it suddenly loomed large (Miller 1995; Weiner 1993). If prospects for major conventional or nuclear war were remote, conflicts within states were expected. One influential writer foresaw clashes of civilizations (Huntington 1993). Conflicts in the post-Cold War era would arise over cultural differences. And, from this questionable premiss, it was not hard to see why security specialists would suddenly start taking international migration seriously.

The second factor was a direct consequence of the collapse of communist regimes. International migration became more of an option for peoples which had lived under communist rule. Indeed, as the Iron Curtain fell, anxiety in Western Europe over mass migration from the former Warsaw Bloc area grew. For the most part, it was misplaced, although millions did exit Eastern Europe in the 1990s. The anxiety best evoked by the German term *Voelkerwanderung* served to heighten awareness of international migration as an important factor affecting international relations. The gap between international migration studies and international relations was apparent in the exaggerated fears of uncontrollable mass movement voiced by some analysts of European and world affairs. Students of international migration suddenly were thrust into the role of security analysts and their assessments were on the mark (Widgren 1990). International migration studies achieved credibility and prominence.

Concomitantly, there was a flowering of international relations theory. Particularly in the United Kingdom, approaches and schools long obscured by realist and neo-realist dominance came into their own. The focus of the so-called English school was upon international society, the norms, patterns, and expectations that regulated intercourse between states and between societies (Evans and Wilson 1992). In this optic, international migration was consequential because it interwove societies in deeply penetrating and inextricable ways. Important dimensions of international society were bilateral accords and multilateral instruments regulating international movements of people.

A confluence of events and scholarly developments threw into question the parting premiss of the realist approach—the primacy of the sovereign state. In Western Europe, the progress of regional integration produced a novelty—a regional entity that transcended its constituent sovereign states. The long monopoly of sovereign states was ended, although sovereignty was far from obsolete and sovereign states were far from *dépassés* as some contended.

The collapse of communism and the crisis of socialism accentuated the power of market forces. A rich vein of international relations writing focused on the growing power and influence of markets and upon the inability of states to subjugate or control markets. States were reduced to tinkering, as it were, at the margins of events and processes that were beyond their control (Cerney 1995). Analysts wrote of the hollowing out and de-territorialization of sovereign states via globalization and transnational business. The sovereign state defined modernity and was being eclipsed by the emergence of late or postmodern society (Ruggie 1993) The obsolescence of sovereignty, in this view, sounded the death knell of realism and neo-realism.

There were excesses in the new and flourishing challenges to the established way of looking at international relations. Sovereignty was not the absolute and immutable attribute common to realists and many of their critics alike. Rather, it has always been mutable and negotiated (Krasner 1993). The creation of the European Union did not signal its demise. Nor did the expansion of market forces necessarily condemn the national state to obsolescence. There was a curious parallelism between the giddy anti-statist ideology of free-market ideologues and the scornful contempt for states and governments displayed by some scholars. States and governments, however, were scarcely obsolete or inconsequential. The sovereign state remained the pre-eminent actor in international relations even if diminished in its prerogatives by worldwide economic developments and the expansion of transnational society. The writing of obituaries for it was premature. Excess and exaggeration was particularly evident in certain writings on international migration and international relations which regarded sovereign states as unable to regulate international migration.

In fact, national states possessed highly variable capacities to regulate international migration (Cornelius et al. 1994). The complexity of international migration, specifically the indeterminacy of illegal migration and illegal alien employment, fuelled political and scholarly debates. The argument that governmental efforts to regulate international migration were illusory because illegal migration persisted despite them was untestable. In the case of transatlantic democracies, expansion and refinement of governmental capacities to deter illegal migration was the norm. The resources committed to enforcement of immigration laws grew enormously but were still often insufficient. Problems and perceptions of ineffective regulation of international migration grew despite enormous expansion of governmental capacity to punish immigration law violations. This paradox underscored the need for greater bilateral and multilateral cooperation on international migration. Intense bilateral and multilateral diplomacy on international migration has become a hallmark of the post-Cold War period. Contrary to those who regard governmental efforts to regulate international migration as illusory, the prevalent assumption appears to be that governments can manage or regulate international migration. But that task is not easy and requires bilateral and multilateral cooperation.

Bilateral cooperation on international migration

Studies of the effects of international migration upon bilateral relationships often emphasize an asymmetry in power between immigration-receiving societies and countries of emigration. Much international migration, of course, arises from socio-economic disparities. If gaps or differentials in wages and annual income can be lowered to the range of one to four or five, most socio-politically problematic international migration will abate (Martin 1997). As a general rule, as testified to by the history of European regional integration, economically driven international migration between countries of similar socio-economic development will be neither extensive nor problematic.

Problems arise in migration between states that are unequally developed often because of the status afforded migrants from the lesser-developed society in a land of immigration, discrepancies between formal policies and immigration realities, or the overall evolution of the economy and of relations between states in an international migration nexus. Economic recession frequently wears out the welcome for international migrants and strains bilateral ties because the poorer emigrant-sending states typically are even more adversely affected by recession than are the better-off immigrant receiving countries. Bilateral tensions may also adversely affect cooperation on international migration issues just as misgivings over international migration can importantly affect an overall bilateral relationship. One of the principal challenges facing policy-makers in the post-Cold War period is management of international migration. The obstacles to successful management are many but they are not insurmountable.

Temporary foreign worker recruitment has figured centrally in many bilateral relationships. In some instances, states have sought to legalize illegal migration by instituting legal recruitment. In other instances, temporary foreign worker recruitment has been viewed as an ephemeral manpower policy adjustment. Decisions to recruit foreign labour often are contested and generally reflect the political influence of employers. However, countries of emigration often advocate such policies since they view them as preferable to illegal migration and as a way to secure employment and wage remittances. The history of temporary foreign worker policies between developed and lesser developed states has been extensively scrutinized. A scholarly consensus has not emerged. Some scholars view such policies as being pragmatic and as having overall positive effects for all involved. Other scholars have been more critical. They emphasize connections between temporary foreign worker recruitment and subsequent illegal migration, the deficiencies of the legal status and protections afforded foreign workers, and a pattern of settlement of temporary foreign workers. Scholars have disagreed over the contributions of foreign worker remittances to development in the countries of emigration. Somewhat paradoxically, political allies of foreign workers in Western democracies have been the most critical of temporary foreign worker policies. Such policies inevitably involve restrictions on residency and employment rights and therefore are problematic in democratic settings.

Whatever the origins of a bilateral immigration nexus, that relationship involves transnational society and often profoundly links more and lesser developed societies. Some such couplings of states institute bilateral commissions to review international migration-related matters of common concern. Some sending countries have created consultative mechanisms to gather information about emigrants and to better articulate and defend their concerns. Homeland states often develop dense webs of consulates available to their citizenries abroad. Policies pertaining to citizenship, naturalization, and political participation by both the immigration-receiving state and the land of emigration can profoundly affect politics in both states and the relationship between them.

Transnational society fosters interdependency between sending countries and immigration-receiving societies. This means that developments in one half of the coupling will usually have an echo in the other half. At times, interdependency can vitally affect security, as when conflicts in countries of origin spill over to the more developed countries. Security, of course, is inclusive of immigrants. Attacks against immigrants have severely strained overall bilateral relations in many instances, including the Franco–Algerian, Turco–German, and US–Mexico cases.

A major concern in post-Cold War scholarship on international relations has been democratization. Some analysts have viewed it as a global imperative (Fukuyama 1993). Studies of democratization, however, pay scant attention to international migration. There is reason to suspect that international migration may importantly affect democratization (Smith 1998). Many of the international migration nexuses involve highly developed democracies with authoritarian or semi-democratic sending countries. In such instances, the freer atmosphere for political debate and expression in the receiving countries can significantly affect politics in the country of origin. Many emigrants are freer to express themselves as aliens abroad than at home. Many homelands fear the subversive effects of emigrant political activities abroad. A host of sensitive bilateral issues can arise in such cases. The receiving governments can marginally influence political outcomes in the homelands depending on the measures or stances adopted towards immigrants and their political expression.

Through naturalization policies, citizenship laws, and policies concerning political participation and representation, many receiving countries can expand the scope of democracy or curtail it. Some immigrant-receiving democracies have enabled resident alien voting in local and regional elections. But many of the exemplary democracies paradoxically house growing populations of aliens who are effectively disenfranchised. Immigrants in highly developed democracies can importantly affect politics. But immigrant voters often appear to vote less than nationals. A major research priority should be better understanding of the effects of immigration upon democratization of origin countries. Many analysts have argued that emigration serves as a political safety valve for many lesser developed countries. However, anti-status quo homeland-oriented political activities by immigrants are commonplace. In some instances, the homeland-oriented politics are revolutionary in nature, in other cases reactionary. There is reason to suspect, though, that exposure to democratic norms and values in the immigrant-receiving countries may encourage democratization in some homelands.

Relatively few scholars have studied bilateral labour agreements. But most of those who have find them skewed in favour of the immigration-receiving countries (Flory 1978). There also has been considerable criticism of the ability, and, in some instances, the willingness of sending countries to protect their emigrants abroad. From the late 1940s through the 1960s, most Western European states signed multiple bilateral labour agreements. Such accords have been rare since the recruitment curbs of the mid-1970s. One of the major exceptions has been the bundle of policies and agreements between the Federal Republic of Germany and several Central and East European countries since 1990. Several hundred thousand foreign workers are admitted under these agreements annually. Most are Polish seasonal workers employed in agriculture and hotels and restaurants (Hoenekopp 1997).

Recent scholarship of international migration in foreign policy and international relations in Europe and North America has advocated more extensive coordination of immigration policy with foreign policy (Teitelbaum and Weiner 1995). The contention is that, despite the important consequences, there is too little systematic thought given to international migration in foreign policy-making. For example, the Federal Republic of Germany unilaterally recognized Slovenia and Croatia for domestic political reasons and gave little or no thought to possible international migration consequences—the refugee flows certain to be triggered by expanded conflict.

Efforts to deter illegal migration, asylum seekers, and refugee flows through measures like border controls and laws against illegal alien employment have been complemented by other measures. Mexico, the USA, and Canada joined in signing the North American Free Trade Agreement. The European Union has created a customs union with Turkey and has signed trade liberalization accords with Tunisia and Morocco. Bilateral or multilateral trade liberalization accords can importantly influence international migration. But it has become quite clear that the influence of immigrant-receiving governments and their policies is marginal as compared to the influence of homeland governments and the macroeconomic policies they pursue (Martin 1997).

Sending country governments tend to view emigration by their nationals to a more highly developed country as a response to labour market needs abroad. The immigration-receiving countries want international migration to conform to democratically mandated laws and policies. This characteristic difference in perceptions renders painstaking progress in bilateral cooperation on international migration. In many instances, however, there is no alternative to cooperation because of the extensiveness and importance of transnational society forged, in part, by international migration. In such cases, successful management of international migration involves much more than decisions to authorize foreign worker recruitment. Some scholars and policy-makers regard international migration realities as givens and argue that policy success depends on recognizing and adapting to those givens. Other policy-makers and scholars regard international migration flows as more fungible and responsive to purposive policies. The complexity of international migration precludes incontrovertible resolution of the debate.

Regional and multilateral cooperation on international migration

The increasing proclivity of national states to cooperate and govern informally and formally through regional and multilateral fora is symptomatic of the underlying changes in international relations which some regard as transformative of the global system. Most transformation theorists regard the sovereign national state as defining the modern era (Ruggie 1993; Onuf 1991). Its eclipse will require different modes of governance from those exemplary of the modern era. For some, then, the intense regional and multilateral diplomacy concerning international migration that has been a hallmark of the post-Cold War period is a precursor and a reflection of system transformation. Most transformation theories do not provide precise benchmarks to delimit evolution from one system to the next. Rather, the transformation is conceived of as a gradual, piecemeal process in which elements of the old will coexist with elements of the new system before transcendence of the old system (Ruggie 1993; Shaw 1997).

In the transatlantic area, informal meetings of representatives of national governments have become a key, but little studied, mode of policy-making. States confront similar challenges and seek common solutions to them. There is awareness that an inability to coordinate and to synchronize policies may adversely affect all the nation states concerned. Concurrently, sovereign states jealously guard their immigration policy prerogatives. Often what emerges are policies of the least common denominator variety. The European Union is the world's most significant experiment in regional integration. Member states differentiate between citizens of the European Union and all others. Regulation of international migration by non-EU citizens is still largely based upon intergovernmental cooperation. Member states' international migration policies have converged in some areas but diverge markedly in others. Efforts to harmonize policies pertaining to international migration and to create a border-free internal European space have lagged due to disjunctures in international migration-related policies and realities in the various member states. The outcome of the Amsterdam Summit in 1998 did not augur well for a European international migration policy in the foreseeable future. Recent historical research on international migration-related policy discussions within the Organization for Economic Cooperation and Development (OECD) and the early European Community concluded that individual states pursued national goals and conceded sovereign prerogatives grudgingly but only to better advance national interests (Romero 1993).

European regional integration has inspired emulation elsewhere. NAFTA was a North American response to the Single European Act of 1986. Immigration issues, however, were expressly avoided in NAFTA negotiations because they were regarded as a 'poison pill', certain to scuttle the negotiations because of the enormous gap in Mexican and US perceptions concerning temporary foreign labour and illegal migration. Paradoxically, both the US and Mexican presidents supported signature of the NAFTA treaty on the grounds that it would significantly reduce illegal migration. Mexican President Salinas argued that Mexico would either export tomatoes or immigrants. Despite the claims made by both presidents, NAFTA was expected to increase migration from Mexico to the USA over the short to medium term. The hope was that trade liberalization and economic reforms in Mexico would attenuate illegal immigration from Mexico to the USA over the long run. The largely unanticipated political developments in Mexico, particularly the rebellion in Chiapas, rendered assessment of NAFTA's effects on international migration even more complicated. A US–Mexico Commission has worked extensively on immigration matters of mutual concern in the 1990s and noteworthy progress on several fronts has been achieved. Mexico's consular protection of Mexican nationals in the USA has been facilitated and there is more cooperation on illegal migration. The advantages and drawbacks of temporary foreign labour policy have been extensively discussed. However, the Clinton Administration has opposed a new guest worker policy.

Sergio Ricca scrutinized African regional cooperation for its effects on international migration up to the 1980s. He found a pattern of states not adhering to provisions of regional instruments pertaining to international migrants. When push comes to shove, African states pursue unilateral policies, often to the detriment of immigrant populations (Ricca 1990). Much the same pattern has occurred in the Arab region where Abdullah Boudahrain has documented a pattern of states ignoring Arab regional instruments pertinent to international migrants (Boudahrain 1985). Mass deportations of international migrants have been recurrent in the Arab world and in Africa.

An International Labour Organisation-led effort in the 1980s to promote Asian–Arab interregional cooperation on international migration collapsed. The displeasure evidenced by several governments and influential personalities over the publication of a critical ILO working paper testified to the sensitivity of governments to criticism of their policies towards migrants even when the criticism was well documented (Zar 1984). The response of some Arab and Asian governments to analysis that revealed shortcomings and abuses in governmental policies has been to remove or muzzle the analysts. Regional and interregional cooperation on international migration is illusory if not based on objective understanding of international migration realities.

Latin America has several intra-regional groupings to facilitate socio-economic and political cooperation. Signature of the Andean Pact in 1979 obliged member states to legalize illegally resident nationals from other member states (Picquet et al. 1986). It was on this basis that the Venezuelan legalization of 1980 was authorized. However, the Southern Common Market (Mercosur) and the Andean Group (GRAN) were not forged with better regulation of international migration specifically in mind. Consequently they have had little effect upon international migration within South America (Kratochwil 1995). In the 1990s, a South Asian bloc of states began discussing ways to facilitate cooperation on international migration. And Southern Africa's regional network of states was recast to facilitate intra-regional cooperation on international migration in the post-apartheid period. New fora proliferated in Europe and the Mediterranean area. Several of these dealt with specific aspects of international migration such as illegal migration and human trafficking. Others were new regional groupings of states, such as the Black Sea-area states, which met to foster regional trade and cooperation, including cooperation on international migration-related questions.

The track record for regional cooperation on international migration has been largely negative. But there are encouraging signs. There appears to be growing awareness of the importance of sharing international migration-related information and instituting and harmonizing statistics on international migration. The OECD's SOPEMI group of international migration experts could and should be emulated in other regions. Most of the world's international migration is South to South rather than South to North. Many individual states possess the wherewithal to pursue unilateral policies. This is most cruelly seen in recurrent mass deportations. But, in most cases, there are mutual benefits to be gained through multilateral cooperation on international migration issues.

International organizations and international migration: towards an international migration regime?

International migration ranks second to oil in terms of importance to the international political economy. An estimated US $70 billion in wages are remitted home by migrant workers each year. Human labour is the most important export for many countries. International migration is the only key part of the international economy that is not coordinated by an international organization (Martin 1997).

In the 1990s, a plethora of international organizations have become more actively engaged on international migration issues, at the behest of their member states. The mandates and roles of several international organizations overlap and the roles of various international organizations require specification and delimitation if redundancy and competition over missions is to be avoided. The growing role of international organizations in international migration does not signal the transcendence of sovereign states because international organizations are created by sovereign states to better pursue their national interests. A founding principle of the United Nations is the inviolability of its sovereign member states.

In the 1980s, there was a great deal of scholarly interest in international regimes. Scholars had broader and narrower conceptions or definitions of what constituted a regime (International Organization 1982). In the looser sense, an international regime refers to perceived constraints on the prerogatives of sovereign states. Many states voluntarily agree to adhere to guidelines and standards on the basis of reciprocity for their nationals in dealings with other states and societies. Treaties are more formalized engagements and take legal precedence. A regime can refer to role-like routinized expectations concerning behaviour as well as to treaty-based commitments.

As Jonas Widgren has noted, many of the elements for an international regime concerning international migration exist. Agencies like the UNHCR, ILO, and IOM have internationally recognized roles and missions (Widgren 1994). There are dozens of regional and multilateral fora working on international migration-related issues. The task for the future is to pull the pieces of the international migration jigsaw puzzle together. This should be pursued on numerous tracks including bilateral, regional, and international diplomacy. Several principles should premiss this diplomacy. First, it should not call into question sovereign states. It is those states which, for better or worse, must legitimize and enforce the policies, rules, and obligations that would be the content of an international regime concerning international migration. Second, the content of such a regime regarding international migration must accord with universal principles of human rights and the foundational principles of key international organizations such as the ILO or the UNHCR which, along with the IOM, would become key components of an international regime pertaining to international migration.

Prospects for the eventual success of ongoing initiatives to foster an international migration regime, such as the New International Regime for Orderly Movements of People (NIROMP) initiative led by Bimal Ghosh, merit the close attention of sovereign states and societies around the world (see Introduction to this volume). If greater cooperation on international migration and refugee questions can be achieved in coming years, prospects for the human condition in the next millennium will brighten considerably. An important immediate priority for states worldwide is harmonization of immigration-related statistics. Progress towards regime formation on other issues usually has been predicated on national governments being able to agree on facts. Unfortunately, credible statistics concerning international migration are not yet available for all areas and countries (Martin 1997; Population Division 1998).

Will the late twentieth-century disarray in multilateral cooperation on international migration give way to a more coherent international system for management of international migration? There are grounds for both optimism and pessimism. There is an embryonic international regime or system for management of international migration. It is centred in the transatlantic area. It has been stressed by late twentieth-century developments like influxes of asylum seekers and the mushrooming growth of other categories of international migrants. And it is threatened by certain systemic developments—growing global inequality in life chances, population imbalances, and the shortcomings in developmental assistance promoting sustainable development. However, international migration was coped with during the crisis period of 1990 to 1995. Sovereign states were not inundated with uncontrollable waves of migrants, as some predicted, in part because many had developed administrative capacities to curb and deter influxes adequately but imperfectly. There was also complementary cooperation in multilateral fora that helped prevent breakdown.

The pessimism arises from the unknown, from uncertainty. And students of system transformation inform us that this is a hallmark of global system transformation. There are so many imponderables—like the future of Chinese emigration—that states will continue doing what they can to exert control over international migration. Indeed, one can reasonably expect many of them to reinforce and expand their efforts in this respect. However, national control measures are only a necessary condition for achievement of cooperative management of international migration. The sufficient condition is expanded and enlightened multilateral initiatives. Unfortunately there is no shared vision, no model to point the way unless it is that of an international regime. Elements of that regime are in place—ILO, UNHCR, IOM, regional pacts like the European Union and fora like the Berlin and Budapest processes, but much remains to be done to ensure that the toward rather than untoward potentiality of international migration shapes future world order.

Some international relations scholars viewed the United States as a hegemon in the post-Cold War period. International relations theory teaches us that hegemons have an overriding interest in the maintenance of systemic order. Yet it is just in the last few years that principal US foreign policy-making institutions have taken international migration seriously (Teitelbaum and Weiner 1995). Meanwhile US domestic political concerns have turned inward-looking, which does not augur well. Can there be expanded and enlightened multilateral initiatives without the United States?

International migration and the entrenchment of the liberal
democratic norm in the post-Cold War order

Analysts like Francis Fukuyama have asserted a durable triumph of liberal democratic values and institutions in the wake of the collapse of most communist governments. Other analysts, such as Samuel Huntington, are less sanguine about the post-Cold War ascendancy of liberal democracy and predict clashes of civilizations, particularly war and conflict over cultural differences both between and within societies.

Despite growing acknowledgement of the importance of international migration and its effects on questions of war and peace, diplomacy and international security, international migration has not figured importantly in scholarly debates over the future of liberal democracy or its diffusion worldwide. This is disappointing because earlier liberal democratic moments, such as the one that followed the First World War, were greatly affected by international migration and how democratic states conducted their immigration policies. Policies of severe restriction and closure, sometimes accompanied by massive deportations of aliens, were part and parcel of the events that brought that liberal democratic moment to an end.

Prospects for the maintenance of the post-Cold War liberal democratic moment, however, appear much brighter then in the past (Green 1997). There is no major counter-project to liberal democratic order as in the past. Some analysts foresee conflict between Islamic lands and Western democracies, but such an outcome is far from preordained. Other analysts worry about ethnic conflicts within societies and spill over to other societies. Diminished prospects for major wars favour maintenance and expansion of liberal democratic governance. Such conflicts can adversely affect the social integration of immigrants from areas affected by major conflict, a spectre clearly raised during the Gulf War of 1991.

Highly durable liberal democratic order can be envisioned. Within this zone, centred in the transatlantic area and regarded by some as an emergent polity in its own right, democratic values, the rule of law, and respect for human rights should be pervasive. The environment will be conducive to maintenance of the legal frameworks that have fostered social integration of legally admitted immigrants in many countries. Indeed, given the social transformations wrought by immigration since the 1970s, it is difficult to see how the acknowledged human right of family life could be ensured in the absence of a legal immigration policy. In this specific sense, maintenance of legal immigration possibilities for purposes of family-related immigration appears imperative. It becomes a litmus test of liberal democracy in a polity that categorically ruled out legal immigration possibilities for immediate family members of citizens or resident aliens would infringe upon their rights. These sovereign states, however, possess the latitude and discretion to determine appropriate procedures and requirements for family-related immigration. Indeed, countries have evolved complicated laws and procedures to accomplish precisely that.

Globalization and greater economic interdependence have meshed sovereign societies and created greater need for orderly movement of persons between societies for economic purposes. The development of global markets has made a legal immigration framework imperative to economic growth and socio-economic well-being. Legal immigrants benefit economies and societies, although their economic effects generally are viewed as marginal in the USA. This assessment is unlikely to change as global economic interdependence progresses. Increasingly, liberal democratic governments view their prerogatives as constrained by market forces. In this optic, a legal immigration framework seems adaptive and conducive to management of effects of globalization and growing economic, social, and political interdependence.

REFERENCES

Axt, H. J. (1997), 'The Impact of German Policy on Refugee Flows from Former Yugoslavia', in R. Muenz and M. Weiner (eds.), *Migrants, Refugees and Foreign Policy*, Providence: Berghahn.

Boudahrain, A. (1985), *Nouvel Ordre social international et migrations*, Paris: L'Harmattan.

Calavita, K. (1984), *U.S. Immigration Law and the Control of Labor: 1820–1924*, London: Academic Press.

Cerney, P. (1995), 'Globalization and the Changing Logic of Collective Action', *International Organization*, 49/4.

Cornelius, W., et al. (1994), *Controlling Immigration: A Global Perspective*, Stanford, Calif.: Stanford University Press.

Cross, G. S. (1983), *Immigrant Workers in Industrial France*, Philadelphia: Temple University Press.

Evans, T., and Wilson, P. (1992), 'Regime Theory and the English School of International Relations', *Millennium*, 21/3.

Flory, M. (1978), 'Ordres juridiques et statut des travailleurs étrangers', in Société Française pour le Droit International (ed.), *Les Travailleurs étrangers et le droit international*, Paris: Éditions A. Pedone.

Fukuyama, F. (1993), *The End of History and the Last Man*, New York: Avon.

Goldgeier, J., and McFaul, M. (1992), 'A Tale of Two Worlds: Core and Periphery in the Post-Cold War Era', *International Organization*, 46/2: 467–91.

Green, D. (1997), 'Comparing Liberal Moments: The International System and Global Outbreaks of Democracy', unpublished International Studies Association—Northeast paper.

Hinsley, F. H. (1963), *Power and the Pursuit of Peace*, Cambridge: Cambridge University Press.

Hoenekopp, E. (1997), 'The New Labor Migration as an Instrument of German Foreign Policy', in R. Muenz and M. Weiner (eds.), *Migrants Refugees and Foreign Policy*, Providence: Berghahn.

Huntington, S. (1993), 'The Clash of Civilizations?', *Foreign Affairs*, Summer.

Hutchinson, J., and Smith, A. D. (eds.) (1994), *Nationalism*, London: Oxford University Press.

Karpat, K. (1996), 'Muslim Migration: A Response to Aldeeb Abu-Salieh', *International Migration Review*, 30/1: 79–89.

Keohane, R., and Nye, J. (1977), *Power and Interdependence*, Boston: Little Brown.

Krasner, S. (1993), 'Westphalia and all that', in J. Goldstein and R. Keohane, (eds.), *Ideas and Foreign Policy: Beliefs, Institutions and Political Change*, Ithaca, NY: Cornell University Press.

Kratochwil, H. (1995), 'Cross-Border Population Movements and Regional Economic Integration in Latin America', *IOM Latin American Migration Journal*, 13/2: 13–21.

Martin, P. (1997), 'Economic Instruments to Affect Countries of Origin', in Münz and M. Weiner (eds.), *Migrants, Refugees and Foreign Policy*, Providence: Berghahn Books.

Miller, M. (1995), 'International Migration and Security: Towards Transatlantic Convergence?', in , L. Tomasied (ed.), *In Defense of the Alien*, New York: Center for Migration Studies, 199–210.

Ministère du Travail (1931), *Recueil de conventions internationales relatives à l'immigration et au traitement de la main-d'œuvre étrangère en France*, Paris: Imprimerie National.

Olsson, Lars (1996), 'Labor Migration as a Prelude to World War I', *International Migration Review*, 30/4 (Winter), 875–900.

Onuf, N. (1991), 'Sovereignty: Outline of a Conceptual History', *Alternatives*, 16/4.

Picquet, M., et al. (1986), 'L'Immigration au Venezuela', *Revue européenne des migrations internationales*, 2/2.

Ricca, S. (1990), *Les Migrations internationales en Afrique*, Paris: L'Harmattan.

Romero, F. (1993), 'Migration as an Issue in European Interdependence and Integration: The Case of Italy', in A. S. Milward et al. (eds.), *The Frontier of National Sovereignty*, London: Routledge, 33–58.

Ruggie, J. (1993), 'Territoriality and Beyond: Problematizing Modernity in International Relations', *International Organization*, 47/1.

Schlaim, A. (1995), *War and Peace in the Middle East*, New York: Penguin.

Shaw, M. (1997), 'The State of Globalization: Towards a Theory of State Transformation', *Review of International Political Economy*, 4/3: 497–513.

Smith, R. (1998), 'Transnational Public Spheres and Changing Practices of Citizenship, Membership and Nation: Comparative Insights from the Mexican and Italian Cases', unpublished paper presented at the Conference on States and Diasporas, Columbia University, New York, 8 May.

Teitelbaum, M. and Weiner, M. (1995), *Threatened Borders, Threatened Peoples*, New York: Willey, Norton.

United Nations (Population Division) (1998), *International Migration Policies*, New York: United Nations.

Waever, O., et al. (1993), *Identity, Migration and the New Security Agenda in Europe*, New York: St Martin's Press.

Weiner, M. (ed.) (1993), *International Migration and Security*, Boulder, Colo.: Westview Press.

Widgren, J. (1990), 'International Migration and Regional Stability', *International Affairs*, 66/4: 749–66.

—— (1994), 'Multilateral Co-operation to Combat Trafficking in Migrants and the Role of International Organizations', Geneva: International Organization for Migration seminar paper.

Zar, Z. (1984), *Recruitment Practices and Working and Living Conditions of Asian Migrant Workers in the Middle East: Problems and Possible Solutions*, Geneva: International Labour Office.

3

Globalization, Sovereignty, and Transnational Regulation: Reshaping the Governance of International Migration

Henk Overbeek

Introduction

Today's international 'regime' covering the trans-border movement of people is inadequate in the face of the challenges posed by the new forms of migration of the past two decades. The legal framework for dealing with refugee movements was essentially a product of the Cold War, reflecting the world's experience with the (European) refugee problems of the 1930s and 1940s caused by Nazism and Stalinism. Policies dealing with labour migration and related issues of family reunification etc. are constructed in strictly national frameworks. Immigration is treated by most states as a threat to their national security or to their socio-economic stability.

If we wish to contemplate, as we should, the contours of a new and comprehensive set of policies and institutional arrangements to deal with transnational mobility of people, we must consider what changes have taken place in the nature of these movements and what the implications of those changes for such a new comprehensive framework. This chapter takes as its axiomatic point of departure the tenet that the global economic and political order is undergoing a far-reaching transformation, which is popularly called *globalization,* or global restructuring. It will be argued that the discussion of new directions in the development of transnational migration policies must take this transformation as its determining context.

This chapter will address the following themes in particular:

1. What is the nature of 'globalization'? What is the underlying dynamic, what are its main manifestations? What if anything is really new about it? How are globalization and regionalization related?
2. In the second section we turn to the question of people's mobility. How does globalization affect and shape contemporary mass movements of people?

3. Then, the question is raised of the transformation of structures of governance nationally and internationally in the age of globalization. How is the exercise of 'sovereignty' reconfigured?
4. In the fourth section we examine how international migration is presently regulated. Can we speak of an international migration regime, and if so what is its nature? Is the existing framework suited to deal with the changing realities of transnational mobility?
5. Finally, we consider the implications of our analysis for the conceptualization of a new comprehensive policy and institutional framework for dealing with mass movements of people.

Globalization

Contemporary movements of people, it is the contention of this chapter, are very intimately linked to the process of what is popularly called 'globalization'. Such developments as the large-scale uprooting of people leading to forced migration (internal displacement and international refugee movements), illegal migration of unskilled manual labour to the growth poles of the global economy, the increased role of criminal organizations in the trafficking of people, the rapidly increasing temporary international mobility of (often highly skilled) service providers, and the globalized management of transnational corporations, are all intimately related to the process of restructuring of the global political economy since the late 1970s.

In much of the literature, 'globalization' is defined in essentially quantitative terms as the increase in cross-border transactions, 'the intensification of economic, political, social, and cultural relations across borders' (Holm and Sørensen 1995: 4). An approach in these terms invites easy empiricist cross-time comparisons which invariably lead to the conclusion that there is nothing very new about globalization: we have seen it all before, and in certain historical periods (e.g. the final decades of the nineteenth century) the world economy was more globalized than it is now.[1]

In this chapter we take the view that globalization must be understood in terms of qualitative practices operating in the global space, rather than in quantitative terms. What is qualitatively new in the present era is above all the progressive incorporation of all of the world's population into interrelated, expanding, and overlapping networks of communication, exchange, and

---

[1] The first contribution to this debate was David Gordon's seminal article (Gordon 1988). More recent contributions along the same line include Hirst and Thompson 1996 and Weiss 1998.

production relations.[2] The deeper essence of this process is that of *commodi-fication*, the transformation of goods, services, and nature (including more and more innate qualities and properties of human beings beginning with their labour power but currently including even their genetic codes) into items that can be privately owned and bought and sold in the market-place. Commodification is a dialectical process, with a destabilizing tension between its two antagonistic poles, i.e. between *privatization*—the commodification of all spheres of human life, the competition of market forces, the individualiza-tion of people—and *socialization*—the progressive replacement of personal bonds by widening circles of impersonal dependence and coherence through division of labour.

The contradictions inherent to commodification and therefore to global-ization account for the latter's uneven character through time and space. A deeper insight into the dialectics of globalization will help us to resolve the old/new dichotomy in the globalization literature: globalization is *at the same* time a familiar phenomenon where there is nothing new under the sun, *and* a qualitatively new phenomenon with commodification reaching into spheres of the social existence of humankind where the market has never penetrated before. It is therefore best to understand the history of globalization as a layered or phased process, with qualitative transformations concentrated in time and space—subsequently to be consolidated, to spread across the globe, and to encounter resistance and activate counter-tendencies. These contradic-tions gradually build up, eventually leading to crisis and transformation.

The major phases of globalization in the history of the world capitalist system have been marked by transformations in the spheres of production and trade relations, in the geographic reach and structure of the system, and in the configuration of governance.

The 'long sixteenth century' (Wallerstein 1974) of the years 1450–1650 saw the dissolution of the European feudal order. This led first of all to the libera-tion of the commercial classes in the towns and the rise (still in rather isolated instances) of capitalist production. The geographic scope of the European order was revolutionized by the spread of *commercial capital* from Western Europe to Asia (the spice trade), the Americas (which were colonized by the Europeans for the purpose of exploiting the gold and silver mines and subse-quently for the establishment of the plantation system) and the western coasts of Africa (pursued for the slave trade). Finally, the dissolution of feudalism led to the rise in Europe of a multitude of sovereign territorial states. This system was consolidated by the Peace of Westphalia (1648).

The second half of the nineteenth century, or more precisely the period

---

[2] This approach to globalization is inspired by such critical studies of the contemporary global political economy as those by Castells (1998), Cox (1987), Mittelman (1996), and van der Pijl (1998).

between the 1840s and the First World War, brought revolutionary changes in the structure of world capitalism. These changes were brought on by the rise of *industrial capital* and the new dynamics this created on the Continent, beginning in Britain, and later on in North America.[3] First, the industrial revolution fundamentally transformed the predominant social relations of production in Europe, dissolving agricultural communities and setting in motion a process of large-scale urbanization. The new need for industrial raw materials from colonial territories and the competitive pressure of the newly emerging industrial rivals to Britain's monopoly provoked an intensification of exploitation in what later became known as the third world, through full colonization, the introduction of various forms of forced contract labour (on the Caribbean plantations as well as in the mining regions in Southern Africa), and the concomitant construction of typical colonial inland infrastructure. The incorporation of most parts of the world into the global market drove commodification to unprecedented heights. The sovereign territorial state, finally, in this period became a truly *national* state, or a 'socialised state' as Nigel Harris calls it (Harris 1995: 5–7). This is the age in which the European populations develop their 'national' consciousness.

The current third phase of globalization is characterized by the rise of *transnational capital*. The antecedents for this phase can be traced to developments in early twentieth-century American capitalism and its post-1945 spread to Western Europe and Japan. This era combined liberalizing world trade and finance with the development of Keynesian welfare states within an essentially national framework, premissed on restricted access to citizenship rights. Labour migration was intensively regulated in the form of *national* guest worker systems such as the Bracero programme for the recruitment of Mexican migrant workers in the USA or the West European recruitment schemes of the 1960s and early 1970s. Foreign direct investment in manufacturing became the leading method for the internationalization of capital.

A dramatic acceleration in the internationalization process followed the deep global recession of the mid-1970s. The response to the crisis on the part of Western capital was to intensify its outward orientation, which resulted in what was dubbed the New International Division of Labour: 'a single world market for labour power, a true world-wide industrial reserve army, and a single world market for production sites' (Fröbel et al. 1977: 30; my translation). This new phase represents a qualitative transition from an *international* to a *global* world.

---

[3] The emergence of *finance capital* (the 'merger' of industrial capital and banking capital) towards the end of the 19th century, as analysed by Hobson, Hilferding, and Lenin, did not undermine the fundamental pre-eminence of industrial capital: the rise of finance in the late 19th century, i.e. the increase in credit and insurance as well as in portfolio and direct investments, was a corollary of the unprecedented growth and spread of industrial capital. That is fundamentally different in the present third phase of globalization.

The importance of this new form of internationalization as contrasted with the earlier phases of globalization in which commercial capital and money capital moved across borders cannot be overstated. Whereas money capital imposes an abstract and indirect discipline on labour, direct investment abroad directly reproduces capitalist relations of production *within* the host countries (Poulantzas 1974).[4] During the whole period since the mid-1980s (with the exception of the early 1990s), while international trade grew faster than global production, foreign direct investment (FDI) grew faster than trade and also outpaced world gross domestic investment (see Table 3.1).

Foreign direct investment has thus become by far the most important engine of accumulation in the global economy. After a slowdown in the early 1990s, direct investments are growing explosively in the most recent years: by 27 per cent in 1997 (UNCTAD 1998), by 39 per cent in 1998 (*Financial Times*, 23 June 1999). As a consequence the share of foreign investment inflows in world gross fixed capital formation has grown rapidly, from 1.1 per cent in 1960 to 2.0 per cent in 1980 and to 7.4 per cent in 1997 (UNCTAD 1994, 1998). By 1997, the total stock of FDI had reached the level of $3.5 trillion.

Foreign direct investment is not undertaken by countries, but by transnational corporations (TNCs, 53,000 of them at the latest count). By 1997 total assets of foreign affiliates of TNCs stood at $12.6 trillion. Sales by foreign subsidiaries reached $9.5 trillion (UNCTAD 1998: 2). In addition to FDI, through strategic alliances and other non-equity arrangements, transnational corporations gain control over assets and markets that are not reflected in the statistics for FDI flows.

The contribution by TNCs to further transnational socialization is greater than that of international trade: if world sales of foreign affiliates of TNCs in 1960 were still smaller than world exports, in 1997 they stood at 148 per cent of world exports (UNCTAD 1998: 2). One-third of world exports are exports of foreign affiliates (ibid. 6). As OECD figures for 1992 indicate, 58 per cent of total US exports were exports by TNCs; in the case of Japan that figure stood at 78 per cent. And the share of *intra-firm trade* in total trade was 23 per cent

---

[4] Financial globalization, i.e. the emergence and growth of global financial markets, is identified by many as the hallmark of globalization. From the perspective of the overall transnationalization of the circuits of productive capital, the role of global finance is in a sense secondary, namely to keep the system together and to lock the spatially dispersed sites of production and accumulation into one global system. However, global financial transactions have far outgrown the dimensions commensurate with this primary role. If we take into account all transactions between all the world's financial institutions (lending, currency transactions, etc.) their volume is now 100 times that of international trade ($4.4 trillion vs. $440 trillion). They have increased from $20 bn. per day in 1973, via $60 bn. in 1983 and $820 bn. in 1992, to $1,200 bn. in 1996 (Oman 1996: 13). Some of the implications of the autonomization of global finance will be taken into consideration below.

TABLE 3.1. *Growth rates of world production, exports, and investments (in %)*

	1980–90	1990–97
world gross domestic product[c]	3.1	2.3
world exports[c]	5.2	7.0
world gross domestic investment[d]	12.5[a]	2.6[b]
foreign direct investment outflows[d]	27.1[a]	15.1[b]

[a]1986–90
[b]1991–5
[c]*source: World Development Report 1998/99* (Washington, DC: World Bank).
[d]*source: World Investment Report 1998* (New York: UNCTAD).

for the USA, and 26 per cent for Japan (OECD 1996: 24). No less than 80 per cent of trade flows in the North American Free Trade Area (NAFTA) are intra-firm flows (Gerbier 1995: 47).

Transnational corporations, we may safely deduce, have a strong impact on the world economy:

they organize the production process internationally: by placing their affiliates world-wide under common governance systems, they interweave production activities located in different countries, create an international intra-firm division of labour and, in the process, internalize a range of international transactions that would otherwise have taken place in the market. (UNCTAD 1994: 9)

Two further trends in the development of FDI must be mentioned because of their special relevance for the specific interpretation of the current phase of globalization developed here.

First, private financial flows to developing countries have far outgrown official development finance. In 1990 official finance accounted for more than half of all flows to developing countries, in 1997 this ratio had dropped to 15 per cent. While the overall inflow of capital increased annually by 16 per cent, official finance fell by 3 per cent annually. This development 'reflects the trend towards liberalisation and globalisation in the areas of investment and finance. Barriers to capital movements have been abolished in many countries and investment decisions are increasingly made on a regional or global scale' (ibid. 13–14).

Second, the rapid expansion of FDI is increasingly tied up with the explosive increase in mergers and acquisitions (M&As) in the world. The total value of cross-border M&As in 1997 was approximately $342 billion (up from less than $100 bn. in 1992), representing 58 per cent of FDI flows (UNCTAD 1998: 19–20), and initial evidence indicates a further rise of these figures to over $500 billion, about 80 per cent in 1998 (*Financial Times*, 23 June 1999, p. 6). Cross-border M&As are mostly concentrated within the developed world, thus tremendously reinforcing the process of *transnationalization*, i.e. the rapidly intensifying interpenetration of the economies (capital markets and labour markets) of the OECD countries.

These data on the concentration of capital within the core area of the world economy do not bring out fully that in fact this process is one of *regionalization*: the largest transnational corporations increasingly build complete integrated production networks within each of the three most important regions, i.e. North America, Western Europe, and East Asia/Pacific, the so-called Triad (UNCTAD 1993). The reasons for this are both general and specific. In general, productive capital is not 'footloose': the relative fixity of productive assets, the skill requirements for the workforce, and the social and political embeddedness of productive capital explain its limited mobility. More specifically, the particular pattern of Triadic concentration is explained by the exigencies of 'flexible accumulation' (just-in-time delivery, small batch production, cultural diversity) and by the desire on the part of TNCs to seek insulation from exchange rate volatility. Politically, 'regionalization' is manifested in the formation of regional blocs: in response to globalization states initiate regional integration schemes (such as the European Union or the larger European Economic Area, NAFTA, Mercosur) which in turn reinforce the incentives for TNCs to establish regionally integrated production networks.

Although many have been tempted in recent years to do so, it would be misleading to understand regionalization as negating globalization. Rather, the two processes are dimensions of a single, multifaceted, process of worldwide social transformation (see Chapter 9 in this volume). This transformation involves the restructuring of relations (economic, political, spatial, sometimes also military) between regional growth centres and their (semi-) peripheries. In the next section, we turn to an examination of the impact of this transformation on people's mobility.

Globalization and migration

At the height of the mid-1970s recession in the Western economies, the phenomenon of runaway industries seemed to herald the end of Fordism, of the welfare state and of full employment. This, in any case, was the prediction made by three German researchers in their study of the new international division of labour (NIDL) (Fröbel et al. 1977). They observed an accelerating relocation of labour-intensive production processes to low-wage countries in Asia and Latin America, matching these countries' strategies of export-oriented industrialization. The conjuncture of three crucial developments made this relocation drive possible:

- an inexhaustible reservoir of cheap labour, which is continuously replenished by an intense rural-urban migration;
- developments in production technology making it possible to separate the labour-intensive parts of the production process from the capital-intensive parts;
- developments in transport and communication technology facilitating the coordination of dispersed production and assembly establishments.

In the words of the authors themselves, 'The conjuncture of these three conditions . . . has created a single world market for labour power, a true world-wide industrial reserve army, and a single world market for production sites' (Fröbel et al. 1977: 30; my translation). The NIDL thesis has attracted a lot of criticism (e.g. Gordon 1988), and subsequent developments have borne out that it is risky to extrapolate on the basis of data from a limited time span. The expectation that industrial production would eventually disappear from the North has not come true. This however does not obliterate the importance of other elements of the work of Fröbel, Heinrichs, and Kreye which are of immediate relevance to this chapter. The work on the NIDL has also drawn attention to the fact that migration is not the only, and for that matter numerically not the most important, way in which national labour forces directly compete with each other: in certain sectors trade, capital flows, and labour migration are feasible alternative modes of accessing the cheap labour power in selected Third World countries (Harris 1995: 21, 160 ff.). This state of affairs is in sharp contrast with the predominant situation from the 1930s until the early 1970s in which labour markets were nationally demarcated and labour could only compete by physically crossing borders. In the age of information and communication technology many sectors of industrial production and commercial service provision can tap labour forces in various parts of the world without the need for migration.[5]

In the core of the global system, in the OECD countries, this development goes hand in hand with a neoliberal offensive of deregulation, liberalization, and flexibilization. While undermining the bargaining power of organized labour and helping to depress wage demands, it simultaneously creates and/or reinforces the demand for various forms of unskilled and semi-skilled workers who are employed under increasingly precarious conditions (Cox 1987; Sassen 1996b; Castells 1998). Governments in the core areas of the global economy seek to compensate for their weaker control over the forces of the market by pursuing projects of 'open regionalism', i.e. forms of

---

[5] In this sense, to give just one concrete example, the threat of KLM to shift its entire automation centre to India, where the necessary specialized labour is available at a tenth of the price in Western Europe, is not a hollow threat but a technically speaking perfectly feasible strategic option. It is the *political* price involved which has so far constrained KLM, but the disciplining effect on KLM's Dutch labour force is considerable.

regional integration aimed at combining further liberalization of the flow of goods and capital with a revival of certain structures of governance of the market. This is how not just the Single Market project in Europe, but also NAFTA, APEC, Mercosur, and several other regional free trade initiatives can be understood.

In more peripheral areas of the world (e.g. Africa, Eastern Europe, Central America), the two most important changes since the mid-1970s (often inter-acting) have been the debt crisis and the ensuing imposition of structural adjustment policies, and the end of the Cold War. The Structural Adjustment Programmes of the IMF and the World Bank, and the withdrawal of, or cutbacks in, military and economic assistance by the superpowers, both resulted in a substantial reduction of external financial resources available for redistribution by the state. This, in turn, seriously affected the ability of govern-ments in many third world states to co-opt rivalling elites into the power struc-ture. In many cases the result was serious social and political crisis, economic disaster, and regime change or state collapse. These complex processes largely explain the surge in forced movements of people since the mid-1970s across the globe, in search of protection and in search of a new and better life (Cohen and Deng 1998; Loescher 1993; UNHCR 1997; Zolberg et al. 1989).

Globalization, in sum, has the double effect of bringing a growing propor-tion of the world population directly into the capitalist labour markets, and of increasingly locking the national and regional labour markets into an inte-grated global labour market. The mechanisms by which this formation of an integrated global labour market takes place are the following:

- incorporation of previously disconnected areas (China, Soviet Union, Eastern Europe, Vietnam) or populations ('indigenous peoples') into the capitalist world market;
- commodification of economic activities previously organized outside the market (through liberalization, privatization, deregulation);
- growing demand for irregular labour in 'post-industrial' economies;
- further proletarianization of the world population (urbanization in the third world, increasing labour market participation rates in the industrial economies); and
- transnational migration (labour migration including brain drain, family reunification and formation, refugee movements); all these forms of migration are enhanced globally by the dramatic fall in the costs of inter-national, and even intercontinental, travel, and by the effects of the newly developed means of communication such as satellite television etc.

Whereas the overall growth of the number of international migrants has followed a fairly even path over time, the growth has been unevenly distrib-uted between developing countries and developed countries. The more rapid growth of the migrant population in the North took place primarily in the

TABLE 3.2. *World migrant population distribution, stock, by major region, 1965–1994*

Region	foreign-born population (millions)				index, 1965=100	% of total population, 1994
	1965	1975	1985	1994		
Developed countries	30.3	38.2	47.8	56.7	187	4.9
North America	12.6	15.0	20.4	25.0	198	8.5
Europe	14.6	19.4	22.8	26.1	179	3.6
Asia-Pacific	3.0	3.8	4.6	5.6	187	1.6
Developing countries	44.9	46.2	57.2	68.4	152	1.5
Sub-Saharan Africa	6.9	10.1	10.3	14.3	207	2.5
Latin America and the Caribbean	5.9	5.7	6.5	7.9	134	1.6
Middle East, South and South-East Asia	31.6	29.8	39.7	45.9	145	1.4
Oceania	0.1	0.1	0.2	0.3	300	4.4
Total	75.2	84.4	105.1	125.0	166	2.2

Source: UNCTAD/IOM 1996, 7.

decade 1965–75, i.e. the last decade of organized guest worker recruitment. After 1975, growth rates in North and South were approximately equal. The difference between North and South is significant, however, in terms of the higher proportion represented by migrants in the overall population of the North (see Table 3.2).

The number of people in search of political asylum has not followed an even growth path over time. In the OECD countries, as the following figure shows, there was a sharp increase in the number of asylum applications in the years 1989–92, and although the numbers have dropped since then, they seem to be stabilizing at a level much higher than before the 'hump' in the early 1990s (see Table 3.3).

Worldwide, people of concern to the United Nations High Commissioner for Refugees numbered 22.7 million at the start of 1997: of these, 58 per cent were refugees, 21 per cent were internally displaced people, and 21 per cent were returnees or 'others of concern' (UNHCR 1997: 2). Of these, 35 per cent are in sub-Saharan Africa, a quarter in North Africa, the Middle East, and Central Asia, and 31 per cent in Europe (a great deal of them from former Yugoslavia) (ibid. 3).

The patterns of regional concentration in the globalization process simultaneously create a framework for the consolidation and intensification of regional migration networks (see also Ghosh, Chapter 9 in this connection). Movements of people are partly occurring in regional contexts as well, not just as a reflection of the emerging new production and labour market structures,

TABLE 3.3. Inflow of asylum seekers (ooos) into selected OECD countries, 1983–1998

	1983	1984	1985	1986	1987	1988	1989	1990	1991	1992	1993	1994	1995	1996	1997	1998
A	6	7	7	9	11	16	21	23	27	16	4	5	6	7	7	14
B	3	4	5	8	6	5	8	13	15	18	27	14	11	12	12	22
CH	8	8	10	9	11	17	25	36	42	18	25	16	17	18	24	41
CZ	–	–	–	–	–	–	–	2	2	1	2	1	1	2	2	4
DK	1	4	9	9	3	5	5	5	5	14	14	7	5	6	5	6
D[a]	20	35	74	100	57	103	121	193	256	438	323	127	130	116	104	99
E[b]	1	1	2	2	3	3	4	9	8	12	13	10	4	4	5	7
F[b]	14	16	26	23	25	32	60	56	47	29	27	26	20	17	21	22
GR	–	–	–	–	6	9	7	4	3	2	1	1	1	2	4	3
H	–	–	–	–	–	–	–	–	–	–	–	–	6	–	1	7
IRL	–	–	–	–	–	–	–	–	–	–	–	–	–	1	4	5
I	3	5	5	7	11	1	2	5	32	3	2	2	2	1	2	7
L	–	–	–	–	–	–	–	–	–	–	–	–	–	–	–	2
N	–	–	1	3	9	7	4	4	5	5	13	3	1	2	2	8
NL	2	3	6	6	14	8	14	21	22	20	35	53	29	23	34	45
PL	–	–	–	–	–	–	–	–	–	–	–	1	1	3	4	3
P	–	–	–	–	–	–	–	–	–	1	2	1	–	–	–	–
S	3	12	15	15	18	20	32	29	27	84	38	19	9	6	10	13
SF	–	–	–	–	–	–	–	3	2	4	2	1	1	1	1	1
UK[c]	4	4	6	6	6	6	17	38	73	32	28	42	44	28	33	58
Sub EUR	65	99	166	197	180	232	320	441	566	697	556	329	288	249	275	367
AUS[b]	–	–	–	–	–	–	1	4	17	4	5	4	5	8	10	8
CDN[b]	5	7	8	23	35	45	20	37	32	38	21	22	26	26	24	25
USA[b]	26	24	17	19	26	61	102	74	56	102	152	143	148	123	80	52
Sub	31	31	25	42	61	106	123	115	105	144	178	169	179	157	114	85
TOTAL	96	130	191	239	241	338	443	556	671	841	734	498	467	406	389	452

[a]Since 1 July 1993, dependants are counted only if an application is filed separately.

[b]Data refer to principal applicants and do not include dependants.

[c]Data include dependants separately from 1995.

Data from: *Migration News Sheet*, various issues (sources: IGC, UNHCR, national data); supplemented with data from SOPEMI 1998. Abbreviations used are as per international motor car registration plates.

TABLE 3.4. *Region of last residence of legal immigrants to the USA, 1901–1996*

Decade	Europe	Asia	Western hemisphere	Other
1901–10	92	4	4	–
1911–20	75	4	20	1
1921–30	60	3	37	–
1931–40	66	3	30	1
1941–50	60	4	34	2
1951–60	53	6	40	1
1961–70	34	13	52	2
1971–80	18	35	44	3
1981–90	10	37	49	3
1991–96	14	32	50	4

Source: 1901–90: Hamilton 1994: 75; 1991–6: OECD SOPEMI 1998: 235.

but also for a series of factors that are migration specific, such as geographic proximity, cultural affinity, historical linkages, and migration chains.

In the case of the United States (see Table 3.4) the twentieth century has shown a very strong tendency towards regional concentration of immigration: immigrants come from neighbouring regions, first of all Mexico, in increasing proportion, while immigration from Europe declined steadily until the 1990s. Immigration from Asia, while rising after the 1940s, reached its peak in the 1980s.[6]

In Western Europe the situation is similar (see Table 3.5). There, more than a third of the foreign residents come from other West European countries, and some 36 per cent come from the Mediterranean countries that were the traditional suppliers of 'guest workers' during the post-war decades. Some 5 per cent come from Central and Eastern Europe, leaving less than one in four who come from further away.

Finally, in Japan, the same situation pertains (Table 3.6). There almost half of the foreign residents are Korean. One-quarter have come from China, Taiwan, and South-East Asia, while one-sixth are immigrants from South America of Japanese descent. All together, less than one-eighth of the foreign residents in Japan are neither from the region nor of Japanese descent.

This relative regional concentration of migration patterns in line with the regionalization of trade, investment, and political relations suggests (a point to which I return later) that the regional context is extremely important when

[6] When reading the table, it must be kept in mind that data for the years 1989–92 are distorted by the fact that under the provisions of the Immigration Reform and Control Act of 1986 some 1.8 million undocumented Mexican residents were granted permanent residence in the USA.

TABLE 3.5. *Foreign residents of Western Europe, 1995 (000s and %)*

| | Country of residence | | | |
| | European Union[a] | | Western Europe[b] | |
	000s	%	000s	%
Total	369,408.2	100.0	381,180.1	100.0
Nationals	351,831.4	95.2	362,083.2	95.0
Non-nationals	17,576.8	100.0	19,096.9	100.0
Western Europe of which:	5,786.9	32.9	6,700.3	35.1
EU-15	5.609.7	31.9	6,511.5	34.1
Other	177.2	1.0	188.8	1.0
Mediterranean of which:	6,492.6	36.9	6,880.7	36.0
Turkey	2,668.8	15.2	2,752.5	14.4
ex-Yugoslavia	1,891.7	10.8	2,183.6	11.4
Morocco	1,034.4	5.9	1,039.9	5.4
Algeria	652.8	3.7	656.0	3.4
Tunisia	244.9	1.4	248.7	1.3
Central and Eastern Europe	983.9	5.6	1,013.2	5.3
of which ex-USSR	197.0	1.1	203.1	1.1
Others	4,313.4	24.5	4,502.7	23.6

[a]The member states of the European Union are: Austria, Belgium, Denmark, Finland, France, Germany, Greece, Ireland, Italy, Luxembourg, the Netherlands, Portugal, Spain, Sweden, and the United Kingdom.
[b]Western Europe is defined here as consisting of Switzerland plus the member states of the European Economic Area, i.e. the fifteen member states of the EU plus Iceland, Liechtenstein, and Norway.

Source: Eurostat, Demographic Statistics 1997, 48–9.

TABLE 3.6 *Foreign population in Japan, 1985–1996 (in 000s and %)*

| Country of origin | 1985 | | 1996 | |
	000s	%	000s	%
Korea	683.3	80.3	657.2	46.6
China/Taiwan	74.9	8.8	234.3	16.6
South-east Asia	20.7	2.4	121.6	8.6
Brazil & Peru	2.5	0.3	238.9	16.9
USA	29.0	3.4	44.2	3.1
Others	40.2	4.7	118.9	8.4
Total	850.6	100.0	1,415.1	100.0

Source: OECD SOPEMI 1998, 253.

thinking about developing new migration policies. It provides the material basis for such policies (i.e. the actual high degree of concentration of many migratory movements within regions), but given the correlation between the different forms of 'regionalization' it is also much more likely that states will be able to reach agreement on such policies given the multitude of possible compensatory concessions in other fields (see also Ghosh, Chapter 9 in this connection). The scope for bargaining is much smaller on a global scale.

Globalization, state, and governance

The impact of globalization processes on the state has unleashed a debate about the question whether the state still matters. Some tend to argue that the end of the nation state is at hand, others have argued that the state has actually been one of the main 'authors' of globalization (Panitch 1996: 84–5). In both cases the issue of state 'sovereignty' is central.

The territorially defined 'sovereign' state in Europe emerged in the seventeenth century: it is a *historical* phenomenon, specific to place and time. And in contradiction with the claims of most rulers (and of realist theory), sovereignty has never been absolute and indivisible. The sovereign state arose out of a situation in which sovereignty over territory and population was shared between the monarchy, the Church, and nobility. From the very moment that the European space was divided into distinct and exclusive territorial sovereignties (states) after the Peace of Westphalia in 1648, these states and their rulers accepted that their sovereignty was less than absolute. It was restrained by international obligations which were deemed necessary to the survival and consolidation of the state system (as they are today through the United Nations Charter, for instance). The idea therefore that sovereignty is total, and is the inalienable eternal right of every state, is a myth: state sovereignty is a historical construct, changing over time and never absolute and indivisible.

In the words of E. H. Carr,

The concept of sovereignty is likely to become in the future even more blurred than it is at present. The term was invented after the break-up of the mediaeval system to describe the independent character of the authority claimed and exercised by states which no longer recognised even the formal overlordship of the Empire. It was never more than a convenient label; and when distinctions began to be made between political, legal and economic sovereignty or between internal and external sovereignty, it was clear that the label had ceased to perform its proper function as a distinguishing mark for a single category of phenomena. (Carr 1964: 230–1)

The critique of the realist conception of sovereignty must be taken a step further by bringing in not only the external dimension, but also the internal

62   *Henk Overbeek*

dimension of sovereignty. The state is not a black box, but a complex set of institutions which emerged out of and is fundamentally part of, a larger social structure. The state's *raison d'état* is not some eternal transhistorical given, but a social construct, underpinned by a particular *historic bloc* (a configuration of class forces) whose uniting ideology defines the general direction of state intervention (Cox 1987), or its 'social purpose' (Ruggie 1998).

The historical rise of the sovereign state is thus one aspect of a comprehensive reorganisation of the forms of social power. [. . .] under this new arrangement, while relations of citizenship and jurisdiction define state borders, any aspects of social life which are mediated by relations of exchange in principle no longer receive a political definition (though they are still overseen by the state in various ways) and hence may extend across these borders. (Rosenberg 1994: 129)

With the rise of capitalism social relations assume a border-crossing, transnational, character in a way that was impossible in the pre-capitalist world where the public and the private were one. In fact, what is presently called 'globalization' represents a new stage in the separation between the public and the private, with exchange relations and the discipline of the market being extended to spheres which were hitherto governed by the public organs of the state. As the economy and with it social relations of production are increasingly dominated by transnational processes, so must the functions of the state dealing with those processes increasingly be performed transnationally to be effective.

The public sphere develops into a power structure with multiple dimensions and functions, not all of which are necessarily linked to the exclusive territoriality of the 'sovereign' state. John Ruggie has called this process 'unbundling' of territoriality:

In the modern international polity an institutional *negation* of exclusive territoriality serves as the means of situating and dealing with those dimensions of collective existence that territorial rulers recognise to be irreducibly transterritorial in character. Nonterritorial functional space is the place wherein international society is anchored. (Ruggie 1993: 165).

Unbundling of territoriality creates a multiplicity of functional systems at different levels which replace the exclusive and unitary state-centred form of territorial sovereignty which had come to define our very conception of state sovereignty. Nowhere is this unbundling further advanced than in the European Union, where the Treaties of Maastricht (1991) and of Amsterdam (1997) have created a multi-layered governance structure with specific roles for supranational, intergovernmental, national, and regional institutions and authorities.

But in other regional contexts and at the global level, too, similar developments are transpiring. Institutions such as the International Monetary Fund and the World Trade Organization have achieved a considerable degree of

autonomy from the national governments that nominally control their exec-
utives, while more informal organizations such as the G7 play a crucial role in
influencing longer-term strategic policy orientations. The emergence of these
new structures, often combining public and private forces, inspired Robert
Cox's famous phrase of a 'global *nébuleuse*' (Cox 1996: 26–7).

The process of unbundling of territoriality also reinforces the increasing
difficulty for political leaders in parliamentary democracies to legitimize the
policies to which they are committing themselves and their countries in the
transnational arena (Zürn 1995: 154). The reduction of democratic control
that is implied by the unbundling of territoriality is called by Stephen Gill the
'New Constitutionalism', 'the move towards construction of legal or constitutional devices to remove or insulate substantially the new economic institutions from popular scrutiny or democratic accountability' (Gill 1992: 165).

This discussion has made it clear that state sovereignty is historically
specific: its meaning changes over time and space. It is no longer, and really
never was, absolute and indivisible. The concept of the sovereignty of the state
continues to be important, if for no other reason than that state leaders invoke
it, but we must distinguish myth from reality: sovereign authority increasingly
resides in a multitude of institutions, some complementing each other, some
contesting the authority of others. The state remains crucial, but if states are
to reassert their authority over the sphere of private exchanges ('the market')
they will have to do so in concert. This is one poignant meaning of the concept
of multilateralism (Cox and Sinclair 1996).

Regulation of world migration

As observed in the introduction to this chapter, global migration is hardly regu-
lated notwithstanding the activities of such organizations as the International
Labour Organisation (ILO), the International Organization for Migration
(IOM), the United Nations High Commissioner for Refugees (UNHCR) and
the Inter-Governmental Consultations on Asylum, Refugees and Migration
(IGC). There are several explanations for this perhaps surprising absence:

- the 'sovereignty' of the state: the sovereign state is assumed to be unwilling to relinquish control over those who cross its borders: 'Since the
  development of the modern state from the fifteenth century onward,
  governments have regarded control over their borders as the core of
  sovereignty' (Weiner 1995: 9);
- the modest scale of international migration: an estimate by the United
  Nations puts the world's foreign-born population for 1994 at 125
  million or 2 per cent of the world's population (see Table 3.2; also
  chapter 1);

- as explained above, unlike other commodities, labour of different countries often does not have to move across borders to compete (Fröbel et al. 1977; Harris 1995);
- finally, during the decades of 'embedded liberalism' states did not need to compete for scarce sources of labour, which was available in surplus quantities (Zolberg 1991: 309, 313–14).

The relative exception to this rule of course is the asylum framework circumscribed by the 1951 Geneva Convention and the 1967 Protocol (Loescher, Chapter 8 in this volume). The approach in the Geneva Convention clearly echoes the circumstances of the immediate post-war years in Europe, coloured as they were by the horrific experiences of Nazism and Stalinism. It replaced the post-First World War emphasis in refugee law on *collective* refugee problems (persecuted nationalities in the remains of the broken-up multinational empires of Russia, Austria–Hungary, and the Ottoman Empire) by the typically bourgeois liberal emphasis on *individual* persecution on the basis of ethnic origin, religious belief, and especially political conviction (Zolberg et al. 1989).

Since the beginning of the 1990s, there has been a dramatic change in the international system as compared to the years between 1945 and 1989. Global restructuring has eroded the inviolability of state sovereignty, the number of international migrants (especially refugees) rose dramatically after 1989, and global competition between labour forces and between states has rapidly increased as a reflection of intensifying global competition among the world's leading TNCs. The existing asylum framework was not equipped to deal with the consequences of state formation and the massive return to the persecution of newly created 'minorities' (Zolberg et al. 1989; Loescher 1993).

In the wake of these changes we can observe a growing trend towards convergence in the modes of migration regulation. This is true first of all because 'all of the world's various migratory streams are interconnected, and the policies of the various states pertaining to them are of necessity interactive' (Zolberg 1993: 54). Likewise, Saskia Sassen concludes that 'we are seeing a *de facto* transnationalising of immigration policy' (Sassen 1996a: 1), in which there is 'a displacement of government functions on to non-governmental or quasi-governmental institutions and criteria for legitimacy' (ibid. 24). Elsewhere, I have called this mode of governance *transnational regulation*, i.e. the governance of transnational activities and processes in ways and through means not reducible to (inter-)state activity alone, and involving a range of private and (semi-)public actors operating in a transnational arena, that is beyond rather than across (international) or above (supranational) national borders (Overbeek 1998: 90–1).

There are, however, no institutionalized governance structures (neither global, nor regional) for the effective regulation of transnational migration.

For instance, although Mexican migration to the USA is a crucial ingredient in the regional political economy and a very sensitive political issue between the two countries, and although the migration question was implicitly at the heart of the initiative to create the North American Free Trade Area (NAFTA), the NAFTA agreement contains only very weak references to the problems of migration (Martin et al., Chapter 6 in this volume). In other regions, too, the seeds of regionalized migration policies are being sown. In South-East Asia calls for regional migration policies are regularly heard in ASEAN, in South America similar concerns are raised in Mercosur, and in Southern Africa the member states of the Southern Africa Development Community have formulated a Protocol on the Facilitation of Movement of Persons (second draft, January 1997). However, these initiatives have yet to produce any tangible results.

Until now, the only operational regional frameworks are the emerging 'Puebla' framework in North and Central America and the more developed one in Europe. The European framework is a hybrid form, combining elements of intergovernmental regulation and more informal transnational coordination (for more detail, see Overbeek 1995, 1996). Let us briefly look at these frameworks in order to gain a better understanding of the direction in which developments are going.

Globalization, as we saw above, is an ambiguous and contradictory process: it produces universalizing as well as localizing tendencies, and in fact implies 'regionalization', i.e. the restructuring of the global political economy into macro-regions. Neoliberal regionalism in fact precisely highlights the essence of these developments: the combination of new forms of 'open regionalism' and neoliberal economic restructuring.

In the case of Europe, regionalism in the sphere of the regulation of migration has taken the form of a sharply restrictive (yet clearly selectively so) immigration regime. In fact, unwanted would-be immigrants travelling from or through states sharing borders with the EU are increasingly faced with a *cordon sanitaire* erected along the outer limits of the Union. To the south, the EU is constructing such a fence via the Euro-Mediterranean Partnership agreements concluded in Barcelona in late 1995, which include readmission agreements, border control cooperation, and aid. To the east, the Central and East European countries (Poland, Czech Republic, Slovakia, Hungary, and Slovenia, as well as Romania and Bulgaria and the Baltic states) have also signed readmission agreements with the EU, incorporated into the Europe Agreements. In exchange, the western states assist their neighbours both technically and financially to cope with the consequences of this policy. The result of this policy is rapidly becoming visible. The number of asylum applications in the countries of the European Union has fallen sharply since 1992. The countries in Central Europe, particularly the economically successful Czech Republic and Poland, have now themselves become attractive to tens of thousands of labour migrants from the Ukraine, Belarus, and beyond (Ghosh 1998).

The next stage in the regionalization process may well be the creation of a European Migration Convention as proposed by Austria (Meissner 1993: 65). A first step was taken in October 1991 in Berlin, when representatives of the European Union and the Visegrad countries, Bulgaria and Romania, agreed to closer cooperation on clandestine migration. This conference was followed by a second ministerial conference on illegal migration in the region held in Budapest in February 1993. As a follow-up to this 'Budapest process' Switzerland and Austria set up the International Centre for Migration Policy Development (ICMPD), located in Vienna (Widgren 1994: 53). The ICMPD serves as the Secretariat for the Budapest Group and prepared the agenda for the third Ministerial Conference of the Budapest Group held in October 1997 in Prague. This conference was attended by thirty-seven European states, the USA, and representatives of ten international organizations concerned in one way or another with the combating of illegal migration and human trafficking. The Budapest process furthermore entails countless informal meetings by Working Groups, Expert Meetings, etc. Although formally an intergovernmental process, the secrecy involved allows the governments concerned considerable freedom of manœuvre (Overbeek 1999).

The 'Puebla Process' started with the 1996 Regional Conference on Migration held at Puebla (Mexico), in which ten North and Central American countries took part (with others present as observers). The initiative dates back to earlier discussion in the region in 1990 (the Punto Arenas agreement) and to the NAFTA agreement. Just as the Budapest Process, the Puebla's Process central concern is the issue of illegal migration and trafficking of migrants. Puebla is linked to the initiative to extend NAFTA into a Free Trade Area of the Americas (FTAA) (see Pellerin 1999).

Immigration policies, it becomes clear, take shape at the intersection of economic and political considerations. If one of the essential functions of the modern state is to 'govern the economy' in order to guarantee the conditions for capital accumulation and the supply of sufficient employment and income opportunities to its population, then the process of global restructuring has made the state into a less and less effective guarantor. At the same time, this growing inability of the national state to provide sufficient employment and income undermines the legitimacy of the political structures. Governments are increasingly subject to contradictory forces and tendencies as a result.

The *economic* imperatives of global restructuring and competition dictate new structures of 'flexible accumulation', with a reduction in the power of organized labour and a deregulation of labour markets. A certain level of irregular immigration is functional for this purpose, which explains why governments are reluctant to sanction the employers of illegal labour (Harris 1995: 25–49). In Germany studies have shown that a 1 per cent increase in the share of less-skilled foreign workers in the labour force leads to a 5.9 per cent fall in the wages of blue-collar workers, and a 3.5 per cent increase in white-collar wages. Similar results emerge from studies in the USA (Ghosh 1999: 18). On the *political* side, the logic of democratic welfare state politics induces politicians to close the borders more tightly in fear of electoral losses. The contradiction is grasped eloquently by Gary Freeman who wrote:

National welfare states are compelled by their logic to be closed systems that seek to insulate themselves from external pressures and that restrict rights and benefits to members. They nonetheless fail to be perfectly bounded in a global economy marked by competition, interdependence and extreme inequality. . . . relatively free movement of labour across national frontiers exposes the tension between closed welfare states and open economies and . . . ultimately, national welfare states cannot coexist with the free movement of labour.' (Freeman 1986: 51)

The consequences of 'open regionalism' and neoliberal restructuring in terms of the degree of democratic control with respect to these developments are worrying, as a small digression on European asylum policies makes clear. The main European instruments developed to deal with the migration 'crisis' of 1989–92 were the Schengen Treaty and the Dublin Convention. The Schengen Execution Agreement of 1990 (which came into effect in March 1995)[7] purports to determine the responsibility for examining asylum requests within Schengenland, which is assigned as a rule to the country of first entry into the EU. The Dublin 'Convention Determining the State Responsible for Examining Applications for Asylum lodged in one of the Member States of the European Communities' does the same, but in this case for all members of the European Union.

These 'common' policies were essentially constituted *outside* the framework of the European Union: European policy in this field was not supranational (communitarian), but intergovernmental. This approach was confirmed in the Treaty on European Union (Maastricht Treaty), where only visa policy was brought under the 'first pillar', the communitarian regime. All other matters concerning immigration and asylum were placed under the Third Pillar, the intergovernmental mechanisms for dealing with matters of domestic security, police, terrorism, etc. (while the Second Pillar, also intergovernmental, deals with foreign policy and defence issues) (Collinson 1993: 110–15). The Treaty of Amsterdam has brought a cosmetic change, but no more than that: immigration and asylum matters have been moved to a separate title on 'Free movement of persons, asylum and immigration' in which Community institutions will have a role. However, decision-making will be subjected to the require-

---

[7] The Schengen agreement was initially concluded between five states (the Benelux, France, and Germany) and has now been joined by all but two EU members (Britain and Ireland will stay out of 'Schengenland') and also by Norway and Iceland.

ment of unanimity which may be changed after five years to a qualified majority rule only if there is unanimity on that change. In fact therefore, the strictly
intergovernmental mode of decision-making has been prolonged for at least
another five years (see van Selm 1998 for details).

Neoliberal restructuring of the global economy involves both the further-
ing of the 'free movement' of goods, services, and capital, and the disciplining
of labour. When considering the question of the governance of migration we
are therefore confronted with a paradox: the free movement of production
factors in liberal practice does not extend to labour (Hollifield, chapter 3 in
this volume): its movement is strictly regulated by the state. This contradiction is compellingly caught by Stephen Gill's phrase 'disciplinary neoliberalism' (Gill 1995). There is clearly a tension here between regulating migration
under the auspices of global neoliberalism on the one hand, and upholding
the values of democratic governance on the other. When we turn to discuss
the contours of a possible new comprehensive framework for the regulation
of global migration in the next section, we shall therefore emphasize the
importance of democratic multilateralism as a safeguard against downward
harmonization through disciplinary neoliberal policy competition.

Reshaping the governance of international migration

The foundation-stone [of this work] is and must remain the State. Respect for its
fundamental sovereignty and integrity are crucial to any common international
progress. The time of absolute and exclusive sovereignty, however, has passed; its
theory was never matched by its reality. It is the task of leaders of States today to
understand this and to find a balance between the needs of good internal governance
and the requirements of an ever more interdependent world. (Boutros Boutros-Ghali,
An Agenda for Peace, 1992)

There are good reasons to be very negative about the prospects for the development of 'a more equitable code of conduct in the sphere of international
migrations' (Zolberg 1991: 320). But even if in the short run the prospects are
not good, it is still worthwhile to reflect on what the analysis presented in this
chapter implies for attempts to find the balance that Boutros-Ghali spoke of.

First, although this volume focuses on ideas for an international migration
policy, it must be made clear that unless such an effort is embedded in a more
general effort to address the underlying causes especially of all forms of involuntary migration, any such effort will inevitably result in the codification of
the existing extremely restrictive immigration practices of most of the countries of immigration. More concretely, this would imply that the international
community must address

- the structural inequities in the global political economy producing

and/or reproducing poverty among two-thirds of the world's population (such as unequal exchange, the dumping of agricultural surpluses, etc.);
- the global arms trade which fuels many of the refugee-producing conflicts around the globe;
- the neo-colonial political interference in (if not initiation of) regional and local conflicts by major powers.

Second, at the level of the global community as a whole, a comprehensive International Migration Framework Convention must be created to set forth and guarantee the general principles governing the regulation of transnational migrations, to ensure a sufficient degree of coordination between regional migration regimes, and to deal with those migratory movements that cannot be covered in a regional setting. There are three major components in such a regime.

The *institutional framework* to be developed at the world (and regional) level must be democratic, i.e. transparent and responsive to the needs of migrants as well as to those of the participating states. This might be accomplished by involving, besides the institution most obviously suited to play a key role here, namely the International Organization for Migration, international non-governmental organizations (humanitarian organizations, representative associations of migrants and refugees, etc.) in the formulation of norms and rules and in the processes of supervision and control (advisory councils, boards of governors, etc.). The Charter of the United Nations provides us with a model: article 71 creates the possibility for ECOSOC to collaborate with NGOs, and the practices developed under this provision of the UN Charter may be adapted to suit the global migration framework.

The *asylum and refugee framework* providing the basis for the existing international refugee regime (i.e. the 1951 Geneva Convention and the 1967 New York Protocol) must be amended to take into account the altered nature of international refugee movements. Here the proposals put forward by Zolberg, Suhrke, and Aguayo (1989) may serve as a starting point. They propose to introduce as the central principle 'the immediacy and degree of life-threatening violence' (p. 270) in order to afford protection to the 'victims' on an equal footing with the more common subjects of present asylum law, the 'activists' and the 'targets'. The United Nations High Commissioner for Refugees (UNHCR) is destined to be the lead global institution here. As regards asylum policies of the OECD countries in particular (this in light of their recent record), it must be emphasized that asylum seekers who are denied recognition as refugees yet are not returned to their home country must be given a legal status enabling them to build a new life rather than be forced to go underground. Otherwise the governments themselves 'produce' illegal migrants.

An equivalent *framework for voluntary migration* (permanent and temporary) must be created in which states undertake to bring their national immigration policies in accordance with an internationally negotiated harmonized set of criteria formulated to safeguard the interests of migrants as well as the interests of the signatory states. The existing provisions of ILO Conventions and the GATS should be incorporated into such a framework, which might also borrow relevant provisions from the Conventions concluded under the authority of the Council of Europe. Although its early conclusion seems increasingly uncertain, the draft Multilateral Agreement on Investments (MAI) contains provisions that have a bearing on the movement of people and consequently further negotiations of an MAI should take into account what has already been achieved in the migration field. Leading roles in this area are for the International Labour Organisation and the International Organization for Migration. One important principle to be followed here is that the legal position of long-term residents must be improved. Both the return of migrants to their home countries and their effective integration into the host society are obstructed by their insecure status (i.e. by the difficulty in many host countries to gain full membership in the welfare state and by the difficulties they encounter upon return to their home country). These problems could be substantially reduced, for instance, by expanding the possibilities for dual citizenship or by allowing reimmigration with full retention of rights in case of failed return migration. Several countries have recently increased these possibilities (e.g. Mexico, Turkey, France, Great Britain, and Brazil) while others contemplate doing so (South Korea, the Philippines), and discussion about these themes especially in the major countries of immigration (the USA and Germany in particular) make it clear that a multilateral approach with a balanced distribution of advantages and costs would greatly enhance the chances of success.

Third, Regional Migration Conventions must provide the institutional and operational settings in which to specify and operationalize the general principles set out in the global frameworks. It would seem that only in regional settings will it be possible to formulate effective instruments to deal with such undesirable developments as the increasing role of organized crime in the trafficking of people (and drugs and arms). As with the Prohibition in the 1930s, an exclusively repressive policy only raises the price of the prohibited good (in this case access to the labour markets of the OECD countries) without substantially reducing the flow.

These regional regimes may be embodied in Regional Migration Conventions, incorporating

- regional development, educational and employment initiatives
- preferential trade agreements
- effective measures against human trafficking

- agreements on the readmission of illegal migrants
- arrangements for temporary labour migration
- quota for permanent migration
- return migration schemes
- improvement of the legal position of migrants in host countries.

In the light of the analysis in earlier sections of this chapter it is important to emphasize the importance of an integral and comprehensive approach. If certain elements, such as the provisions relating to the entry of temporary labour, are realized in isolation from the other elements and principles, this is bound to serve only the interests of the employers looking for cheap workers. Public governance of these processes must guarantee the balance between the various elements of the Conventions.

Finally, let us return to the point of departure of this contribution: *commodification*. This chapter's unspoken thesis has been that there is a possibly irreconcilable tension between unchecked *commodification* on the one hand and humankind's *emancipation* from bondage and deprivation on the other. To guard against the risk that orderly regulation of migration privileges further commodification over emancipation, it is essential to stress the need for transparency and accountability in the institutional set-up and for consensual multilateralism instead of de facto bilateralism. Karl Polanyi was right to see that capitalism oscillates between *laissez-faire* and *social protection* (Polanyi 1957). The forces profiting from laissez-faire as we have seen can fend for themselves. It is the ordinary people of the world who need the protection of democratic public institutions, both at the national and at the global level.

REFERENCES

In the text there are references to two migration news journals: *Migration News Sheet* which is published monthly by the Churches' Commission for Migrants in Europe (CCME) in Brussels, and *Migration News*, which is produced monthly by the University of California at Davis and may be accessed via Internet on the Migration News Home Page: http://migration.ucdavis.edu

Carr, E. H. (1964), *The Twenty Years' Crisis 1919–1939: An Introduction to the Study of International Relations*, New York: Harper & Row, orig. edn. 1939, 1945.
Castells, M. (1998), *The Information Age: Economy, Society and Culture III: End of Millennium*, Oxford: Blackwell Publishers.
Cohen, R., and Deng, F (1998), *Masses in Flight: The Global Crisis of Internal Displacement*, Washington, DC: Brookings Institution.
Collinson, S. (1993), *Europe and International Migration*, London: RIIA/Pinter.

Cox, R.W. (1987), *Production, Power and World Order: Social Forces in the Making of History*, New York: Columbia University Press.

Cox, R.W. (1996), 'A Perspective on Globalization', in Mittelman, J. 1996: 21–30.

—— and Sinclair, T. J. (1996), *Approaches to World Order*, Cambridge: Cambridge University Press.

ECRE/ENAR/MPG (1999), *Guarding Standards—Shaping the Agenda*, Brussels: European Council on Refugees and Exiles/European Network against Racism/Migration Policy Group.

Freeman, G. P. (1986), 'Migration and the Political Economy of the Welfare State', *Annals of the American Academy, AAPSS*, 485: 51–63.

Fröbel, F., Heinrichs, J., and Kreye, O. (1977), *Die neue internationale Arbeitsteilung: Strukturelle Arbeitslosigkeit in den Industrieländern und die Industrialisierung der Entwicklungsländer*, Hamburg: Rowohlt.

Gerbier, B. (1995), 'Globalisation ou régionalisation?', *Économies et Sociétés*, Hors Série no. 33, 11/95, 29–55.

Ghosh, B. (1998), 'East West Migration: Trends and Policy Perspectives', paper prepared for the Conference on 'Europe: The New Melting Pot', Nanovic Institute for European Studies, University of Notre Dame, Indiana, 22–4 Mar. 1998.

—— (1999), 'Challenges and Opportunities of Economic Globalisation: Some Implications for Labour, Industry and Nation-States', paper prepared for the Bundesanstalt für Arbeit Workshop on 'Internationalisierung der Arbeitsmärkte', 27–8 Apr., Frankfurt a/M.

Gill, S. R. (1992), 'The Emerging World Order and European Change: The Political Economy of European Union', in R. Miliband and L. V. Panitch (eds.), *Socialist Register 1992*, London: Merlin Press, 157–95.

—— (1995), 'Globalisation, Market Civilisation, and Disciplinary Neoliberalism', *Millennium: Journal of International Studies*, 24/3: 399–423.

Gordon, D. M. (1988), 'The New Global Economy: New Edifice or Crumbling Foundations?', *New Left Review*, 168 (Mar.–Apr.), 24–64.

Hamilton, K. A. (ed.) (1994), *Migration and the New Europe*, Washington, DC: Center for Strategic and International Studies.

Harris, N. (1995), *The New Untouchables: Immigration and the New World Worker*, London: Penguin Books.

Hirst, P., and Thompson, G. (1996), *Globalization in Question: The International Economy and the Possibilities of Governance*, Cambridge: Polity Press.

Holm, H.-H., and Sørensen, G. (eds.) (1995), *Whose World Order? Uneven Globalization and the End of the Cold War*, Boulder, Colo.: Westview Press.

Loescher, G. (1993), *Beyond Charity: International Cooperation and the Global Refugee Crisis*, Oxford: Oxford University Press.

Luciani, L. (ed.) (1993), *Migration Policies in Europe and the United States*, The Hague: Kluwer.

Meissner, D., et al. (1993), *International Migration Challenges in a New Era: Policy Perspectives and Priorities for Europe, Japan, North America and the International Community*, The Triangle Papers No. 44, New York/Paris/Tokyo: The Trilateral Commission.

Mittelman, J. H. (ed.) (1996), *Globalization: Critical Reflections*, International Political Economy Yearbook vol. 9, Boulder, Colo: Lynne Rienner Publ.

Niessen, J., and Mochel, F. (1999), *EU External Relations and International Migration*, Brussels: Migration Policy Group.

OECD (1996), *OECD Economic Outlook*, No. 60, Paris: OECD.

OECD SOPEMI (1998), *Trends in International Migration*, Paris: OECD.

Oman, C. (1996), *The Policy Challenges of Globalisation and Regionalisation*, OECD Development Centre Policy Brief No. 11, Paris: OECD.

Overbeek, H. W. (1995), 'Globalization and the Restructuring of the European Labour Markets: The Role of Migration', in M. Simai (ed.), *Global Employment: An International Investigation into the Future of Work*, London: Zed Books and United Nations University Press, 204–18.

—— (1996), 'L'Europe en quête d'une politique en matière de migration: les contraintes de la mondialisation et de la restructuration des marchés du travail', *Études internationales*, 27/1 (Mar.), 53–80.

—— (1998), 'Global Restructuring and Neoliberal Labor-Market Regulation in Europe', *International Journal of Political Economy*, 28/1 (Spring), 54–99.

—— (1999), *The Budapest Process: Internationalization of Migration Controls*, paper presented at the 40th Annual Conference of the International Studies Association, 16–20 Feb., Washington. DC.

Panitch, L. V. (1996), 'Rethinking the Role of the State', in Mittelman 1996: 83–113.

Pellerin, H. (1999), 'The Cart before the Horse? The Coordination of Migration Policies in the Americas and the Neoliberal Economic Project of Integration', *Review of International Political Economy*, 6, forthcoming.

Polanyi, K. (1957), *The Great Transformation: The Political and Economic Origins of Our Time*, Boston: Beacon Press, orig. edn. 1944.

Poulantzas, N. (1974), *Les Classes sociales dans le capitalisme aujourd'hui*, Paris: Le Seuil.

Pijl, K. van der (1998), *Transnational Classes and International Relations*, London/New York: Routledge.

Rosenberg, J. (1994), *The Empire of Civil Society: A Critique of the Realist Theory of International Relations*, London/New York: Verso.

Ruggie, J. G. (1989), 'International Structure and International Transformation: Space, Time, and Method', in E.-O. Czempiel and J. N. Rosenau (eds.), *Global Changes and Theoretical Challenges: Approaches to World Politics for the 1990s*, Lexington, Mass.: Lexington Books, 21–35.

—— (1993), 'Territoriality and beyond: Problematizing Modernity in International Relations', *International Organization*, 47/1: 139–74.

—— (1998), *Constructing the World Polity: Essays on International Institutionalization*, London/New York: Routledge.

Sassen, S. (1996a), *Transnational Economies and National Migration Policies*, Amsterdam: IMES.

—— (1996b), *Losing Control? Sovereignty in an Age of Globalization*, New York: Columbia University Press.

Selm, J. van (1998), 'Asylum in the Amsterdam Treaty: A Harmonious Future?', *Journal of Ethnic and Migration Studies*, 24/4 (Oct.), 627–38.

United Nations Conference on Trade and Development (UNCTAD) (1993), *World Investment Report 1993: Transnational Corporations and Integrated International Production*, New York/Geneva: United Nations.

—— (1994), *Transnational Corporations, Employment and the Workplace: An Executive Summary*, New York/Geneva: United Nations.

United Nations Conference on Trade and Development (UNCTAD) (1998), *World Investment Report 1998: Trends and Determinants*, New York/Geneva: United Nations.

UNCTAD/IOM (1996), *Foreign Direct Investment, Trade, Aid and Migration*, Geneva: United Nations, Current Studies Series A No. 29, Unctad/DTCI/27.

United Nations High Commissioner for Refugees (1997), *The State of the World's Refugees: A Humanitarian Agenda*, Oxford: Oxford University Press.

Wallerstein, I. (1974), *The Modern World System I: Capitalist Agriculture and the Origins of the European World-Economy in the Sixteenth Century*, New York: Academic Press.

Weiner, M. (1995), *The Global Migration Crisis: Challenge to States and to Human Rights*, New York: HarperCollins College Publishers.

Weiss, L. (1998), *The Myth of the Powerless State: Governing the Economy in a Global Era*, Cambridge: Polity Press.

Widgren, J. (1994), 'Shaping a Multilateral Response to Future Migrations', in Hamilton 1994: 37–55.

World Bank (1999), *World Development Report 1998/99: Knowledge for Development*, Washington: World Bank.

Zolberg, A. R. (1991), 'Bounded States in a Global Market: The Uses of International Labor Migrations', in P. Bourdieu and J. S. Coleman (eds.), *Social Theory for a Changing Society*, Boulder, Colo.: Westview Press, 301–25.

—— (1993), 'Are the Industrial Countries under Siege?', in L. Luciani (ed.), *Migration Policies in Europe and the United States*, The Hague: Kluwer, 53–81.

—— Suhrke, A., and Aguayo, S. (1989), *Escape from Violence: Conflict and the Refugee Crisis in the Developing World*, Oxford: Oxford University Press.

Zürn, Michael (1995), 'The Challenge of Globalization and Individualization: A View from Europe', in Holm and Sörensen 1995: 137–64.

4

Migration and the 'New' International Order: The Missing Regime

James F. Hollifield

Introduction

From the founding of the Bretton Woods exchange rate system (1944) through the conclusion of the last (Uruguay) round of GATT talks in the 1990s, the post-war international order has been marked by multilateralism and the building of liberal regimes for trade and finance. These regimes in turn have reduced the risks of openness for national economies and they have stimulated international exchange across the board. Like trade, portfolio, and foreign direct investment, international migration has increased dramatically in the post-war period; but, with the notable exception of refugees, no liberal regime for migration has emerged. Why has migration continued at such high levels in the absence of a regime and in the face of cyclical downturns?

Economists have long argued that exposure to trade leads to increased competition and efficiency, resulting in greater specialization in production, and a wider and cheaper range of goods available to consumers. Likewise, mobility of productive factors (labour and capital) and the reduction of trans-action costs are seen as essential to the smooth functioning of markets. In the case of trade, the GATT regime was constructed through a multilateral process with most favoured nation status (MFN), non-discrimination, and reciprocity as the organizing principles. In the case of international finance, exchange rate stability has been pursued unilaterally (by the USA during the early Bretton Woods period) and multilaterally through the IMF and World Bank. Both institutions have worked to solve problems of liquidity and adjustment as they arise. In each case, the international community seems to have accepted these goals/goods as indivisible, and herculean political efforts have been made to solve free rider problems.

An earlier version of this chapter was published in the *UCLA Journal of International Law & Foreign Affairs*. 3/2 (Fall/Winter 1998–9), 595–636.

Even though similar economic efficiency arguments can be made in favour of international mobility of skilled and unskilled labour, no liberal regime for international labour migration has emerged. Nation states are reluctant to expose their economies and societies to exogenous, competitive pressures, more so in the area of migration than in the areas of trade and finance. It is only at certain points in time and under certain political-economic conditions that states have been willing to take the risk of being more open. How can we explain the opening and closing of borders over time, and does openness to labour migration co-vary with openness to trade and investment? Is international labour migration simply a function of the ongoing process of globalization of economies and societies, or is it linked to changes in international and domestic politics?

This chapter argues that openness to migration is heavily dependent upon (1) ideational and institutional factors, especially rights, which influence citizenship and national identity, (2) domestic political alignments and interests that are determined in part by factor proportions and intensities in economic production, and (3) the structure of the international system, including the presence or absence of international regimes. In contrast to transnational or globalization arguments about the weakening of the sovereignty of the nation state, this chapter offers evidence in support of a (modified) neoliberal argument, which stresses the role of institutions and rights; but without abandoning the central precepts of realist theory that states are rational actors and that they will pursue their interests within the confines of the international system, which is structured by the distribution of power. Finally, the chapter develops a model of strategic interaction and decision-making in order to specify and compare the conditions under which a new international regime for the orderly movement of people (NIROMP) might be developed.

Regulating international trade and migration

The first rule of political economy is that markets do not and cannot exist in the absence of regulation. This is true at the national as well as the international level. But intervention to establish and maintain markets for goods, services, capital, *and labour* is more complicated at the international level, because no central authority exists to guarantee contracts, ensure exchange rate stability, and maintain free trade. The economic historian, Charles Kindleberger, who served as a staff economist for the Marshall Plan, was one of the first to point out the importance of having a leader in the international economy willing to shoulder the responsibility for establishing and maintaining a free trading system.[1]

---

[1] See Kindleberger 1973.Kindleberger's argument evolved into what is now called 'hege-

Another difficulty of sustaining international markets arises from the collective action problem of finding a basis for cooperation among a diverse group of states in an ever changing international system. With the collapse of the Bretton Woods system, the decline of American hegemony in the 1970s, and the end of the Cold War in the 1990s, multilateralism[2] has replaced reliance on American political and economic power as the cornerstone of the international political economy. Likewise, as Ronald Rogowski and others have demonstrated (Rogowski 1989; Milner 1997), trade can have a dramatic effect on domestic political alignments, making it difficult to maintain support for international economic policies, even in the most outward-looking states, like Great Britain in the nineteenth century or the USA in the post-Second World War period.

Nevertheless, liberal states have found ways to overcome these hurdles, primarily through multilateralism and the building of international institutions, which help to lock even the most protectionist states into a more open world economy. Constant political battles are fought to prevent and defeat isolationist and protectionist coalitions. Why do states and their political leaders do this? Simply put, because they recognize the enormous advantages of free trade and open investment regimes. In the 1990s, many recalcitrant third world states have jumped on the free trade band wagon, despite the tremendous asymmetries in the world economy between the richest and poorest states.

But if the logic of trade and finance is one of openness, the logic of migration tends to be one of closure. From a political standpoint, international migration is the mirror image of international trade and finance. The wealthier states push hard to keep the lines of trade and investment open, while the poorer states are more sceptical, fearing dependency. With migration, it is the opposite: by and large, the wealthier states push hard to keep foreigners out, usually for reasons of national security or identity; whereas many poorer states want to export people, to reap the benefit of remittances or simply to maintain a social safety valve.

Yet from an economic standpoint, it is exceedingly difficult to separate trade and investment from migration. The movement of goods, services, and capital increasingly entails the movement of labour, especially but not exclusively on the high end of the labour market. Conventional economic wisdom

---

monic stability theory', where in the words of Robert Keohane 'hegemonic structures of power, dominated by a single country, are most conducive to the development of strong international regimes whose rules are relatively precise and well obeyed . . . the decline of hegemonic structures of power can be expected to presage a decline in the strength of corresponding international economic regimes.' Quoted in Gilpin 1986: 72.

[2] John Ruggie defines multilateralism in terms of three criteria: indivisibility, generalized principles of conduct, and diffuse reciprocity. Ruggie 1993, Part I.

has it that in the long run, trade can substitute for migration, through a process of factor-price equalization.[3] But in the short run, historical and empirical studies demonstrate that free trade can lead to increased migration, especially when disparities in wages and incomes are very high, as between the USA and Mexico, for example (Martin 1995). Although paradoxical, the reasons for this are simple: when backward economies are exposed to strong exogenous competitive pressures, the agricultural sector can collapse, leading to a rural exodus, swelling the population of cities, and increasing pressures to emigrate. Likewise, increased trade in services leads to high-end migration, because technical and professional staff are integral parts of the service. The relationship between trade and migration is in fact very complex; and restrictions on one can lead to increased pressure on the other. With greater economic interdependence, migration has become more transnational, as individuals and groups move back and forth across national boundaries, blurring the distinction between the home and host societies.

Sorting out winners and losers from migration is at least as complicated in the case of migration as in the case of trade. We can start from the basic premiss that migration is heavily dependent on factor proportions and intensities, and that groups will support or oppose migration depending upon whether they represent scarce or abundant factors. This is the political corollary of economic, push-pull arguments, which hold that cross-border movements of people have a strong economic dimension and that such movements are basically a function of demand-pull and supply-push factors.[4] There is little doubt that people move in search of better opportunities—however defined—and that the existence of markets, and information or kinship networks is a necessary condition for migration to occur. But the sufficient conditions for migration are political. States must be willing to open their borders for exit and entry; and such openness is not simply a function of interest group politics or cost-benefit analysis. Institutions play a crucial role in determining openness or closure.

As we can see in Table 4.1, there has been a continuous increase in the world migrant population, both in developed and developing countries and across regions, since 1945. This increase parallels similar increases in the volume of world trade and foreign investment,[5] despite the absence of an international migration regime. It would be tempting to conclude that migration is simply a part of the inexorable process of globalization and that states

---

[3] This is the Stolper-Samuelson theorem. Stolper and Samuelson 1941. Also Mundell, 1957.

[4] For a more in-depth discussion of the political economy of international migration, see Hollifield 1992a and Cornelius et al. 1994: 6–11.

[5] For the trends in trade, foreign direct investment, and migration, see UNCTAD 1995. Cf. also Rogowski 1989.

TABLE 4.1. *World migrant population, 1965–1994*

Region	1965	1975	1985	1990	1994	As % of total pop. 1994
Developed countries	30.3	38.2	47.8	54.1	56.7	4.9
North America	12.6	15.0	20.4	23.9	25.0	8.5
(refugees)					(0.7)	
Europe	14.6	19.4	22.8	24.9	26.1	3.6
(refugees)					(1.9)	
Asia	3.0	3.8	4.6	5.3	5.6	1.6
(refugees)					(0.05)	
LDCs	44.9	46.2	57.2	65.6	68.4	1.5
Sub-Saharan Africa	6.9	10.1	10.3	13.6	14.3	2.5
(refugees)					(6.8)	
Latin America	5.9	5.7	6.5	7.5	7.9	1.6
(refugees)					(0.1)	
Mid-East, South, and South-East Asia	31.6	29.8	39.7	43.8	45.9	1.4
(refugees)					(5.0)	
Oceania	0.1	0.1	0.2	0.3	0.3	1.4
(refugees)					(0.05)	4.4
Total	75.2	84.4	105.1	119.6	125.0	2.2
(refugees)					(14.5)	

Source: International Organization for Migration and UNCTAD. Millions of foreign born.

have little control over these movements of people.[6] The corollary of this globalization thesis is that migration will continue so long as there are economic imbalances in the international economy, or until the process of factor-price equalization is complete. But I shall argue that such a conclusion is not only simple and premature, but wrong. We must look more closely at political, institutional, and structural factors that govern international migration, ever mindful of the fact that economic pressures for migration are strong and will remain so for the foreseeable future. To do this, I propose (1) to examine some competing explanations for the continuous rise in international migration and (2) to develop a model of strategic interaction and decision-making to explain the conditions under which an international migration regime might develop.

[6] On the globalization thesis, see Sassen 1991 and 1996. On migration, globalization, and the rights of foreigners cf. Soysal 1994 and Jacobson 1996.

Realism and national security arguments

The most venerable theory of international relations is political realism. Robert Keohane succinctly summarizes the assumptions of this theory as follows: '(1) states (or city-states) are the key units of action; (2) they seek power, either as an end in itself or as a means to other ends; and (3) they behave in ways that are, by and large, rational, and therefore comprehensible to outsiders in rational terms' (Keohane 1986: 7). At first blush, political realism would seem to tell us little about international migration, other than the fact that states are sovereign, power-seeking units, which act in their own self-interest. As such, one would expect states to protect their sovereignty and maximize their power, by opening or closing their borders when it is in their national interest to do so. But this argument is not only dangerously close to being a tautology, it begs the question of why states at certain points in time open or close their borders.

As is often the case with such pure realist arguments, we are thrown back into an ad hoc analysis of state rationality, seeking to determine, for example, when it is in a state's national interest to open its borders and when it is not, or whether out- or in-migration will enhance the state's power and contribute to its national security. Neo-realist theory, which builds upon the basic assumptions of political realism, is somewhat more sophisticated and may offer us more insights into why states open and close their borders. The father of neorealism, Kenneth Waltz places great emphasis on the systemic nature of international politics, and the fact that the system is structured by anarchy and state behaviour is conditioned by the distribution of power within this anarchic system (Waltz 1979). States, according to Waltz, are caught in an inescapable security dilemma. Any policy which has a national security dimension must be made in response to the structure of the international system, if a state is to survive in a world characterized by anarchy and the 'war of all against all'. Using this perspective as a starting point, we must ask ourselves (1) whether or not international migration has a national security dimension and (2) to what extent are migration and migration policy structurally determined?

The second question may be somewhat easier to answer than the first, simply because we have seen a massive change in the international system with the end of the Cold War in 1990. If Waltz is correct, such a dramatic shift from a bipolar world to one characterized by unipolarity—the USA is the sole remaining superpower—should have an impact on migration and on the making of migration policy. This of course assumes that migration is a matter of 'high politics' and that the national security interests of states are at issue. What hypotheses can we derive from this theory? The first and most obvious concerns the effects of the end of the Cold War on East–West migration and refugee movements in particular. With more openness in the international system, we would expect migration to increase; but it may no longer be in the interest of the Western democracies to support a liberal international regime for refugees.

Prior to the end of the Cold War, the Western democracies, led by the USA, constructed a liberal regime for refugees, built on the 1951 Geneva Convention and the United Nations High Commissioner for Refugees. The principles of this regime are well known. They are (1) asylum (based on a well-founded fear of individual persecution), (2) *non-refoulement*, (3) protection, (4) non-discrimination, (5) international cooperation, and (6) a commitment to search for solutions to the problem of refugees. Arguably this regime was created in response to the horrors of the Second World War, which left millions of refugees and displaced persons scattered throughout Europe; but it was also a construct of the Cold War.[7] It was designed, in the late 1940s and early 1950s, to facilitate the flight of individuals from communist regimes. For the period from roughly 1950 to 1990, much of the openness of liberal democracies to migration can be explained with reference to the bipolar structure of the international system. Liberal states in particular felt compelled to cooperate in the building and maintenance of the refugee regime.

Following the realist logic, we would expect liberal states to back away from their commitments to asylum with the end of the Cold War; and overall levels of immigration should decline. Certainly, there is ample evidence in the 1990s that the commitment of liberal states to the international refugee regime, if not to human rights, has weakened. The Schengen Agreement in Europe suspended *non-refoulement* for those asylum seekers who transit through a 'safe' third country. The 1993 amendment of article 16 of the German Basic Law/Constitution eliminated the blanket right to asylum in that country. The 1996 immigration reforms in the United States restricted due process and equal protection for asylum seekers; and earlier the American President revoked the special status of Cuban refugees, who until 1995 enjoyed an automatic right to asylum. All of these changes indicate that liberal states are adjusting to new geopolitical realities and attempting to restrict migration from formerly communist states. It is no longer in the strategic interests of liberal states to promote refugee migration. But the larger question remains: will international migration decrease significantly now that the Cold War is over? It may be too early to tell. A quick glance at the numbers in Table 4.1, however, indicates little change in world migration, as late as 1994.

If we return to the more difficult question of whether or not migration can be defined as a national security issue, we quickly run into the limitations of

---

[7] The origins of the asylum regime actually date from the period immediately following the First World War and the creation of the League of Nations. See Goodwin-Gill 1996.

realist and neo-realist arguments. Perhaps the most eloquent argument in favour of treating migration as a national security issue has been made by Myron Weiner, who contends that migration can destabilize societies and regimes, especially in weaker third world states, but also in the more advanced industrial democracies (Weiner 1995). Third world states are particularly vulnerable, because their legitimacy may already be precarious and they do not have the political or economic capacity to absorb large numbers of immigrants in short periods of time. If we look again at Table 4.1, we can see that Weiner has a point. The number of migrants is much larger in developing than in developed countries, 68.4 compared to 56.7 million, as of 1994. The refugee crisis in the great lakes region of central Africa in the mid-1990s resulted in the destabilization of the Mobutu regime in Zaire, demonstrating how threatening such massive flows of refugees (in this case Hutus fleeing Rwanda) can be for some states. The fledgling democracy in Macedonia also was sorely tested by the exodus of ethnic Albanians from Kosovo during the 1999 Balkan War.

But Weiner extends his national security argument to the advanced industrial democracies, by pointing out that the fear of immigration among native populations should not be dismissed as merely irrational or xenophobic. Immigration, he contends, is threatening to many groups and individuals in these countries, whether on economic (foreigners take jobs from natives) or cultural (foreigners threaten the political and cultural cohesion of society and the nation) grounds. Again, if we look at Table 4.1, we can see that the number of migrants as a proportion of the total population is more than twice as high in 1994 in the developed (4.9 per cent) as opposed to the developing world (1.3 per cent). The numbers alone may contribute to some xenophobia. From Weiner's national security perspective, immigration can lead to crises of absorption wherein societies can be further divided and destabilized. He cites the example of racist violence in the newly unified Germany as an example of the dangers of too much migration in too short a period of time. Looking at the USA, Arthur Schlesinger Jr. and Samuel Huntington echo Weiner's concern for the solidarity and stability of Western democracies, when faced with large waves of immigration.[8] In addition to this 'cultural threat', migration also raises concerns about terrorism and drug trafficking, as well as environmental degradation that may result from overpopulation. Each of these 'threats' can and have been used by politicians as a justification for restricting international migration.

Some human capital arguments reflect the same national security logic,

[8] See Schlesinger 1992 and Huntington 1996: p. 45. Huntington writes 'Promoting the coherence of the West means . . . controlling immigration from non-Western societies, as every major European country has done and as the United States is beginning to do, and ensuring the assimilation into Western culture of the immigrants who are admitted.'

namely a concern for the power, wealth, and sovereignty of the nation state. A classic example is to be found in the works of George Borjas, who poses the question succinctly in the title of his best-known book, *Friends or Strangers*? His argument is that immigration policy should be driven by national economic interests, and these should determine whether migrants are friends or strangers. As an economist, Borjas uses a strict cost-benefit calculus to determine if migrants have the requisite skills (human capital) needed by the national economy (Borjas 1990). He goes on to argue that the American economy no longer needs a large pool of unskilled and uneducated (largely Mexican) immigrants, and every effort should be made to restrict the entry of this group. The argument suggests that waves of low-skilled immigration will contribute to inequalities in American society and further weaken the national economy. The realist element in this type of economic reasoning is not so clear as in Weiner's political formulation. If we adopt a strictly cost-benefit rationale, the interests involved in making immigration policy begin to look more like they belong in the realm of low rather than high politics; and it becomes increasingly difficult to make a national security argument for restriction.

For every economist like Borjas who makes an argument against immigration, we can find another economist (like the late Julian Simon) who makes an argument in favour of increased immigration (Simon 1989). Like any public policy in a democracy, immigration policy is to a large extent interest driven. A political scientist, Gary Freeman, has constructed a rational-choice/pluralist framework for explaining the difficulties that liberal democracies encounter in their attempts to restrict immigration. He argues that even though it may be in the national interest to restrict low-skilled immigration, this has been difficult because powerful business interests, ethnic lobbies, intellectuals, and others have captured the state, making it virtually impossible for governments to carry out what is (in his view) clearly in the interest of the nation and society as a whole, and what is demanded by the electorate and by public opinion (Freeman 1995: 881–97; Joppke 1998a: 266–93; see also chapter 3 in this volume).

All of these interest-based arguments (Borjas, Simon, Freeman) point to the difficulties of reducing migration to a national security issue. They also indicate the extent to which national security itself is a social construct. In the 'constructivist' perspective, the interests and identities of states are heavily influenced by a range of sociological factors; and they are constructed by the actors involved.[9] They are not—as realists would have us believe—purely a function of international systemic or structural factors, such as the distribution of power within the system. This would be doubly true for international migration, as compared to issues of trade and finance; because migration

---

[9] For a summary of the constructivist theory of international relations and national security, see Katzenstein 1996, especially the introduction by Katzenstein, pp. 1–32.

involves the movement of animate rather than inanimate commodities. Unlike goods and capital, people/foreigners have the potential to immediately and radically transform the culture and politics of societies in which they arrive.[10] Hence, as Myron Weiner has pointed out, migration *can* threaten the national security of the nation state. It is therefore not surprising that political debates over defining the national interest with respect to migration can be intense. But, no matter how hard we try, it is impossible to remove cultural and social factors from these debates, or to reduce the terms of the debate to a cost-benefit calculation. As Max Weber and Claude Lévi-Strauss remind us, all actions are not strictly economic or instrumental (Weber 1947; Lévi-Strauss 1966). Subjective and normative elements figure heavily in the construction of interests and national security.

Does this mean that we can dispense with realist perspectives on international migration? I shall argue that we cannot, for two reasons. First, we must recognize the constraints that structural factors impose upon states in their formulation of migration policies and their willingness to allow entry and exit. Migration policies are inextricably linked with foreign policies. The end of the Cold War and its impact on the international refugee regime is a case in point. Formerly communist states of the East stopped restricting exit, which compelled liberal democratic states in the West to impose new restrictions on entry. Secondly, we must recognize the primacy of sovereignty in international relations. With few exceptions, since the Peace of Westphalia in 1648, sovereignty and non-interference in the internal affairs of other states have been the central organizing principles of international relations—principles that are codified in international law.

The globalization thesis

The globalization thesis stems largely from works in economic sociology and the sociology of international relations, although some economists subscribe to it.[11] Globalization arguments stand at the other extreme from realism, which stresses the role of the nation state as the primary decision-making unit in international relations. The globalization thesis comes in a variety of shapes

[10] As Yossi Shain and Rey Koslowski have pointed out, international migration can create divided loyalties and transnational political communities. Shain stresses the rise of political diaspora, whereas Koslowski focuses on the emergence of dual nationality as a sign of the weakening of the nation-state. See Schain 1989 and Koslowski 1996.

[11] For an interesting and pithy critique of globalization by an economist, who names names, see Krugman 1996. Krugman is particularly disturbed by globalization arguments that stress the need for nations to be more competitive, which can quickly lead into zero-sum or mercantilist thinking about trade and other forms of international exchange.

and sizes, but they all share a common assumption: the regulatory power (and sovereignty) of the national state has been weakened by transnational, social, and economic forces, ranging from the internationalization of capital, to the rise of transnational communities, to the increasing importance of human rights in international relations. The nation state is no longer the sole, legitimate actor in international relations, if it ever was. Rather, the tables have been turned against the state, which is unable to control either transnational corporations—especially banks which move vast sums of capital around the globe—or migrants, who move in search of employment opportunities. The internationalization of capital, we are told, has provoked a radical restructuring of production, as national economies move up (or down) in the international product cycle. Production itself has been decentralized with the rise of new centres of power and wealth, which Saskia Sassen has dubbed 'the global city' (Sassen 1991; see also Henk Overbeek, chapter 3 in this volume).

According to Sassen and others, the rise of transnational economies has resulted in the creation of transnational communities, as workers are forced to move from one state to another in search of employment, often leaving family members behind. Such communities can be found at both the high and low end of the labour market, as individuals move with more or less ease from one national society to another. A great deal of research has been done to document this practice among Mexican immigrants to the United States. Douglas Massey was one of the first to point out the importance of transnational social networks in linking communities in the country of origin to those in the country of destination. These kinship and informational networks helped to instil confidence in potential migrants, thus raising their propensity to migrate and, in effect, lowering transaction costs for international migration.[12] Alejandro Portes argues that migrants have learned to use this 'transnational space' as a way to get around national, regulatory obstacles to their social mobility. He goes on to point out that changes in Mexican law to permit dual nationality may reinforce this type of behaviour, leading to ever larger transnational communities (Portes 1996; Portes and Bach 1985).

The rapid decline in transaction costs and the ease of communication and transportation have combined to render national migration policies obsolete. Indeed, the entire regulatory framework of the state with respect to labour and business has been shaken by the process of globalization. To compete in the new international market-place, business and governments in the OECD countries have been forced to deregulate and liberalize labour and capital markets, whereas less developed states have been thrown into debt crises, leading to the imposition of painful policies of structural adjustment, which in

---

[12] See Massey et al. 1987. For a cogent review of transnationalism and migration theory, see Portes 1997: 799–825.

turn cause more migration from poor to rich states.[13] A case in point is the financial crisis in Mexico in the mid-1990s, which led to the devaluation of the peso and a surge in emigration to the United States in the latter part of the decade (US Commission on Immigration Reform 1997).

Politics and the state have been factored out of international relations in these types of globalization arguments, most of which are inspired by world systems theory (Wallerstein 1974). Following on this apolitical logic, both trade and migration, which are closely linked, are largely a function of changes in the international division of labour; and states play at best only a marginal role in determining economic and social outcomes. The prime agents of globalization are transnational corporations and transnational communities, if not individual migrants themselves.[14] If states have such a minor role to play, any discussion of national interests, national security, sovereignty, or even citizenship would seem to be beside the point. But at least one group of sociologists has tried to bring politics and law, if not the nation state, back into the picture.

Recent works by Yasemin Soysal and David Jacobson focus on the evolution of rights for immigrants and foreigners. Both authors posit the rise of a kind of postnational regime for human rights wherein migrants are able to attain a legal status that somehow surpasses citizenship, which remains grounded in the logic of the nation state (Soysal 1994; Jacobson 1996). Jacobson, more so than Soysal, argues that individual migrants have achieved an international legal personality by virtue of various human rights conventions, and both authors view these developments as presenting a distinctive challenge to traditional definitions of sovereignty and citizenship. But Soysal in particular is careful not to use the term postnational or transnational citizenship, opting instead for the expression postnational membership. Wrestling with the contradictory nature of her argument, Soysal writes: 'Incongruously, inasmuch as the ascription and codification of rights move beyond national frames of reference, post-national rights remain organized at the national level ... the exercise of universalistic rights is tied to specific states and their institutions' (Soysal 1994).

Another sociologist, Rainer Bauböck is less circumspect. He argues simply that, given the dynamics of economic globalization, a new transnational/political citizenship is necessary and inevitable (Bauböck 1994). Bauböck draws on political and moral philosophy, especially Kant, in making his argument in favour of transnational citizenship. Like Soysal, he relies heavily on

---

[13] See Sassen 1996. Also Holm and Sörensen 1995. For a critique of the globalization perspective on migration, see Joppke (1998*b*).

[14] James Rosenau takes the globalization argument to its logical extreme, postulating the 'individualization of the world' and the rise of 'post-international politics'. See Rosenau 1990.

the recent history of international migration in Europe and the experience of the European Community/Union to demonstrate that migration has accompanied the process of economic growth and integration in Europe, and that these migrants, many of whom were guest workers, have achieved a rather unique status as transnational citizens. What all three of these authors (Soysal, Jacobson, and Bauböck) are attempting to do is to give some type of political and legal content to world systems and globalization arguments. But like Saskia Sassen, they see the nation state as essentially outmoded and incapable of keeping pace with changes in the world economy.

What do these theories tell us about migration policy (the opening and closing of societies) and the more or less continuous rise in international migration in the post-war period. At first glance, they would seem to account rather well for the rise in migration. Even though many of the globalization arguments, which draw heavily upon world systems theory, are neo-Marxist in orientation, they share many assumptions with conventional, neoclassical (push-pull) theories of migration. The first and most obvious assumption is that migration is caused primarily by dualities in the international economy. So long as these dualities persist, there will be pressures for individuals to move across national boundaries in search of better opportunities. But whereas many neoclassical economists (like the late Julian Simon) see this as pareto optimal—creating a rising tide that will lift all boats—many globalization theorists (like Sassen and Portes) view migration as further exacerbating dualities both in the international economy and in national labour markets. This variant of the globalization thesis is very close to the old Marxist argument that capitalism needs an industrial reserve army to surmount periodic crises in the process of accumulation.[15] As migration networks become more sophisticated and transnational communities grow in scope and complexity, migration should continue to increase, barring some unforeseen and dramatic fall in the demand for immigrant labour. Even then, some globalization theorists, like Wayne Cornelius, would argue that the demand for foreign labour is 'structurally embedded' in the more advanced industrial societies, which cannot function without access to a cheap and pliable foreign work force (Cornelius 1998).

The second (crucial) assumption that globalization theorists share with neoclassical economists is the relatively marginal role of the state in governing and structuring international migration. States can act to distort or delay the development of international markets (for goods, services, capital, and labour), but they cannot stop it. With respect to migration, national regulatory regimes and municipal law in general simply must accommodate the development of international markets for skilled and unskilled workers. To

---

[15] A version of the industrial reserve army argument can be found in Piore 1979. For a critique of this argument, see Hollifield 1992a: 19 ff.

talk about the opening and closing of societies is simply a non-starter in a 'global village'. Likewise, citizenship and rights can no longer be understood in their traditional national contexts. If we take the example of post-war West Germany, nationality and citizenship laws date from 1913 and, until the reforms of 1999, they retained kinship or blood (*jus sanguinis*) as the principal criterion for naturalization (Brubaker 1992: 165 ff.). But the very restrictionist citizenship regime did not prevent Germany from becoming the largest immigration country in Europe. Globalization theorists, like Sassen, Portes, and Soysal can explain this anomaly by reference to the structural demand for foreign labour in advanced industrial societies, the growth of networks and transnational communities, and the rise of postnational membership, which is closely tied to human rights regimes—what Soysal calls universal personhood. National citizenship and regulatory regimes would seem to explain little in the variation of migration flows or the openness (or closure) of German society.

A more fully developed critique of these arguments will be provided in the conclusion. But what can we retain at this point from globalization, as opposed to realist, arguments? The biggest shortcoming of the globalization thesis—in contrast to realism—is the weakness or in some cases the absence of any political explanation. The locus of power and change is in society and the economy. There is no place for states and national regulation in this framework. Almost everything is socially and economically determined. The next section reviews neoliberal arguments, which, unlike realism, leave room for economic explanations and, unlike globalization theory, neoliberal theory also leaves room for politics and the state in explanations for the rise of international migration.

Neoliberalism and international regimes

Neoliberal arguments, often referred to among international relations theorists as liberal institutionalism, are heavily rationalist and they have some things in common with neorealism. Both schools of thought stress the primacy of interests, the major difference being that neoliberals want to disaggregate the 'national interest', and to look at the multiplicity of social and economic groups which compete to influence the state. For neoliberals, both national and international politics can be reduced to an economic game, and ultimately to a problem of collective action. To understand this (means-ends) game, all that is needed is to correctly identify the interests and preferences of social, economic, and political actors.[16] Not surprisingly, neoliberal theorists

[16] A representative example of neoliberal theorizing can be found in Milner 1997: 33–66.

focus almost exclusively on politics and policy in liberal states, where the competition among groups is relatively open and unfettered by authoritarianism and corruption. Studying competition among groups at the domestic level, as well as the allocational and distributional consequences of policy, presents a clearer picture of why states behave the way they do in the international arena, whether in the areas of trade, finance, or migration.

Since this approach incorporates both economic and political analysis, it has come to be called international political economy (IPE). IPE theorists are very interested in the connections between domestic and international politics. In addition to focusing on domestic interests, they also stress the importance of institutions in determining policy outcomes. For one of the original IPE theorists, Robert Keohane, institutions hold the key to explaining the puzzle of conflict and cooperation in international relations, especially with the weakening of American hegemony in the last decades of the twentieth century. Along with Joseph Nye, Keohane argued that increases in economic interdependence in the post-war period have had a profound impact on international relations, altering the way states behave and the way in which they think about and use power (Keohane and Nye 1977). In the nuclear age and with growing interdependence, it became increasingly difficult for states to rely on traditional military power in order to guarantee their security; because security was tied more and more to economic power, and nuclear weapons fundamentally altered the nature of warfare. The challenge for states (especially liberal states) was how to construct a new world order to promote national interests that were tied ever more closely to international trade and investment, if not to migration.

In the first two decades after the Second World War, this problem was solved essentially by the United States, which took it upon itself to reflate the world economy and to provide liquidity for problems of structural adjustment. This approach to international political economy was dubbed hegemonic stability (Kindleberger 1973; Gilpin 1986). But with the gradual decline of American economic dominance in the 1970s, the problem arose of how to organize world markets in the absence of a hegemon. The answer would be found, according to Robert Keohane, John Ruggie, and others, in multilateralism and the building of international institutions and regimes (like GATT and the IMF) to solve the problems of international cooperation and collective action (Keohane and Milner 1996). As the Cold War waned in the 1980s, the entire field of international relations shifted dramatically away from the study of national security towards the study of international economics, especially issues of trade and finance. In the last decades of the twentieth century, even domestic politics, according to IPE theorists, has been thoroughly internationalized.[17]

---

[17] See Keohane and Milner 1996.

Despite the fact that international migration would seem to lend itself to neoliberal arguments (migration has a strong political-economic dimension and it clearly contributes to the internationalization of domestic politics), very little has been written about it from this perspective.[18] The reasons for this are fairly simple. Until recently, there was little demand for international policy in the area of migration, with the major exception of refugees, noted above. Even for the refugee regime, the numbers were relatively modest until the 1980s, and the incentives for cooperation among liberal states were closely linked to the Cold War and the bipolar structure of the international system. From the late 1940s to the 1970s, liberal states had little incentive to cooperate or to build regimes for managing labour migration; because there was an unlimited supply of (unskilled) labour available, which could be recruited through bilateral agreements with the sending countries. The German *Gastarbeiter* (1960s) and the American *bracero* (1940s to the 1960s) programmes are classic examples of these types of bilateral accords. We did, however, see more innovation in the area of refugee policy, especially in Europe where states came together to find ways to slow the influx of asylum seekers. The Dublin Convention and the Schengen Accords have helped to harmonize asylum policy in Western Europe, creating a border-free Europe, but one where every member state is responsible for policing a common external border.

But the situation with respect to international labour migration has not changed that much in the 1980s and 1990s, despite the end of the Cold War. There is still an unlimited and rapidly growing supply of cheap labour available in developing countries. What has changed, however, are the goals of immigration and refugee policies among the OECD states. The demand now is for policies to control, manage, or stop migration and refugee flows. The Cold War refugee regime, specifically UNHCR, has come under enormous pressure to manage various refugee crises, from the Cambodians in Thailand, to the Kurds in Iraq, to the Hutus in Zaire (now the Republic of Congo), to the Albanians fleeing Kosovo. Existing international organizations for dealing with economic migration, such as the IOM and the ILO in Geneva, have not been besieged by demands for action. With the major exception of Western Europe, which has developed a regional regime for migration, there has been little effort to regulate international labour migration on a multilateral basis.

What can neoliberal theory tell us about the development of international migration and the willingness of states to risk exposing their economies to cooperate in building a new international regime for the movement of people (NIROMP)? The *first hypothesis* that we can derive from neoliberal theory is

---

[18] For an early attempt to use the IPE framework for understanding migration, see Hollifield, 1992*b*: 568–95. For a more recent and purely IPE study of migration, see Kessler 1997.

that states are more willing to risk opening their economies to trade (and by extension migration), if there is some type of international regime (or hegemonic power) that can regulate these flows and solve collective action and free rider problems. However, as I have pointed out above, there is no regime for regulating migration that comes close to the type of regime that exists (GATT/WTO) for trade, or for international finance (IMF/World Bank). Yet we know that migration has increased steadily throughout the post-war period, in the absence of a regime or any type of effective multilateral process. The EU and Schengen group are exceptions. If we accept the realist assumption that states are unitary, sovereign actors, capable of closing as well as opening their economies, then other (political) factors must be at work, driving the increases in migration and maintaining a degree of openness to migration, at least among the advanced industrial democracies.

The *second hypothesis* that can be derived from neoliberal theory for explaining the rise of international migration focuses on domestic coalitions. The maintenance of a relatively open (non-mercantilist) world economy is heavily dependent on coalitions of powerful interests in the most dominant, liberal states. In *Resisting Protectionism*, Helen Milner—a prominent neoliberal theorist—demonstrates how advanced industrial states in the 1970s were able to resist the kind of beggar-thy-neighbour policies that were adopted in the 1920s and 1930s. She argues that growing interdependence (multinationality and export dependence) helped to solidify free trade coalitions among the OECD states in the postwar period, thus preventing a retreat into protectionism following the economic downturns of the 1970s and 1980s (Milner 1988: 18–44). Government leaders in a range of industrial nations were willing (and able) to resist strong political pressures for protectionism in the 1970s in large part because a powerful constellation of business interests contributed to a substantial realignment within these societies, and in some cases polities themselves were (creatively) redesigned by political entrepreneurs to facilitate the maintenance and strengthening of these new (free trade) coalitions.[19] Of course, free trade interests were bolstered by the existence of an international trade regime (GATT) in the 1970s.

Therefore, from a neoliberal perspective, the central question with respect to migration is how did pro-immigration coalitions in the key OECD states form, and will they be able to maintain legal immigration regimes with the end of the Cold War and in the absence of a strong international migration regime? We should not discount the importance of international systemic constraints, like the end of the Cold War, which clearly has had an impact on political coalitions and alignments in all of the liberal democracies. The Cold War's demise had a profound impact on coalitions supporting open migration policies, even

---

[19] This argument, similar to Milner's, is made by Michael Lusztig (1996).

more so than in the area of trade. The major difference between trade and migration is in the nature and types of the coalitions that form to support or oppose them. Although related, in the sense that strong economic liberals tend to support both free trade and more open migration policies,[20] there is a much stronger ideational and cultural dimension involved in the making of pro-migration coalitions than is the case with free trade coalitions, which tend to be based more narrowly on economic interests.

Free trade policies clearly have important political and social effects, but the arguments about comparative advantage and tariff policies tend to be heavily economic, and interest groups are organized along sectoral or class lines. With respect to trade, individuals and groups tend to follow their market interests; but in the making of migration policies, this is not always the case. If a state can be sure of reciprocity, i.e. that other states will abide by the MFN principle, then it is easier to convince a sceptical public to support free trade. With migration, on the other hand, economic arguments (about the costs and benefits of migration) tend to be overshadowed by political, cultural, and ideological arguments that cut across class lines. National identities and founding myths, what I have called elsewhere 'national models', come into play in the making and unmaking of coalitions for admissionist or restrictionist migration policies (Hollifield 1997a, 28–69; Hollifield 1997b). Debates about migration in the liberal-democratic (OECD) states revolve as much if not more so around issues of rights (see below) and national identity than around issues of markets or social class. The coalitions that form to support more open migration policies are often rights-markets (left-right) coalitions; and debates about sovereignty and control of borders are reduced to debates about national identity—a fungible concept that reflects values, morality, and culture, rather than a strictly instrumental, economic calculus.

If we take a neoliberal approach to understanding the rise of migration in the post-war era, we are thrown back into an analysis of three factors, which together drive national migration policies. The first of these factors is ideational, historical, and cultural. Migration policy, especially in the big three liberal republics (the United States, France, and Germany), is heavily influenced by national (or founding) myths, which are codified in citizenship and nationality laws (Hollifield 1997a, 1997b; Brubaker 1992). These myths and the national identity are fungible, subject to manipulation, and they involve strong elements of symbolic politics. They are reflected in constitutional law and can be analysed from a historical, sociological, legal, and political standpoint.

Citizenship, like society or the economy, is subject to exogenous shocks; and immigration, as Myron Weiner and Rey Koslowski have pointed out, can

---

[20] For more evidence on the relation between free trade and pro-immigration coalitions in the USA, see Hollifield and Zuk (1998). Cf. also Kessler 1997.

change the composition of societies, alter political coalitions, transform citizenship and the national identity. The argument therefore can be made, following Koslowski, that migration contributes to the internationalization of domestic politics and economics. Multiculturalism is the functional equivalent of multinationalism. If the rise of multinational corporations, as Milner and others have argued, contributed to the creation of new free trade coalitions, then the rise of immigration and multiculturalism has contributed to new pro-immigration coalitions. As foreigners gain a legal foothold in liberal societies, rights accrue to them, and they become political actors capable of shaping both policy and polity.[21]

But there is clearly a second factor involved in building pro-migration coalitions. As Gary Freeman argues, businesses that are dependent on foreign labour—whether skilled, as in the case of the software industry, or unskilled, as in the case of construction trades or agriculture—can form powerful lobbies; and under the right conditions, they can capture parts of the state in order to maintain access to a vital input (Freeman 1995; Joppke 1998*a*). The political and economic history of Western states, since the late nineteenth century when the transaction costs of migration were drastically reduced, is replete with examples of businesses working with, around, through, or against the state to import labour (Cornelius et al. 1994). Economic interests are always at play in the making of migration policy, because the profits to be had from importing labour are great (demand-pull forces are strong), and there is an abundant supply of cheap labour available. Cutting off access to foreign labour for businesses that are heavily dependent upon it is the same thing as imposing high tariffs on imported raw materials. The industries affected will howl. Both policies are protectionist and they have profound allocational effects, often leading to increases in irregular migration.

In the post-war period, the third and most important factor in building pro-migration (as opposed to free trade) coalitions is institutional. Perhaps the most famous and oft-quoted statement about European guest worker programmes was made by the Swiss novelist Max Frisch, who said 'we asked for workers and human beings came'. Unlike capital or goods, migrants, as individuals and sometimes as groups (e.g. Cubans in the USA, ethnic Germans and Jewish immigrants in Germany) can acquire legal rights and protections under the aegis of liberal constitutions and statutory law. Even when they are not admitted immediately to full citizenship, migrants acquire the rights of membership, which can, depending upon the state, include basic civil rights, a package of social or welfare rights, and even political or voting rights.[22] What is important to keep in mind, however, is that these rights are

---

[21] Here the early, path-breaking works of 1981 and Schmitter 1979 are very instructive.

[22] In the Netherlands and Sweden, for example, resident aliens have voting rights in local elections. Cf. Hollifield 1992*a*, Soysa 1994, and Jacobson 1996.

anchored in national legal systems; and, although they may flow from constitutional law, they also depend upon increasingly fragile political coalitions,
involving left- and right-wing liberals. With the end of the Cold War, these
'strange bedfellow' coalitions have become more difficult to sustain, even in
the area of political asylum, a principle which is supported by international
law.[23] As the coalitions weaken, we would expect to see a concomitant decline
in support for admissionist immigration and refugee policies.

But rights have a very long half-life in liberal democracies. Once they are
extended and institutionalized, it is extemely difficult to roll them back. Most
democracies—especially those like the USA, France, and Germany, which
have republican traditions and strong elements of separation of powers—
have a variety of judicial checks that limit the ability of executive and legisla-
tive authorities to alter civil, social, and political rights. To understand the
'limits of immigration control' in liberal democracies, as well as the mix of
internal and external strategies for control, we must have a clear understanding of the evolution of rights-based politics and of the way in which rights are
institutionalized.[24] Even if rights-markets coalitions supporting immigration
weaken, this does not mean that migration and refugee policies will change
overnight, or that liberal states can quickly and effectively seal their borders.

To conclude, the neoliberal approach requires us, in the first instance, to
look at international institutions and regimes, and secondly at the types of
coalitions that form to support more open migration regimes. I have identified three factors that influence coalition building: (1) ideational and cultural
factors which are closely linked to formal-legal definitions of citizenship; (2)
economic interests, which are linked to factor proportions and intensities, i.e.
land, labour, capital ratios; and (3) rights, which often flow from liberal-
republican constitutions. The following sections of the chapter will develop
this neoliberal framework, offering a critique of realist and globalization arguments.

Risking migration

Of the three analytical perspectives on migration and international relations
that we have reviewed so far, neoliberalism comes closest to answering the
question of why states risk migration. But, as I indicated above, we cannot
ignore structural or systemic factors, like the end of the Cold War, which can

[23] Aristide Zolberg was one of the first to point to the 'strange bedfellows' phenomenon.
See Zolberg 1992. Also Tichenor 1994: 333–62.

[24] On this point, see the introduction in Cornelius et al. 1994. Also Hollifield 1999:
59–96.

influence the propensity of states to support liberal international regimes. In the absence of a threat or a hegemon to unite liberal states and help them overcome collective action problems, multilaterlism is one way for states to cooperate and to build a migration/refugee regime. Following the work of John Ruggie (1993: 3–47) we can identify three tenets of multilateralism. The first of these is *indivisibility*, which is another way of saying that *the object of multilateral regulation should take the form of a public good*. Unless it is a hegemon, a single state or even a small group of states cannot provide this good for the international community. The costs and benefits of its provision must be shared relatively equally among states. The second tenet of multilateralism is principles or *norms of conduct*, which can alter the behaviour of states. The fewer principles or norms there are, the greater will be the likelihood that states will respect them and change their behaviour. The most difficult problem in any multilateral regime is to find a single compelling principle (or at least a very small number of interrelated norms or principles) *'around which actor expectations can converge'*.[25] Finally, Ruggie points to *diffuse reciprocity*, meaning that *states must be convinced that everyone will respect the rules of 'the game'*, thus making it possible for governments to persuade a sceptical or even hostile public to accept the short-term political and economic costs of establishing the regime, in order to reap the long-term gains.

Using this neoliberal framework, we can ask what are the possibilities of building an effective international migration regime? What would be the incentives to participate in such a regime? Can states overcome their misgivings, which may include loss of sovereignty, threats to national security and identity, and changes in the composition of the citizenry. On the first point—indivisibility—we must ask if migration can be defined as an international public good. As pointed out above, this is problematic, especially if we compare migration and trade. During the post-war period, a consensus emerged, thanks to American leadership and following the doctrine of comparative advantage, that an open trading regime would promote world prosperity and peace. The motto of the immediate post-war period was 'peace through trade'. The GATT system was created to ensure that the costs and benefits of free trade would be shared equally; and this allowed the leading liberal states (especially the USA) gradually to overcome the hostility and scepticism of weaker developing states. Free trade would lead not only to specialization in production, increased output, and pareto-optimal economic outcomes, it also would promote interdependence and a more peaceful world.

This type of economic reasoning, however, does not work well in the area of migration, because the asymmetries between developed and developing countries are too great. It is only at certain points in time (such as the turn of

---

[25] Multilateralism is obviously closely related to the notion of an international regime, as defined by Krasner 1982: 185–205.

the century in America, the period of reconstruction in Europe after the Second World War, or the period of very high growth in Asia in the 1970s and 1980s) that the interests of developing and developed states converge. Developing states almost always have an incentive to export surplus populations, whereas developed states only periodically have an interest in admitting large numbers of foreign workers. So the history of migration has tended to be one of fits and starts, of peaks and valleys, which tended to follow the business cycle. But there is strong evidence that this dynamic may have been broken in the post-war period, at least for certain 'core' liberal states in America and Europe (Hollifield and Zuk 1998). We can see this in the rates of world migration (Table 4.1), which have been rising continuously since 1945. So, if migration does not follow the business cycle, then what is driving it? The answer in a word is rights. As the world has become more open, more democratic, and more liberal, people are freer to move than ever before in history. This has placed great strains on liberal states, especially on the institution of citizenship. Liberal states are caught on the horns of a dilemma or, what I have called elsewhere, a liberal paradox (Hollifield 1992*a*, 222 ff.; Weiner 1995: 112 ff.). In liberal political and economic systems, there is a constant tension between markets and rights, or liberty and equality. Rules of the market require openness and factor mobility; whereas rules of the liberal polity, especially citizenship, require some degree of closure, mainly to have a clear definition of the citizenry and to protect the sanctity of the social contract—the legal cornerstone of every liberal polity. Equal protection and due process cannot be extended to everyone without undermining the legitimacy of the liberal state itself. How can states solve this dilemma and escape from this paradox? Constructing an international migration regime, as the members of the European Union have done, is one way out.

But, if migration is to be defined as an international public good, it cannot be defined purely in economic terms, even though mobility of productive factors (like free trade) is recognized in economic theory to be pareto optimal. In order to regulate migration on a unilateral basis, liberal states must adopt draconian (illiberal) policies that may threaten the foundations of the liberal state itself. It is not efficient or desirable in a liberal state to close or seal borders. This would be the ultimate strategy for external control. Likewise, strategies for internal control, including heavy regulation of labour markets, limiting civil rights and liberties for foreigners and citizens, and tampering with founding myths (e.g. weakening birthright citizenship) also threaten the liberal state; and such measures can fan the flames of racism and xenophobia by further stigmatizing foreigners. Establishing a multilateral process for regulating and controlling immigration offers one way to get out of this dilemma. But to accomplish this, control must be redefined on a multilateral basis as the 'orderly movement of people' (Ghosh 1998). Orderly movements imply respect for the rule of law and state sovereignty, which are fundamental principles in every liberal state.

The problem remains of how to set up generalized principles of conduct in the area of migration. Various conventions exist, many put forward by the UN and its agencies (UNHCR, IOM, and ILO), to safeguard the rights of migrant workers and to establish standards for the treatment of these workers and their families.[26] Likewise, the GATT rounds have including some discussion and side agreements dealing with certain forms of high-end migration. The General Agreement on Trade in Services (GATS) is a case in point (Bhagwati et al. 1996; Ghosh 1997). But none of these agreements has achieved the status of a full-blown international migration regime, capable of altering the behaviour of states. It is only with respect to asylum that a quasi-effective international regime has emerged in the post-war period, with a single guiding principle, namely 'a well founded fear of persecution'. Likewise, the freedom of movement clauses of the various treaties of European Union have resulted in the construction of a regional migration regime, for EU member states; and the Schengen group has evolved a set of rules for dealing with migration of third country nationals, specifically asylum seekers.

In such a regional context, where the asymmetries are less pronounced than in the international system, it is easier to solve the problems of reciprocity and collective action. Rules can be adopted and formalized through already established institutional procedures. At the international level, what we have seen instead is a proliferation of very weak rules, norms, and procedures, resulting in a kind of fragmented and ineffective regime (Ghosh 1998; see also chapters by Ghosh in this volume). Moreover, the primary concern of the most powerful liberal states is not to facilitate the orderly movement of people (even paying tourists), or to promote international factor mobility. Rather the concern is for control, which has as many different meanings as there are states. The challenge, therefore, for any state or organization attempting to construct an international migration regime will be to *define control in such a way that it is indivisible*, can serve as a generalized norm or principle of conduct, and so that it can lead to diffuse reciprocity. This is no mean feat, because heretofore international migration has been regulated almost exclusively on a bilateral basis, if not through some type of imperial hierarchy. In fact, we still see both regulatory systems at work today. It is only among the OECD states that freedom of movement (but not settlement) has been more or less achieved, especially for the highly skilled. Between the core liberal states in the international system and the less developed countries, movement of populations is still governed by a system of imperial hierarchy, which is in many ways more one-sided (unilateral) today that it was during the colonial era.[27]

---

[26] International Organization for Migration (Geneva: IOM, 1994). See also the special issue of the *International Migration Review* on the UN convention on the Rights of Migrant Workers and the Families, 25/737 (1991).

[27] In the case of the British Commonwealth, for example, freedom of movement for

To better understand the difficulties of international cooperation to regulate migration I have constructed a typology of international regimes. This typology, depicted in Figure 4.1, points to a clear distinction between the regulation of capital, goods, and services on the one hand, and migrant labour or refugees (people) on the other hand. When it comes to regulating trade and capital flows—an essential function of the international political economy—multilateralism (on the y-axis) is strongest and most heavily institutionalized in the area of finance. Even though the institutions dealing with international finance are far from perfect, the IMF and the World Bank have become the bulwarks of stable exchange rates, without which international trade and investment would be difficult and extremely risky. The GATT/WTO regime for trade also is heavily institutionalized, but the multilateral basis of this regime is, I would argue, weaker than that for finance. The need for strong currencies and stable exchange rates is felt much more acutely by states than the need for free trade. Nonetheless, both of these institutions have evolved together in the post-war period. Powerful market incentives, as well as formal enforcement mechanisms in the case of WTO, compel states to 'play by the rules' (Goldstein 1993: 201–32).

Of the two 'regimes' dealing with migration, one for labour migrants and the other for refugees, clearly the refugee regime, which is institutionalized through the UNHCR, is the more effective, for reasons I have spelled out above. I put the term regimes in quotes, because the 'labour regime' is quite ineffective. The rules for entry and exit of economic migrants are controlled by nation states, not by international organizations like the UN, the IOM, or the ILO. Again the major exception is the EU; but the EU regime for international labour migration functions only for nationals of the member states, *not* (or at least not yet) for third country nationals (Guiraudon 1998). Even for the Schengen states—referred to in the British press derisively as Schengenland—third country nationals do not have freedom of movement. Only Schengen nationals have this right. Schengen does, however, function as a multilateral regime for asylum; and it is a very restrictive regime, designed to help member states restrict refugee migration and prevent 'asylum shopping'. Refugees have the right to request asylum in the first Schengen state in which they arrive—consistent with the Geneva Convention; but, if they transit through a 'safe' third country, then they can be *refoulés* (sent back to that

colonial subjects was greater prior to the granting of independence. From the 1960s until the passage of the British National Act in 1981, there was a gradual restriction of immigration from the so-called New Commonwealth states. The 1981 Act effectively shut out people of colour from British citizenship. See Layton-Henry 1994. Certainly the same could be said of the relationship between France and its former colonies in Africa, except for the fact that the French have never completely shut former colonial subjects out of French citizenship *de jure*, although *de facto* one could argue that it is extremely difficult for North and West Africans to immigrate and naturalize. See Hollifield 1994.

Institutions

		(Weak)		(Strong)
M				
u				
l	**S**	Refugees and Political Asylum		Finance
t	**t**			
i	**r**	(UNHCR)		(IMF and World Bank)
l	**o**			
a	**n**			
t	**g**			
e				
r				
a		International Labour Migration		Trade
l				
i				
s	**W**			
m	**e**	(ILO and IOM)		(Gatt/WTO)
	a			
	k			

FIG. 4.1. A typology of international regimes

third country). The result has been to forge a more or less common asylum policy in Schengenland, and to turn all adjoining states into buffer states. The important point is that these West European states, together with the USA and other liberal democracies, are respecting the letter if not the spirit of international refugee law. Although the principles of the refugee regime are widely recognized, as an institution the UNHCR remains weak and heavily dependent on a few 'client states', especially Sweden, the Netherlands, and other small European social democracies. The Japanese contribute a lot of money to the UNHCR and the Americans support it and use it as a tool for managing refugee crises around the world, especially when American national interests are involved.

Unlike the refugee regime, the 'regime' for international labour migration is weakly institutionalized (depicted on the x-axis) with no central norm, and its principal organs, ILO and IOM, based in Geneva, have little regulatory or institutional capacity. For the developed states in particular, the costs of participating in a regime for international migration would seem to outweigh the benefits; and a short-term strategy of unilateral or bilateral regulation of migration is preferred to a long-term, multilateral strategy. This is less true for the refugee regime, because the more powerful liberal states need this regime for situational exigencies—to manage massive refugee flows that can destabilize governments and in some cases entire regions. When such crises strike close to home, as in the 1999 Balkan War, the utility of the refugee regime goes up exponentially. But when the crisis is past, it drops again.

To date, unwanted labour migrations might be considered more of a nuisance, especially from a political standpoint; but they are not fundamentally threatening, therefore they can be handled unilaterally and on an ad hoc basis. The pay-off from international cooperation in the area of unwanted labour migration is negative and there are numerous opportunities for defection. The possibilities for monitoring, enforcement, or developing some principle of non-discrimination are minimal at this point in time. We are therefore thrown back onto the domestic level in our search for an explanation of why states risk migration; and the three factors outlined above—cultural and ideational, economic interests, and rights—must be studied on a case-by-case basis to explain why states open and close their borders.

Yet an international market for labour exists and it is growing. If the first rule of political economy is that markets beget regulation, then some type of international regime is likely to develop. What will be the parameters of such a regime and how will it evolve? International relations theory, especially neoliberal/rationalist arguments, offer some clues.

Strategies for developing a NIROMP

One of the principal effects of economic interdependence is to compel states to cooperate (Keohane and Nye 1977; Milner 1988). Increasing international migration (see Table 4.1) is one indicator of interdependence and it shows no signs of abating. As the international market for skilled and unskilled labour grows in the coming decades, pressures for creating an international regime will increase. Following the work of Lisa Martin and drawing on the preceding review of international relations theory (Martin 1993; Ruggie 1993: 91–121) we can identify two ways in which states can overcome coordination problems with respect to migration. In the absence of trust and reciprocity (e.g. the developed states do not trust less developed states to help control borders and deter irregular migration), there are two ways for states to solve the coordination problem: (1) through *centralization of regulatory power* and the pooling of sovereignty, and (2) *suasion* or, as Martin puts it 'tactical issue linkage' (Martin 1993: 104).

We already have seen an example of the first strategy at the regional level in Europe. The EU and to a lesser extent the Schengen regimes were built through a process of centralization and pooling of sovereignty. But, as I have pointed out above, this was fairly easy to do in the European context, because of the symmetry (of interests and power) within this region and the existence of an institutional framework (the EC or EU). It would be much more difficult to centralize control of migration in the Americas or Asia, where the asymmetries (of interest and power) are much greater, and levels of political and economic development vary tremendously from one state to another. It is unlikely that regional trade regimes like NAFTA or the APEC will lead quickly to cooperation in the area of migration. But the beginnings of collaborative arrangements are there, just as they were in Europe with the ECSC in the early 1950s. The regional option—multilateralism for a relevant group of states—is one way to overcome collective action problems and to begin a process of centralization. Most international regimes have had a long gestation period, beginning as bilateral or regional agreements. It is unlikely, however, that an international migration regime could be built following the example of the ITO/GATT/WTO. It is too difficult to fulfil the prerequisites of multilateralism: indivisibility, generalized principles of conduct, and diffuse reciprocity (see above). The norm of non-discrimination (equivalent of MFN) does not exist; and there are no mechanisms for punishing free riders and no way of resolving disputes. In short, as depicted in Figure 4.1 above, the basis for multilateralism is weak and there is only a very weak institutional framework.

With the tremendous asymmetry of interests and power between developed (migration receiving) and less developed (migration sending) countries, suasion may be the only viable strategy for overcoming collective action problems, whether at the regional or international level. Lisa Martin points to a number of ways in which suasion can help to solve coordination problems (Martin 1993: 104–6). *Step one* is to develop a '*dominant strategy*', which can only be accomplished by the most powerful states, using international organizations to persuade or coerce smaller and weaker states. In the NIROMP framework, *orderly movement of people*, defined in terms of rule of law and respect for state sovereignty, should be the principal objective of hegemonic, liberal states.

Step two is to persuade other states to accept the dominant strategy. This will necessitate '*tactical issue linkage*', which involves identifying issues and interests not necessarily related to migration (such as MFN, for example) and using these as leverage to compel or coerce states to accept the dominant strategy. This is, in effect, an 'international logroll'. Such tactics will have only the appearance of multilateralism, at least initially. Tactical issue linkage was considered in negotiations between the USA and Mexico over the NAFTA agreement, and migration issues have figured prominently in negotiations between the EU and prospective EU members in East Central Europe.

In such instances reciprocity is specific rather than diffuse. Individual states may be rewarded for their cooperation in controlling emigration. Again we have seen many bilateral examples of this type of strategic interaction between the states of Western and Eastern Europe. The post-unification German governments have cut a number of deals with East Central European states to gain their cooperation in the fight against irregular migration. In the case of Poland, this has involved investments and debt relief, as well as greater freedom of movement for Polish nationals in Germany. But liberal-democratic states may face a problem of credibility in pursuing these types of strategies. They need international organizations to give them greater credibility (cover) and to facilitate these logrolls.

The *third step* for hegemonic states is to *move from what is an essentially one-sided, manipulative game to a multilateral process, and eventually to institutionalize this process.* The long-term benefits of such a strategy for receiving states are obvious. It will be less costly to build an international regime than to fight every step of the way with every sending state, relying only on unilateral or bilateral agreements. This may entail some short-term loss of control (larger numbers of visas, higher quotas, etc. for the sending states) in exchange for long-term stability and more orderly/regular migration. The ultimate pay-off for liberal states is the establishment of a liberal world order based upon rule of law, respect for state sovereignty, ease of travel, and the smoother functioning of international labour markets. The pay-off for sending states is greater freedom of movement for their nationals, greater foreign reserves, and a more favourable balance of payments (thanks to remittances), and increases in cultural and economic exchange, including technology transfers.

As I argued above, however, changes in the international system with the end of the Cold War have altered this game in several ways. First, it has made defection easier. Since 1990, states are more likely to pursue beggar-thy-neighbour policies by closing their borders and not cooperating with neighbouring states in the making of migration and refugee policies. The Schengen process itself is a kind of beggar-thy-neighbour policy on a regional scale. Secondly, the new post-Cold War configurations of interests and power, both at the international and domestic level, make it more difficult to pursue a multilateral strategy for controlling international migration. Rights-markets coalitions have been breaking apart in the dominant liberal states, increasing polarization and politicization over immigration and refugee issues. Yet at the same time, liberalization and democratization in formerly authoritarian states in the East and the South have dramatically reduced the transaction costs for emigration (Hollifield and Jillson 1999). Initially this caused panic in Western Europe where there was a fear of mass migrations from east to west. Headlines screamed 'The Russians are Coming!'[28] Even though these massive flows did not materialize, western states began to hunker down and search for ways to reduce or stop immigration. The time horizons of almost all western democracies suddenly were much shorter, because of these changes in domestic and international politics. Migration came to be perceived as a greater threat to national security (Huntington 1996).

If the USA were to defect from the liberal refugee and migration 'regimes',

---

[28] This was the leader in *The Economist*, for example.

such as they are, it could mean the collapse of these regimes. In game theoretic terms, such a defection would fundamentally alter the equilibrium outcome, and it would be potentially very costly to all states and to the international community. At least as far as migration is concerned, the process of globalization of exchange could be quickly and dramatically reversed. As happened in the area of international finance with the collapse of the Bretton Woods system in the early 1970s and in the area of trade with the Latin debt crisis of the 1980s and the Asian crisis of the 1990s, to prevent the collapse of liberal migration and refugee 'regimes', the US and other liberal states must pursue an aggressive strategy of multilateralism, taking the short-term political heat, for long-term political stability and economic gain. Without the kind of leadership exhibited in the areas of international trade and finance, irregular migrations will increase and become ever more threatening, leading more states to close their borders.

Conclusion: the myth of globalization

The two central questions posed in this chapter are (1) how can we explain the continuous rise in international migration in the post-Second World War period and (2) why are states willing to risk migration? Several hypotheses, derived from international relations theory, were advanced. The first of these is the realist or national security argument, that states open and close their borders in response to changes in the structure of the international system. The problem with this argument is that such structural change (i.e. shifts in the distribution of power) is relatively rare. But such a change did occur in 1990 with the end of the Cold War, and there is considerable evidence that the willingness of (liberal) states to risk migration declined dramatically in the 1990s. Coalitions of left- and right-wing liberals, what I termed rights-markets coalitions, which had flourished during much of the Cold War period, suddenly came under pressure; and they have fallen apart in many liberal societies. But we have not seen a concomitant decline in the rate of international migration.

An alternative hypothesis is offered by what I call globalization theory, derived largely from world systems arguments. According to the globalization thesis, migration is largely a function of changes in the international division of labour, and restructuring of the global economy, which entails rapid and massive movements of productive factors, including capital and labour. Globalization is a social and economic imperative and even the most powerful states are incapable of regulating flows of capital, goods, services, information, and people. The result has been the rise of new global centres of production, what Saskia Sassen calls the 'global city', which is outside of the regulatory reach of the state. The demand for (skilled and unskilled) foreign labour is embedded in the economies of the advanced industrial societies.

In such pure globalization arguments, it makes little sense to study either domestic or international politics, as a way of understanding increases in international exchange, whether in the areas of finance, trade, or migration. Sovereignty is an antiquated concept and we must think about the global economy in terms of postnationalism. Yasemin Soysal, David Jacobson, and Rainer Bauböck have argued that, with respect to migration, the globalization of the economy has created a new kind of postnational membership, or in Bauböck's terms, a transnational citizenship. Rights, according to Jacobson, now extend across borders. Such political developments are the logical counterpart of globalization.

The globalization thesis, in which outcomes are socially and economically determined, stands at the opposite extreme of realism, in which outcomes are politically determined. A third perspective, neoliberalism, accepts the continuing importance of the nation state in international relations. But neoliberals argue that economic interdependence has altered the way in which states think about and use their power. Rather than relying on traditional military means to pursue their national interest, liberal states are increasingly drawn into 'collaboration games' in order to regulate the international economy and reduce the risks associated with trade in particular. This desire to reduce risks and lower transaction costs has led the most powerful states to construct international regimes for trade and finance. Unlike the neorealists, neoliberal theorists do not consider the unitary actor assumption to be sacrosanct; and they are willing to look at domestic politics, especially at the types of coalitions and institutions that may facilitate openness and increase the demand for international cooperation.

Following the neoliberal and neorealist arguments, I have argued that the rise in migration in the post-war period is closely linked to three factors: (1) the structure of the international system, including the distribution of power and the presence or absence of international regimes; (2) domestic political coalitions, based on economic interests (factor proportions and intensities) and rights (which flow from liberal constitutions and laws); finally, a third factor is ideational, cultural, and legal—what Rogers Brubaker calls 'traditions of citizenship and nationhood'. During the Cold War, liberal states were more willing to risk migration, because of the bipolar nature of the international system, which prevented large-scale emigration from communist states and helped to solidify rights-markets coalitions in liberal states. The end of the Cold War has radically altered the configuration of power and interests, both at the national and international level, and it has changed the dynamic of collaboration games, especially with respect to migration. States are still willing to risk trade and the institutions for maintaining stable exchange rates, specifically the IMF, are supported by a coalition of liberal states, led by the

United States. There is evidence, however, that multilateralism in these areas (trade and finance) is under increasing political pressure, especially in the USA. A new isolationism and protectionism are stirring.

The logic of cooperation is different for trade and migration. Liberal states work hard to keep trade and investment flowing in the world economy; and they increasingly work hard to keep migration, including refugees, bottled up in less developed (sending) countries. The international trade regime (WTO) is based squarely on the doctrine of comparative advantage and the principle of non-discrimination (MFN). Free trade has come to be accepted by a wide range of states as an international public good. Ironically, following the Stolper-Samuelson theorem of factor-price equalization, trade (and FDI) are often touted as the solution to the problem of unwanted migration. According to this theorem, trade can substitute for migration in the long term. Nevertheless, migration continues in the short term and may actually be increased when less developed economies are exposed to strong exogenous shocks of trade and foreign investment.

No organizing principle has emerged as a basis for international coopera- tion to regulate migration. The international refugee regime, based on a well- founded fear of persecution, and the EU regime, based on freedom of move- ment for nationals of member states, are the exceptions. The primary reason for the lack of cooperation and the absence of an international regime in the area of migration is the tremendous asymmetries between interests and power in the international system. The challenge for proponents of an international migration regime is to find (1) an organizing principle and (2) a strategy for overcoming collaboration problems in this area. In the penultimate section of this chapter, I suggested a principle, namely rule of law and orderly movement of peoples, and several strategies for overcoming asymmetries of interest and building a regime, including centralization of authority to promote trust, provide information, and enforcement mechanisms. The problem with this strategy is that it requires continuous and strong intervention by a hegemon or group of hegemonic states. A more likely strategy is suasion, which involves tactical issue linkage and international logrolls. Linking unrelated issues to cooperation in controlling emigration.

The central argument in this chapter is that states will not continue to risk migration in the post-Cold War era, without some type of international regu- latory framework. If, as I and many others have argued, migration is closely linked to trade and investment, both economically (in the sense that trade and investment require factor mobility) and politically (in the sense that the same coalitions which support free trade and open investment regimes tend to support more open migration regimes), then any weakening on the part of liberal states in their commitment to support orderly movements of people could threaten the 'new liberal world order'. This argument is at odds with the globalization thesis, inasmuch as I see politics and the nation state as crucial to the stability of the global economy, especially with the end of the Cold War. To paraphrase Karl Polanyi, without the 'continuous, centrally organized, and controlled intervention' of the most powerful liberal states, the 'simple and natural liberty' of the global economy will not survive (Polanyi 1957: 140). Globalization is a myth, insofar as it ignores the imperatives of politics and power, which are still vested in the nation state.

REFERENCES

Bauböck, R. (1994), *Transnational Citizenship: Membership Rights in International Migration,* London: Edward Elgar.

Bhagwati, J. N., Panagariya, A. and Kosters, M. (eds.) (1996), *The Economics of Preferential Trade Agreements,* Washington, DC: AEI Press.

Borjas, G. J. (1990), *Friends or Strangers: The Impact of Immigrants on the U.S. Economy,* New York: Basic Books.

Brubaker, R. (1992), *Citizenship and Nationhood in France and Germany,* Cambridge, Mass.: Harvard University Press, 1992.

Commission on Immigration Reform (1997), *Binational Study on Migration between Mexico and the United States,* Washington, DC: Commission on Immigration Reform.

Cornelius, W. A. (1998), 'The Structural Embeddedness of Demand for Immigrant Labor in California and Japan', paper prepared for a meeting of the University of California Comparative Immigration and Integration Program, San Diego.

—— Martin, P. L. and Hollifield, J. F., (eds.) (1994), *Controlling Immigration: A Global Perspective,* Stanford, Calif.: Stanford University Press.

Freeman, G. P. (1995), 'Modes of Immigration Politics in the Liberal Democratic States', *International Migration Review,* 29.

Ghosh, B. (1997), *Gains from Global Linkages: Trade in Services and Movements of Persons,* London: Macmillan.

—— (1998), *Huddled Masses and Uncertain Shores: Insights into Irregular Migration,* The Hague: Kluwer International.

Gilpin, R. (1986), *The Political Economy of International Relations,* Princeton: Princeton University Press.

Goldstein, J. (1993), 'Creating the GATT Rules: Politics, Institutions and American Policy', in Ruggie 1993.

Goodwin-Gill, G. S. (1996), *The Refugee in International Law,* Oxford: Clarendon Press.

Guiraudon, V (1998), 'Third Country Nationals and European Law: Obstacles to Rights', *Journal of Ethnic Studies,* 24/4.

Hollifield, J. F. (1992*a*), *Immigrants, Markets, and States,* Cambridge, Mass.: Harvard University Press.

—— (1992*b*), 'Migration and International Relations: Cooperation and Control in the European Community', *International Migration Review,* 26/2.

—— (1994), 'Immigration and Republicanism in France: The Hidden Consensus', in Cornelius et al., 1994: 143–76.

—— (1997a), 'Immigration and Integration in Western Europe: A Comparative Analysis', in Emek Uçarer and Donald Puchala (eds.), *Immigration into Western Societies: Problems and Policies*, London: Pinter, 28–69.

—— (1997b), *Immigration et L'état nation: à la recherche d'un modèle national*, Paris: L'Harmattan.

—— (1999), 'Ideas, Institutions, and Civil Society: On the Limits of Immigration Control,' in T. Hammar and G. Brochmann (eds.), *Mechanisms of Immigration Control: A Comparative Analysis of European Regulation Policies*, Oxford: Berg, 59–96.

—— and Jillson, C. C. (eds.) (1999), *Pathways to Democracy: The Political Economy of Democratic Transitions*, New York: Routledge.

—— and Zuk, G. (1998), 'Immigrants, Markets, and Rights', in H. Kurthen, and J. Fijalkowski (eds.), *Immigration and the Welfare State: Germany and the United States in Comparison*, Stanford, Calif.: JAI Press.

Holm, H. H., and Sörensen, G. (eds.) (1995), *Whose World Order: Uneven Globalization and the End of the Cold War*, Boulder, Colo.: Westview.

Huntington, S. P. (1996), 'The West and the World', *Foreign Affairs* (Nov./Dec.).

International Organization for Migration (1994), 'International Responses to Trafficking in Migrants and the Safeguarding of Migrant Rights', Geneva: IOM.

Jacobson, D. (1996) *Rights across Borders: Immigration and the Decline of Citizenship*, Baltimore: Johns Hopkins University Press.

Joppke, C. (1998a) 'Why Liberal States Accept Unwanted Immigration', *World Politics*, 50: 266–93.

—— (1998b), *Challenge to the Nation-State: Immigration in Western Europe and the United States*, New York: Oxford University Press.

Katzenstein, P. J. (ed.) (1996), *The Culture of National Security: Norms and Identity in World Politics*, New York: Columbia University Press.

Keohane, R. O. (1984), *After Hegemony: Cooperation and Discord in the World Economy*, Princeton: Princeton University Press.

—— (ed.) (1986), *Neorealism and Its Critics*, New York: Columbia University Press.

—— and Milner, H. V. (1996), *Internationalization of Domestic Politics*, New York: Cambridge University Press.

—— and Nye, J. S. (1977), *Power and Interdependence: World Politics in Transition*, Boston: Little Brown.

Kessler, A. E. (1997), 'Trade Theory, Political Incentives, and the Political Economy of American Immigration Restriction, 1975–1924', Paper delivered at the Annual Meeting of the American Political Science Association, Washington, DC, August 1997.

Kindleberger, C. P. (1973), *The World in Depression, 1929–1939*, Berkeley and Los Angeles: University of California Press.

Koslowski, R. (1996), 'Migration, the Globalization of Domestic Politics and International Relations Theory', paper presented at the International Studies Association Meeting, San Diego, March 1996.

Krasner, S. (ed.) (1982), 'International Regimes', *International Organization*, 36: 185–205.

Krugman, P. (1996), *Pop Internationalism*, Cambridge, Mass.: MIT Press.

Layton-Henry, Z. (1994) 'Britain: The Would-Be Zero Immigration Country', in Cornelius et al. 1994: 273–96.

Lévi-Strauss, C. (1966), *The Savage Mind*, Chicago: University of Chicago Press.

Lusztig, M. (1996), *Risking Free Trade: The Politics of Trade in Britain, Canada, Mexico, and the United States*, Pittsburgh: University of Pittsburgh Press.

Martin, L. (1993), 'The Rational State Choice of Multilateralism', in Ruggie 1993: 91–121.

Martin, P. L. (1995), *Migration and NAFTA*, Washington, DC: Institute for International Economics.

Massey, D., et al. (1987), *Return to Atzlan*, Berkeley and Los Angeles: University of California Press, 1987.

Miller, M. J. (1981), *Foreign Workers in Western Europe: An Emerging Political Force*, New York: Praeger.

Milner, H. (1988), *Resisting Protectionism: Global Industries and the Politics of International Trade*, Princeton: Princeton University Press.

—— (1997), *Interests, Institutions, and Information: Domestic Politics and International Relations*, Princeton: Princeton University Press.

Mundell, R. A. (1957), 'International Trade and Factor Mobility', *American Economic Review*, 47: 321–35.

Piore, M. J. (1979), *Birds of Passage: Migrant Labor in Industrial Societies*, Cambridge: Cambridge University Press.

Polanyi, K. (1957), *The Great Transformation: The Political and Economic Origins of Our Time*, Boston: Beacon Press.

Portes, A. (1996), 'Transnational communities: their emergence and significance in the contemporary world system', in R. P. Korzeniewicz and W. C. Smith (eds.) *Latin America in the World Economy*, Westport, Conn.: Greenwood Press.

—— (1997), 'Immigration Theory for a New Century: Some Problems and Opportunities', *International Migration Review*, 31: 799–825.

—— and Bach, R. L. (1985), *Latin Journey: Cuban and Mexican Immigrants in the United States*, Berkeley and Los Angeles: University of California Press.

Rogowski, R. (1989), *Commerce and Coalitions: How Trade Affects Domestic Political Alignments*, Princeton: Princeton University Press.

Rosenau, J. (1990), *Turbulence in World Politics: A Theory of Change and Continuity*, Princeton: Princeton University Press.

Ruggie J. G. (ed.) (1993), *Multilateralism Matters: The Theory and Practice of an Institutional Form*, New York: Columbia University Press.

Sassen, S. (1991), *The Global City: New York, London, Tokyo*, Princeton: Princeton University Press.

—— (1996), *Losing Control? Sovereignty in an Age of Globalization*, New York: Columbia University Press.

Schain, Y. (1989), *The Frontier of Loyalty: Political Exiles in the Age of the Nation-State*, Middleton, Conn: Wesleyan University Press.

Schlesinger Jr., A. (1992), *The Disuniting of America: Reflections on a Multicultural Society*, New York: Norton.

Schmitter, B. E. (1979), 'Immigration and Citizenship in West Germany and Switzerland', unpublished Ph.D. Dissertation, University of Chicago.

Simon, J. L. (1989), *The Economic Consequences of Immigration*, New York: Blackwell.

Soysal, Y. (1994), *The Limits of Citizenship*, Chicago: University of Chicago Press.

Stolper, W. F. and Samuelson, P. A. (1941), 'Protection and Real Wages', *Review of Economic Studies*, 9: 58–73.

Tichenor, D. J. (1994), 'The Politics of Immigration Reform in the United States, 1981–1990', *Polity*, 26/3: 333–62.

UNCTAD (1995), *Foreign Direct Investment, Trade, Aid and Migration*, Current Studies Series A No. 29, Geneva: International Organization for Migration.

Wallerstein, I. (1974), *The Modern World System*, New York: Academic Press.

Waltz, K. (1979), *Theory of International Politics*, Reading, Mass.: Addison-Wesley.

Weber, M. (1947), *The Theory of Social and Economic Organization*, New York: Oxford University Press.

Weiner, M. (1995), *The Global Migration Crisis: Challenge to States and to Human Rights*, New York: Harper Collins.

Zolberg, A. (1992), 'Reforming the Back Door: Perspectives historiques sur la réforme de la politique américaine d'immigration', in Costa-Lascoux and P. Weil (eds.), *Logiques d'état et immigration*, Paris: Éditions Kimé.

5

Why do we Need a General Agreement on Movements of People (GAMP)?

Thomas Straubhaar

Introduction

The twentieth century began worldwide with the (partly artificial) making of nation states.[1] It is about to end with the slow, incremental but ongoing erosion of nation states power. Nation states have been very efficient as institutions to minimize transaction costs in the area of industrialization.[1] In a world of increasing globalization for more and more business activities, however, the politically defined territoriality of nation states comes under growing economic pressure. Several nation states have broken up into parts (like the Soviet Union or Yugoslavia). Others have started to congregate in regional integration blocs (like NAFTA, EU, ASEAN, Mercosur). Many national borders have been abolished and some integrated areas without national borders have arisen (like the EU).

In a globalizing world, many 'national' problems lose their 'national' dimension. They spill over national borders and become 'international'. The same is true for *public goods*.[2] Some public goods get an 'international public

Thanks are due to the editor, Bimal Ghosh, for his valuable comments on earlier drafts and to the participants of the preparatory meetings in Geneva in September 1997 and Arrabida in June 1999.

[1] 'Transaction costs arise from the transfer of ownership or, more generally, of property rights. They are a concomitant feature of decentralized ownership rights, private property and exchange... Transaction costs, like production costs, are a catch-all term for a heterogeneous assortment of inputs. The parties to a contract have to find each other, they have to communicate and to exchange information. The goods must be described, inspected, weighed and measured. Contracts are drawn up, lawyers may be consulted, title is transferred and records have to be kept. In some cases, compliance needs to be enforced through legal action and breach of contract may lead to litigation' (Niehans 1987: 676). In short: transaction costs are all additional costs of market activities that are not included in the production costs.

[2] Public goods are characterized by some degree of non-rivalry in consumption *and* the

goods' character.[3] Consequently, national laws are increasingly being replaced by international laws or regulations. There is an augmenting body of international organizations which deal with 'international public goods'. Popular examples are the United Nations (for security affairs), the World Bank/IMF (for financial affairs), or the World Trade Organization (for trade affairs). These international regimes are intended to optimize benefits from the interplay of national actors in a global game.

However, there is one issue that is only reluctantly dealt with in an international framework. Migration has been and is seen as a (probably *the*) fundamental national topic. Nation states and their governments can hardly imagine relinquishing the right to decide autonomously who should belong to them and who must stay outside. Questions of entry, stay, and membership (i.e. nationality and citizenship) touch the soul of nations. Consequently nation states and their governments are only partly and slowly willing to delegate authority for these fundamental issues to international regimes. The NIROMP (new international regime for orderly movements of people) project is one of the first attempts to provide a common framework to make international movements of persons more orderly, manageable, and efficient for both sending and receiving countries. Complementary to the other chapters in this volume, I focus on some economic aspects of an international migration arrangement.

My contribution argues that *global games need global rules*. The era of globalization calls for an international framework to regulate international movements of people efficiently. This is due to the fact that in 1990 about 120 million people were living outside the country of their birth (see Chapter 1, Table 1.1—the number may now have increased to above 130 milliion). Taken in absolute numbers this is close to the population size of Nigeria which is the tenth biggest country worldwide. 'More than ever before, migration is a global phenomenon' (Weiner 1996: 128). In the up-coming century of cyberspace, migrants might even be described as an incarnation of the 'virtual citizen'

impossibility of excluding somebody from consuming them. They also include goods and services that private markets fail to supply efficiently because they are subject to strong scale economies (generating a 'natural monopoly') or subject to severe externalities (i.e. indirect effects of economic transactions on people not directly involved in this activity). Examples include codes of law and regulation, telecommunication and transportation networks, technical infrastructure, educational affairs, and many others.

[3] The term 'international public goods' has been used by Charles Kindleberger (1986) in his presidential address to the American Economic Association. It means that matters of national politics or market failures have now become topics of international concern with their repercussions easily crossing national territories. Popular examples for such 'international externalities' (i.e. individual behaviour (in)directly affects the welfare of others in other countries) are peacekeeping, environmental damage (ozone layer, air pollution, ovefishing, etc.) or macroeconomic instability but they can also be found in migration issues as we shall see later.

meaning that they are almost perfectly adapted to a spaceless, borderless, territory-less world of the future.

Migration has become one of the most discussed *political* topics. The border-less nation of international migrants grows fast. Not surprisingly, citizens of old 'traditional' territory-bounded nation states in Europe and North America fear being overrun by herds of people from Africa or Latin America. An all-too-familiar chorus (especially by those eager to exploit the issue for electoral gain), quickly declared international migration as a security threat that leads to unjus-tified, exaggerated, and dangerous perpetuation of 'myths and half-truth lend-ing them the status of conventional wisdom' (Papademetriou 1997).

In line with the basic idea of the NIROMP project, I discuss the *economic necessity* of a shift from national migration politics to an international regime. The basic idea is very simple: as an economist, I find many convincing theo-retical arguments and much empirical evidence that international movements of people are welfare increasing for the sending area and the receiving area as well. However, due to the relative heterogeneity of the labour force (skilled/unskilled, employed/unemployed, old/young, male/female) a fully liberalized international labour market by itself would not lead to an optimal allocation of the workforce. The main reason for this assumption lies in the *asymmetric macroeconomic incentives* behind cross-border movements of people. Regions with a labour surplus prefer the emigration of low-skilled unemployed or underemployed workers and are eager to keep their brightest minds. Regions with a demand for immigrants would prefer high-skilled workers that are valued complements to the native labour force but they would dislike unskilled people that might crowd out native workers into unemployment or that might just consume (national) public goods (like streets, schools, hospitals) without paying a cost-covering fee. Consequently, an international framework should seek to avoid brain drain effects in the emigration country and crowding out effects in the immigration area.

In what follows, the first section gives an overview of what globalization means and offers a short survey about some recent migration trends. I then ask why and how we should regulate international migration. The fourth section develops some basic elements of a General Agreement on Movements of People (GAMP) and this is followed by a conclusion.

Migration patterns at the dawn of the twenty-first century

The twentieth century has been the century of *globalization*. Fundamental technological innovations after the Second World War have effectively changed 'One Earth' into 'One World'. The basic trigger of this process has been the tremendous technological innovations in microelectronics in the last decades. On the whole, they have considerably narrowed 'space' and shortened 'time'. Transaction and communication costs of worldwide business and long-distance travelling have decreased substantially.[4] International economic activities have become even cheaper because many of the costly impediments of artificial barriers to trade have been removed (like tariffs in the WTO framework); or some past political conflicts have diminished in intensity or even completely disappeared (like the Cold War and apartheid in South Africa).

International trade has rapidly increased over the last decades. About one-quarter of all produced goods and services are exported at the end of the 1990s, up from one-eighth in 1970 (data from World Bank 1999: 229 and World Bank 1995: 51). However, much more important is that the degree of spatial mobility has become much higher for *factors of production* (i.e. labour and capital). The fall in transaction and transportation costs has made international migration a cheaper and consequently more attractive option for more people around the globe than ever before in human history.

Goods and factor markets have become much closer and better interlinked. Previously segmented, national factor markets have opened up to 'global' capital and labour markets with all forms of country-crossing cooperation. Workers and funds have the technical opportunities to move over longer distances more easily and more rapidly than in the past. It takes only a few hours to travel to any corners of the earth. Consequently, a global labour market emerges. It must be said that this 'globalization' takes different forms. As explained below, depending on their individual characteristics, workers are interlinked directly over international migration flows or indirectly over worldwide trade in goods and services.

(*a*) Relatively *unskilled 'blue-collar' workers* are affected by the 'globalization' phenomenon through two different independent channels: they are *indirectly* challenged by 'cheap' imports of (standardized) goods; this might happen especially in the traded, industrialized sectors (i.e. toys or textiles); or they are *directly* challenged by 'cheap' labour immigration; this might happen especially in the non-traded, service-oriented sectors (i.e. construction, restaurants, tourism). 'Globalization' in this unskilled segment of the labour market means an almost unlimited supply of workers and a relative scarcity of complementary production factors (i.e. (human) capital). The consequence is tough competition and a pressure or tendency towards worldwide equalization of real wages (i.e. purchasing power corrected incomes per hour) for the unskilled labour force.

---

[4] The *World Development Report* 1995 (World Bank 1995: 51) shows for example that the costs of a three-minute New York-to-London telephone call has dropped from an index of 100 in 1940 to an index of 1 in 2000. Similar cost reductions appear for long-distance transportation of people or freights.

(*b*) For the relatively *higher skilled 'white-collar' specialists* 'globalization' means the opportunity to search worldwide for the most attractive complementary production factors. They can communicate, cooperate, and sell their knowhow around the globe—sometimes within 'cyberspace' or within the 'virtual company' and this often means without even leaving their home town. Consequently, they will choose their main place of residence according to the expectations of return on their human capital investments. This might also mean that the quality of life with regard to *consumption* could be better for this choice than the local possibilities of *production.*

It is remarkable enough that a large part of workers need not move internationally in order to access the worldwide, interlinked labour market. The indirect competition over worldwide trade in goods and services (and over electronic commerce and virtual service-exchange) without cross-border mobility of workers explains why even a small proportion of internationally mobile people has such a tremendous effect on the earnings of lower-skilled workers.

It must be mentioned, however, that despite the increasing globalization of economic activities, and despite the much lower transportation and travelling costs, international movement of people is still the exception and not the rule.[5] Only 2 per cent of the world's population live outside their home countries. This empirical fact contradicts the popular judgements and prejudice. It can be claimed that for most people 'staying' is a preferred option compared to 'going'. Thus, people are mostly bound to their places of origin. This has something to do with non-transferable location-specific advantages. They are not only economic, but also, and perhaps more importantly, cultural, linguistic, social, and political. During periods of immobility at a particular location, individuals invest in the accumulation of location-specific skills, abilities, and assets (this also includes the learning of local habits, values, and customs). Some of these abilities, and assets cannot be transferred easily to different locations. A rather extreme example of non-transferable abilities is the skills of an Australian aborigine who is an expert at surviving in the desert. He will find it difficult, however, to employ these skills in westernized and urbanized parts of the world where they are of little value.[6]

There are also less spectacular examples, even with respect to groups of individuals who are usually assumed to have a high propensity to migrate. High-school graduates for example, when trying to find a job in their home

---

[5] Consequently, we have to look more carefully to the economics of *immobility*. Why do people prefer to stay even if the average standard of living is much higher in other countries? In Fischer et al. 1998 we develop an '*insider advantage approach*' to explain the economic rationality behind the preference for immobility.

[6] For a related case study see P. Hoagan, *Crocodile Dundee*, Alice Springs/Hollywood, 1985 (film).

town, are likely to have location-specific assets simply by knowing many of their fellow citizens and by being accustomed to the peculiarities of their town. Like the aborigine, they are unable to transfer these assets, which in turn is likely to reduce their willingness to take up residence in a different macro-level unit. This applies to an even higher degree to people in a later stage of their life. Not only are they likely to have a stronger personal attachment to a particular place, but over time they have usually also collected a much larger amount of information and abilities than the high-school graduates mentioned above. This increases the costs which arise from the devaluation of these assets when moving to a different place of residence.

All in all, *location-specific insider advantages* contribute to an understanding of why most people stay immobile even under conditions of important national and regional disparities. It implies that people do not move because the loss of location-specific assets and abilities as a result of migration would be too severe and because immobility allows for the accumulation of insider advantages. With regard to recent migration patterns the interesting point is that 'globalization' allows people to 'stay' geographically but to 'go' functionally. This means that workers can do their (mostly service-related) business worldwide using the internet or in cyberspace without ever leaving their home.

It is also remarkable that the majority of international movements of people are not global but local. Most of the world's migration flows occur within culturally homogeneous areas and separate geographical regions, for example within South and East Asia, Africa, or Latin America (see also Ghosh, Chapter 9 in this connection). Furthermore, international migration is often due to consequences of the moving of national borders for political reasons rather than the movement of people. 'Borders crossing people' takes place almost as often as 'people crossing borders'. Very recent examples are the collapse of the Soviet Union and Yugoslavia and the building up of new countries in Eastern Europe. But in many cases the construction of new nation states in Asia, Africa, or Latin America has also followed arbitrary and artificial borderlines. Thus, people are suddenly 'non-citizens' even though they have not even moved an inch.

Both empirical facts—the relatively strong preference for immobility and the rather local dimension to international labour migration—should make nation states in the northern hemisphere well aware that the fears of mass migration from the South are highly exaggerated. To bring it to the point, many (if not most) fears of globalization do not stem primarily from direct cross-border movements of people. They are provoked much more by the indirect consequences of international (increasingly electronic) trade in goods and services that sometimes come together with the suppliers of specific services. Much more than the traditional permanent migration flows, some other new cross-border mobility patterns challenge the relatively higher-developed immigration countries in Europe and North America. These, of course, have much to do with globalization and the lower transportation and transaction costs for international movements of people:

(*a*) An increasing number of cross-border migration is *temporary* which means seasonally or even weekly or daily. More people from further geographical areas can afford to commute over longer distances back and forth across borders for shorter periods of time. These migration flows are not recorded in official statistics because they do not fulfil the duration criteria of at least six continuous months. Some of these daily commuting cross-border movements cannot even be recorded at all for practical reasons. Just to give an example: the Tijuana–San Diego border in San Ysidro is crossed by much more than 100,000 people daily and it would be simply too costly to record them all in detail.

(*b*) Temporary migration has become more important in *service-related activities*. In many cases 'trade in services' is embodied in 'movements of persons'. Popular examples of such cross-border activities of men-bounded service activities are managers, scientists, consultants, computer specialists, but also artists, sportsmen, hair dressers, street cleaners, dress makers, or cashiers. Remarkably enough, these service-related international movements also appear within the group of high-skilled workers. Besides participants in business meetings or people negotiating contracts, this also includes intra-company transferees, corporate trainees, service sellers, or individual service providers and specialists on specific assignments (see Ghosh 1997 for more details).

(*c*) The international intra-firm movements are of special and growing economic interest. Multinational companies send their employees abroad. They take advantage of this internal labour market to transfer internationally firm-specific skills and knowledge.[7] Internal labour markets allow lower transaction costs related to hiring processes as compared to external labour markets (for example screening costs to learn about the motivation and skills of new employees or turnover costs to provide new employees with firm-specific rules and division of activities). They are of special interest for the relatively higher-skilled workers (managers, specialists, technicians). The cross-border intra-firm mobility of highly skilled technical and managerial

---

[7] The principle of internal labour markets goes back to the work by Doeringer and Piore (1971). It describes the reasons why firms cover job openings by workers already employed within the company. Besides the transferability and protection of firm-specific skills and knowledge these reasons include the information about the workers abilities and motivation (i.e. the screening has already been done before) and the savings of search and turnover costs. Internal labour markets are characterized by the fact that they do not follow the supply-demand mechanisms of external labour markets. They are planned and administered by firm-specific rules and procedures and the outcome (i.e. the individual wages) might deviate substantially from market equilibria (see Williamson 1975 for more details).

experts might be a very efficient strategy to transfer firm-specific knowhow from headquarters to the subsidiaries and vice versa.

(*d*) Network or chain migration has increased (see Bauer and Zimmermann 1997). This means that the flow of immigrants into a certain country depends on the stock of immigrants from the same country of origin who already live there. It sounds quite logical that it is much easier for a foreigner to get a job from an earlier arrived fellow-countryman. Economically, this has something to do with the international transferability of country-specific skills or knowledge that allows people to move physically but to keep their location-specific insider advantages. Just to give an example: normally an Anatolian cook cannot transfer his or her knowledge of cooking special Turkish food to a traditional German *Bierstube*. Rather he would have to start as a dish washer in Bayern and has to learn how to cook German *Knödel*. However, if he works for an Anatolian restaurant in Berlin, he can do almost the same job as back home in Turkey.

(*e*) In many cases, especially in Europe, migratory flows are increasingly dominated by rights acquired by former legal immigrants (i.e. family reunification) and by humanitarian reasons (refugees and asylum seekers). These two channels function largely as a substitute for direct demand-determined, labour-market oriented immigration, which has been made considerably more difficult since the beginning of the 1980s. Asylum seekers might stay even after the fundamentals in their home countries have changed and a safe return would be possible. They might build up networks and act as channels for further immigration flows.

(*f*) Another supply-driven channel that acts as a substitute for demand-determined legal labour migration is *irregular migration*. The latter has become an issue of heated public debate in Europe and North America and it is politicized by right-wing parties such as the 'Front National' in France, the 'Freiheitlichen' in Austria, the 'Republicans' in Germany, or the 'Save our State' movements in California. Illegal migrants break laws and rules and clearly provoke the credibility of judicial systems and the confidence in the power and authority of constitutional settings. They also challenge the public transfer system. Illegal foreign workers do not generally pay direct income taxes, but they often use public goods or publicly subsidized services like schooling or medical treatments for their children. Illegals compete with legals for job opportunities but have the possibility to avoid certain obligations, costs, taxes, and fees compulsory for the legal workers. These legal, economic, and social provocations make it easy to understand why politicians and their voters are not willing to accept the phenomenon of illegal migration.[8]

---

[8] But regardless of these negative impacts on the host society, illegal migration exists and it is growing all over the world. And this is not only due to the vehement and irreversible will of hopeless and desperate people from poor regions to enter the holy land of

The fundamental challenge of these contemporary international migration patterns is that they follow a rather *self-feeding self-enforced dynamic*. Network migration, rights-driven humanitarian migration (like family reunification, asylum seekers, or refugees) and also much of illegal immigration is supply driven. Contrary to the labour market-driven demand-determined economic migration the supply-driven migration cannot be controlled and regulated by (traditional) national laws and rules of the immigration country. In a very simple-minded view 'it just happens' (of course it is also very much driven by some vested interest groups in the destination area!). How can and how should nation states react to this growing complexity of contemporary migration patterns? The following sections will provide some guidelines.

Why should we regulate international migration at all?

The history of mankind is a history of migration. However, it has always been a hotly debated controversy whether migration is a good or bad phenomenon and whether and how it should be regulated to improve its benefits and lower its potential negative impacts. Questions like the following ones may arise in such a context: what costs and benefits do we exactly focus on? Is unrestricted international migration good or bad for the sending or the host society and what about the migrants themselves? Did the Red Indians for example make a big mistake by not preventing the Palefaces from immigrating? Obviously, answers to such questions differ according to subjective, individual evaluations. What makes the answer even more difficult is the fact that all impacts of international migration are not time invariant. They depend on the stage of economic development, changing economic business cycles, the intensity of social changes, and other non-economic factors.

Openness increases the efficiency of international production, it promotes economic wealth in all locations, and it stimulates economic convergence between the economic areas involved. This is one of the few iron laws of economics. It has led national economies to lower their protective restrictions

---

wealth and glory. There is also a need and demand for illegal immigrants. Some people (like house owners needing some help in cleaning and maintenance) and economic groups (like restaurant owners or farmers) benefit from illegal migrants (see Ghosh, chapter 1 in this volume). They try to avoid direct labour costs, indirect social payments, and costly regulations. The supply of and demand for illegal foreign workers create an economic market for illegal migration and a political market for the supply and demand of border controls and labour market regulations. Consequently, the phenomenon of illegal migration has to be analysed within an economic framework but also with an understanding of the political economy behind the setting of laws and rules. For a further analysis of the (politico-)economics of illegal migration see Jahn and Straubhaar (1998; also Ghosh 1998).

on international trade in goods by joining the GATT (now WTO). Lately, the GATT has expanded to include measures that facilitate the international trade in services within the newly established General Agreement on Trade in Services—GATS (see Ghosh 1997 for details). With regard to international cross-border movements of people, national governments are much less positive in their evaluations. It turns out, that 'man in his elemental state is a peasant with a possessive love of his own turf; a mercantilist who favors exports over imports; a Populist who distrusts banks, especially foreign banks; a monopolist who abhors competition; a xenophobe who feels threatened by strangers and foreigners' (Kindleberger 1984: 39). Of course, this negative evaluation of international movements of persons has something to do with the (supposed) effects on the host society.

In a very simplified world scenario with assumptions such as economically identical people who act individually and independently from each other and perfect and fully competitive markets with no common or public goods and no redistribution of income by some taxes or social benefits, *migration would be a positive mechanism*. In such a framework, migration is an arbitrage phenomenon that overcomes local surpluses or scarcities in factor endowments. In a world with no national borders and no limits to the internationally free movement of labour, migration is welfare improving for the world as a whole. This is one of the clear results of the positive theory of international trade.

However, this is a very aggregated *cosmopolitan* view. The problem with such a perception is that it does take into account the distribution of the gains from free migration. Additionally, the positive evaluation of migration effects is much more complex if we abandon the neoclassical framework used above. If we allow for unequal distribution of capital (wealthy and poor people), segmented labour markets (skilled and unskilled workers), and unemployment, or if we consider the existence of public goods, free migration of labour could also lead to negative effects—at least for some specific factors or groups. Just to give an example, imagine a blue-collar worker in the German 'Ruhrpot' area. Unlike the well-trained neoclassical economist, he or she is bound to express concern about immigration-induced unemployment, wage reductions, and a general deterioration of national welfare. The opposing attitudes result primarily from differences in perspectives. While the economist's enthusiasm is based on a certain long-term, allocational efficiency school of thinking, the blue-collar worker's fears are based on a short-term, distribution-oriented perspective.[9]

---

[9] Economists differentiate between *allocation* and *distribution* effects of migration. *Allocation* has something to do with the geographical organization of the production. It involves the macroeconomic efficient mix and use of input-factors. *Distribution* refers to the various payments to different factors of production (capital, skilled, or unskilled labour). It involves primarily microeconomic benefits and personal damages that are subject to more or less individual evaluations.

An evaluation of the effects of migration becomes even more complex if we include *externalities* of migration. In standard textbooks, economists differentiate between pecuniary and non-pecuniary (called 'technological') externalities.[10]

The *pecuniary* externalities of migration draw attention to the fact that macroeconomic allocational efficiency almost always has some negatively evaluated consequences on an individual microeconomic level. While the reallocation effects of migration are clearly positive on the whole, there will be winners and losers in the immigration and emigration countries. To the degree that labour markets are segmented, competition between natives and immigrants for employment opportunities leads to distribution effects within the host country. Those who have invested capital in the immigration economy gain, because labour becomes less scarce and therefore the average wage level will fall and the capital rent will increase. The part of the native labour force that can be regarded as being complementary to the immigrating labour force might reach a higher productivity and could be better off with rather than without migration. However, the other part of the native labour force that can be substituted by immigrating workers will become more abundant and their average wage level will fall. Finally, it is also possible that an immigrant will push a native out of the labour market and thus make him unemployed.[11]

Of course, we could show theoretically that the winners from migration (i.e. the capitalists and the complementary domestic labour force) could more than fully compensate the losers (i.e. the unskilled). We could also argue that in most cases unemployment is the consequence of labour market inflexibilities, wage rigidities, and structural inefficiencies. We could convincingly demonstrate that all these deficiencies have little to do with immigration and that immigrants actually contribute to *cure* these weaknesses. We could even repeat that most of the labour market pressure of globalization stems from the import of foreign goods and services and only partly from cross-border movements of persons. But all these valid arguments in favour of immigration do

---

[10] Positive externalities are the effects of subjects' actions that positively influence other subjects' actions without them having to do (or pay) anything for it. *Pecuniary* externalities are well taken by price-quantity market mechanisms. They occur through competition between different individuals for the same good or factor. If a customer asks for some bread another customer is affected by this demand because prices of bread might go up if customers compete with each other. *Non-pecuniary* or *technological* externalities are not internalized by the market. They occur in form of (indirect) spill-over effects to people not directly involved in specific market activities.

[11] Most of these *pecuniary* externalities of immigration tend to be the other way around if we flip the coin and look at the impacts of *emigration* for the sending countries. Emigration also has (pecuniary) external effects on those left behind, because labour becomes more scarce and capital becomes relatively more abundant. Therefore the capital–labour ratio increases in the emigration country.

not outweigh the individual evaluation of those citizens who are directly concerned (the unemployed or the ones crowded out from well-protected jobs into strongly competitive jobs or even into unemployment). Their *perception* is that a world with no immigrants would be a better world![12]

In contrast to pecuniary externalities, technological externalities of migration arise if some neoclassical assumptions do not hold. For the sake of simplicity, I summarize all types of market failure under the category technological externality and, therefore, I do not differentiate between institutionally induced types of market failure. It is a common feature of technological externalities that migration under such conditions does not only have distribution but also allocation implications. Within the context of migration the special focus is on indivisibilities, positive externalities from skilled labour, unemployment, and publicly provided education.

(*a*) Indivisibilities violate the neoclassical assumption of constant returns to scale.[13] Markusen (1988) models a two-country world in which both countries produce a modern human capital-intensive good under increasing returns to scale and a traditional good under constant returns in autarchy. If free trade is allowed the larger country will specialize in the production of the modern good and thereby cause the wages of skilled labour to diverge, which

---

[12] Following 'the logic of collective action' by Mancur Olson (1965, 1987) the fight against immigration led by vested interest groups of people negatively concerned should not really surprise. The losers are a more homogeneous, smaller group with a lot to lose for the single member while the potential winners are a much more heterogeneous, larger group with a relatively small gain for a single member.

[13] 'Constant economies of scale' means that it needs the double amount of all production factor inputs (i.e. labour *and* capital) to exactly double the output produced. Each single input, however, yields decreasing partial returns to scale, i.e. the more one increases the input of one single factor while leaving the other inputs constant, the less is this factor's marginal return. 'Increasing returns to scale (IRS)' implies that the larger the total amount of inputs, the higher their productivity. What does that mean for migration? Imagine two originally separated regions South and North which are identical in everything but the size of their economy. Due to the simple difference in economic output produced and the existence of IRS, the compensation of input factors in the bigger region (North) will be higher than in the smaller one (i.e. the South). If we now allow people to migrate from the South to the North where they get better compensation for their work, migration will no longer even out differences in factor payments but increase the scope for economies of scale in the 'northern' economy even further. The process of widening wage and interest-rate gaps between area of emigration and area of immigration does not stop until scarce location-specific factors in the area of immigration and corresponding redistribution effects eventually level out South to North differences in mobile factor's return to an extent that mobile factors no longer consider it worthwhile to move. Note that migration by IRS widens the development gap between the economically more important area and the less important area. Who benefits from economies of scale depends on what area is economically more important initially. Immigration into the initially bigger area strengthens its position as the core economy, while the smaller economy loses competitiveness.

in turn creates strong migration incentives. Thus, the outflow of skilled labour will make the small country smaller leading it to specialize in the production of a traditional good. The emigration of skilled labour exerts a negative effect on per capita income. The same line of argumentation is pursued by Krugman (1991*a*, 1991*b*) who models the emergence of a diverging centre-periphery pattern through migration: since the production function exhibits increasing returns to scale in the input of labour large-scale emigration is likely to occur. This mass emigration clearly benefits the immigration area (i.e. the centre) but leaves the remaining immobile factors of production worse off (in the periphery) and thereby contributes to income divergence.

(*b*) The second kind of market failure is associated with the migration of skilled workers and has something to do with the *positive externalities* stemming from human capital.[14] Depending on the extent to which the production and training of human capital (i.e. schooling and professional or academic education) has been financed by public subsidies, the emigration country loses human capital as soon as skilled or educated people leave their country of origin. This is the so-called *brain drain* as it was discussed by Jagdish Bhagwati (1976*a*, 1976*b*, 1985*a*, 1985*b*) and other scholars (Bhagwati and Dellalfar 1973; Bhagwati and Hamada 1974; Bhagwati and Wilson 1989).[15] This implies that (according to the theory of public goods) the production of human capital in the emigration countries might be too low relative to a world without migration.

(*c*) Following more recent theoretical approaches, in particular the New Growth Theory and the New Economic Geography, free movement of labour might increase the tendency towards *polarization* in economic development, with fast-growing centres and a slow-growing periphery.[16] This is the *dynamic*

---

[14] In more technical terms, the basic argument goes that the technology which determines the productivity of input factors is dependent on the available amount of 'human capital'. The higher the human capital stock, i.e. the total amount of (educated) knowledge, the higher the input factors' output production (given an efficient distribution of inputs). Input factors are assumed to exhibit constant private returns to scale and decreasing partial marginal productivities. They may substitute each other and are paid according to their marginal productivity. Given this set-up, however, markets fail, because they compensate people who invest in skills only for the partial marginal productivity of their human capital, not for the collective external effect of their skills on the technology. This is an important problem because in such a situation, the accumulation of human capital may become an 'engine of growth' that explains persistent differences in growth paths.

[15] The so-called 'brain-drain' discussion about the potentially deteriorating effects of migration on the development of emigration countries has been triggered by the observation that migrants from 'Southern' countries frequently belong to the most highly skilled of their societies.

[16] 'New Growth Theory' and 'New Economic Geography' mean—in a nutshell—that at least one of the standard neoclassical assumptions is relaxed (i.e. identical production technologies, constant economies of scale in production, efficient markets, and the absence of positive or negative externalities of production). Probably the most important change of

analysis of the brain drain phenomenon (actually, this is the polarization effect or *vicious circle* effect of migration already well known by Gunnar Myrdal 1956, 1957, or Albert Hirschman 1958). Centres may acquire absolute economic advantages because geographically concentrated, qualified labour may accumulate knowledge more efficiently and benefit from more learning-by-doing opportunities. Provided such absolute advantages exist, the more favourable conditions within the economic centres allows highly qualified labour to be more efficient and productive than in the periphery. As a result, skilled workers may experience large wage increases by migrating to such centres. Because the centres' advantageous economic position is due to endowments of human-capital intensive labour and location of knowledge-intensive production, immigration of highly qualified labour may increase wage differentials. A dynamic process would then lead to more and more emigration from the lower developed regions to the higher developed core.

Summing up, on theoretical grounds there is a strong argument that the emigration of skilled labour will harm those left behind whereas the emigration of unskilled labour will be beneficial for the sending country. The migration of highly skilled labour might lead to a divergence between the centre and the periphery ('the Mezzogiorno Problem'). Unless policy measures are introduced to offset the effects of migration of skilled workers, polarization effects may become self-sustaining and peripheral regions may find it very difficult to recover economically.

Finally, there are some unalterable prejudices and myths about *non-economic externalities* of migration. Some natives dislike more or less arbitrarily and subjectively the presence of foreigners. They (emotionally) feel negatively touched by some so-called social externalities of foreigners in their utility function.[17] Consequently they lobby against foreigners even if immigrants would create positive economic benefits to the economy as a whole.

the New Growth Theory is that it attempts to *endogenously* determine the rate of technological progress, whereas the rate of technological progress has traditionally been regarded as exogenously given in the neoclassical models. This gives rise to interesting links between the flow of *skilled* migrants and long-run *growth*. For review articles on New Growth Theory see e.g. Romer 1994, Grossmann and Helpman 1994, and Pack 1994; on New Trade Theory see Krugman's introduction in Krugman and Smith 1994. *The* pioneering work in 'New Economic Geography' is Krugman 1991*a*. This is a very valuable collection of fundamental ideas which is also accessible to non-economists.

[17] Social externalities of migration are a more or less completely arbitrary individual evaluation of some personal feelings about immigrants. Consequently, they are hardly (if at all) measurable or comparable. ' "Social externalities" is the term some economists use to dress up anything from urban crowding to xenophobia. It might be argued that the profession would be better served if, rather than providing technical cover for essentially political arguments, economists devoted their time to systematically measuring any negative externalities and, if they fail to turn up, arguing strongly against basing policy advice upon their existence' (Eichengreen 1994: 19).

Negative perceptions of immigration are also combined with regard to the impacts of immigrants on *public coffers*. Whether immigration is a financial relief or a burden for the social distribution system of the host country is not clear at all. Central to this point are the contributions of immigrants to social security and distribution systems and the amount of social security and welfare benefits migrants receive. The issue of 'who is financing or subsidizing whom' can therefore only be estimated *empirically*. But, the empirical results are not clear-cut at all (see Straubhaar and Weber 1994). Again economic business cycles, changes in politics and other non-economic factors make the impacts of immigration on public coffers extremely time variant. Furthermore, whether tax and social security payments of immigrants (government revenue) are set off against monetary and real transfer receipts (government expenditure) is very sensitive to the migration policy and to the process of selecting immigrants. It is clear, however, that the contribution of immigrants to the public coffer is the higher the younger and better educated they are.

To sum up, we see that within a theoretical world of neoclassical models migration is a *positive* arbitrage phenomenon. However, the more we relax the neoclassical assumptions (either by good theoretical reasons or by empirical evidence) we might see that migration does not lead to economic convergence but rather to divergence between sending and receiving areas. Without political corrections free movement of persons might lead to a polarized development process with rich centres and poor peripheries. Consequently, it is wise to think about interventions that could help avoid such an outcome of international migration.

How should we regulate international migration?

The twentieth century has been the century of national migration policies. Nation states all over the globe have initiated rules and regulations to discriminate between members (citizens, nationals) and non-members (aliens, foreigners). It has become and is an undisputed basic principle of international law that national governments have the sovereignty to decide which and how many non-nationals or non-citizens they allow to enter, stay, and work within their territory. Nation states would lose one of their most fundamental constitutive rights if they ceased to set rules about what aliens are allowed to do (rights), what they are required to do (duties), and what they should do (orders). Consequently politicians all over the world are very anxious to keep control on entrance, residence, and economic behaviour of non-nationals. They are well aware that their voters would not like the idea of a migration policy that maintains wide open doors to foreigners (see the reasons mentioned in the preceding section).

Nation, citizenship, and *community* are extremely sensitive values of human life. Michael Walzer (1983: 31) has expressed it very succinctly: 'The primary good that we distribute to one another is membership in some human community. Men and women without membership anywhere are stateless persons.' Being a member of a nation state is something very valuable. This is one reason why people are not willing to share their community with everybody and why they do not stand for open door migration policies.

However, in today's globalized world the concepts of 'nation' and 'citizenship' become more blurred than ever before. Societies are confronted with tendencies towards individualization. More and more, the frontiers of economic relationships and emotional community do not correspond with national territories. Solidarity and social responsibility can hardly be enforced anymore by institutions such as national governments. People would just leave the territories that exercise excessive governmental power. Indeed, the new dimension of globalization is that mobile factors of production can fulfil their wishes. They are enabled to search worldwide for locations which promise a good quality of life and a high standard of living.

Globalization might be the (macro)economic counterpart of (micro)sociological individualization. It weakens traditional social obligations and provides people with a much higher degree of independence. It diminishes the power of institutions and strengthens the position of the individual. The power of 'voting with one's feet' raises and increasingly protects individuals from governmental arbitrariness and discrimination. The possibility to leave generates a sort of permanent direct international democracy.

From the point of view of mobile people nation states can be seen as *clubs*.[18] Like clubs, nation states compete for high potential members. They have to offer attractive 'club facilities' to catch and keep mobile people. They have to produce a bundle of common 'club' goods and offer them to their citizens for taxes, fees, and direct payments. National governments have to provide efficiently (i.e. with minimal costs) those club goods which are demanded by the majority of the club members (i.e. voters of national

---

[18] The club theory originally developed by Buchanan (1965) and Samuelson (1954, 1969) provides an evident framework to sharpen thoughts about the target of economic policy-making in a globalizing environment. The club theory complements the theory of 'pure' public goods. *Club goods* are distinguished from private goods by their general non-rivalry in consumption within a specific capacity (in this regard they are similar to public goods). However after the capacity has been reached, they might be subject to congestion costs. But contrary to public goods (and similar to private goods), individuals (non-members) may be excluded from the consumption of club goods. Nations might be seen as territory-bounded clubs of people who share a certain homogeneity in their preferences. Using an available geographical endowment with fixed local attributes immobile club members have to offer complementary goods and services to attract and keep mobile parts of the value added chain (especially skilled workers and capital). A successful club will try to maximize the per capita value of club members.

governments). The use of such goods is tied to certain conditions which are again set by the majority of the club members (i.e. citizens) and might be formalized in club rules (called constitutions, national laws, or regulations).

The analogy of 'nations' as 'clubs' gains special interest when looking at the admission procedure for new members. The access to national citizenship follows administrative rules such as the *jus sanguinis* or the *jus solis* principle or specific bureaucratic selections. Citizenship gives more or less free and guaranteed access to all sorts of monetary and real transfers provided by nation states. These include not only benefits from various kinds of social networks but also the use of so-called public goods.

In my club analogy *citizenship* becomes equivalent to a *club-membership*. However, access to a club involves fewer emotions and more economic rationality than access to a nation! The 'golden rule' is that new members should be allowed to enter and stay if their marginal contribution to the financing of the club goods (fees, positive external effects) is larger than their marginal (congestion) costs for the old members.

Now it might become more obvious why voters do not appreciate an unrestricted immigration policy: immigrants and citizens basically compete for common national club goods and for pieces of the national redistribution cake. The effects of immigration on common national club goods turns out to be even more explosive if natives are crowded out from the use of the common club goods—which might be the case in social housing, basic medical treatment, recreation areas, or public places (these effects might be called congestion or negative agglomeration effects). The situation is quite comparable to normal clubs, like sporting clubs etc. These would also not give free access to their facilities to new members.

A large increase in the costs for common (national) club goods is caused primarily by the more intensive use and a corresponding rise in maintenance costs or by additional, necessary capital investment due to a newly immigrating population (demographic capital-widening). In such a case the old members will significantly increase the admission fee to the 'club'. New members are accepted as far as marginal benefits of immigration (positive external spill-over effects, taxes, fees, or other contributions to the financing of the common club goods) are evaluated to be higher than the marginal costs of new members (measured in negative external or congestion effects on old members). If a potential new members' characteristics are very attractive and dwarf the additional costs from migration, it is conceivable that a monetary incentive will be given and the welfare services will be improved. Indeed, we already see such financial incentives to attract mobile factors in the case of foreign direct investments by multinational companies. Such capital inflows are subsidized by cheap complementary immobile factors like real estate or by a waiver of taxation.

As can be imagined, most of the club goods effects described above for the immigration country are mirrored in the sending country. Emigration countries lose some of their club members. This is economically harmless or even beneficial to the extent that emigrants may have been unemployed. For an old question still remains valid: 'What is the most effective use to make of existing labor, to employ it abroad or leave it unemployed at home?' (Kindleberger 1967.) The emigration of unemployed, underemployed, or easily replaced workers, who consume more than they produce frees a part of the national income for alternative use. It saves the sending country the current and future social support for people who do not contribute to the national product. Therefore, it leaves the national product unchanged, while the average product per capita of the remaining will rise.

Considerable controversy exists about the validity of these assumptions concerning the positive labour market effects of emigration. Briefly, it can be shown by most empirical evidence that emigrants are typically younger, better educated, less risk averse, and more achievement-oriented than the average population in the sending areas (see Straubhaar 1988). Therefore, the assumption has a high probability that emigrants had been employed and that their marginal product was higher than the average product (that means that emigration lowers the average income per capita of those left behind). To the extent that (formerly employed) emigrants cannot be fully replaced by unemployed persons, emigration has a negative impact. This loss is even higher when the emigrants have generated positive externalities (this means that their private earnings have been lower than their social value added). Just to give an example: if a medical doctor leaves a hospital in India to go to the United States the whole hospital might be in danger and the nurses, assistants, and even the bed-makers might lose their jobs because the key factor (i.e. the surgeon) is missing.

Clubs losing their most valuable members cannot survive economically in the long run. Especially if the emigrants are the net payers (i.e. the younger, better qualified, skilled specialists and managers). So, emigration countries are challenged to keep their brightest citizens. They have to avoid a *brain drain* and to offer attractive local club goods (low taxes, cheap complementary factors of production like infrastructure, construction sites, and good business opportunities).

The club analogy of nation states might look a bit unrealistic. However, all over the world nation states regulate international migration according to their interests. Emigration countries try to keep their skilled citizens back home, immigration countries try to avoid front-door immigration of lower qualified people i.e. the legal entrance and residence of new members with a high probability of being net receivers of common club goods.

In a world with national migration regimes, the different strategies vary significantly. We find immigration barriers for some people (i.e. the unskilled workers) and emigration restrictions for other people (i.e. the skilled workers) and end up in a situation very far from unrestricted international migration. But these nationally divided club policies lead to a polarized development and a *suboptimal* human capital production. The countries of emigration might not invest as much public subsidies for education and human capital development because they are afraid of the loss by a brain drain. The countries of immigration might have incentives for relatively low human capital investments because they could profit from the brain drain and import human capital that has been publicly subsidized elsewhere.

As regards the international movements of lower-skilled people, immigration policies of the developed countries are largely reactive and defensive. It is widely recognized that the restrictive attitude against blue-collar immigration is not successful. In almost all major industrialized democracies a wide and growing gap between the goals of national immigration policy and the actual outcomes emerges. This 'gap hypothesis' of declining efficacy of immigration policies has been supported empirically for nine industrialized democracies (Cornelius et al. 1994).[19] Very often national migration policies act according to a short-term 'muddling through' behaviour. They can be seen as 'a matter of waiting to see what will happen next while issuing ad hoc regulations' (Kubat 1993). Of course this is mainly due to the fact that for tactical reasons politicians have to protect first the interests of their voters (i.e. the citizens). This often makes it necessary (from their point of view) to act immediately in favour of some vested interest groups.[20]

National politics has become more and more ineffective for a rising number of political and economic issues. The main reason for the failure of national migration policies is the loss of effective capacity to control today's migration flows on a national level. Once national governments close the *front door* of legal immigration more or less strictly, most of the entries take place through the *side* (asylum seekers, refugees, family reunification) or *back door* (illegals). In many cases the petition for asylum constitutes a reactive substitute for the stopping of legal, economically motivated immigration. Similarly,

---

[19] The most illustrative example is Germany. The official German position denies that Germany is a country of immigration. Still, immigration to Germany in the last decades has reached an enormous size. 'Germany emerges as the principal immigration country in Europe with inflows of about 800,000 foreigners in both 1994 and 1995' (OECD, SOPEMI 1997: 14).

[20] National migration policies are the result of a complex political-economic powerplay. The players belong to the governments, the national bureaucracies and the political parties and all of them try to maximize their vested group-specific or individual interests. Without going into detail about the theory of the rent-seeking process of politicians, bureaucrats, and lobbyist groups within the political process, we could take it as a rule of thumb that the more the political support for restrictions on immigration, the worse is the current economic situation.

illegal immigration has been a response to the demand of labour markets for cheap, unqualified labour that is not met by the domestic workforce for several reasons (regulations, minimum wages, insufficient qualifications).

The inefficiency and inefficacy of national migration policies has made it clear that an independent procedure by single nation states is no longer adequate. In a world with declining costs for international movements, 'national' clubs come under increasing pressure. Independently designed and performed national migration policies become more and more unfeasible. The fundamental challenge is that territory-bounded national clubs are no longer transaction-cost-minimizing institutional solutions. They are now replaced by functional clubs. These new and sometimes spontaneous arrangements beyond nation states take many forms. In politics supranational organizations (like the European Union) or international organizations (like the UN) take over national competence. The WTO, IMF, World Bank, and other international agreements replace national laws and regulations. In the microeconomic perspective, multinational firms try to internalize efficiently the advantages of globalization. In the areas bordering national frontiers 'functional' local cross-border arrangements rule the daily life problems of commuting, environmental protection, waste dumping or medical treatment. What is labelled as *globalization*—i.e. the increasing openness of goods and factor markets and the higher mobility of people—urges the political circles to react properly. Policies bound to their national territories are not sufficiently able to regulate activities with external effects that overlap several countries. What is needed is a transnational framework to balance the basic allocation benefits of free international migration with the controversial distribution and external effects of cross-border movements. How such an international regime might be structured is explained in the next section.

What should a GAMP look like?

Free international movements of people are economically efficient in most but not in all cases. As long as they involve a reallocation of labour—lowering a surplus here and bridging a gap there—they increase the average per capita income in both sending and receiving countries. However, under certain conditions—indicated above—they can cause serious repercussions for all the countries involved. Immigration of low-skilled workers might provoke further unemployment and crowding-out effects in the consumption of common club goods. Emigration of higher-skilled workers might lead to a brain drain that is negative for those left behind. As a result, some countries would like to allow the entrance of high-skilled people but restrict all other immigration. Other countries would prefer to restrict the emigration of their brightest citizens but would favour the exit of lower qualified and unemployed people. These diverging interests reveal the importance of an international framework for cross-border movements of people. Such an arrangement would seek to achieve some convergence in the otherwise diametrically opposed goals of national migration policies of sending and receiving countries. If we maintain conflicting national policies of this kind, we might end up with economically inefficient national interventions that excessively restrict the free entry and exit of people.

Based on the above, I propose the idea of a GAMP—a General Agreement on Movements of People. Of course the GAMP is the labour market analogy of the GATT for goods and the GATS for services. It expands the idea of open markets to include the issue of free movement for workers. It should deal with all international externalities and market failures of cross-border movements of people. It has to be seen as a complement to the 'GATT for International Direct Investment' as suggested by Charles Kindleberger (1984) many years ago but yet to be realized.

The GAMP intends to provide an international regime for the movement of people across countries. It stems from the conviction that in general, the free international movement of people—like the free movement of goods and capital—is beneficial for all parties involved (i.e. the migrants, the country of origin, and the country of destination). Consequently, it strives first and foremost for liberalization of the movement of people and towards a general acceptance of the free entry and exit of migrants.

However, I have already mentioned the several valid economic reasons which indicate that fully liberalized cross-border movements of workers could also lead to some inefficiency. To avoid brain drain in the emigration countries and congestion effects in the immigrating areas the GAMP should consist of two separate but interdependent parts, i.e. a political part and an economic part (for an overview see Figure 5.1):

(*a*) The *political section* aims at avoiding politically induced (mass) migration. It is part of the international law system including international political relations, human rights, and international security. It follows two principles: first, all people have the right to stay in their home countries and second, governments remain responsible for the consequences of 'bad' governance which may provoke mass migration of their citizens. It also includes the obligation for a country to stay open for its citizens who wish to return home. International asylum and refugee law is part of this section, which would ensure that everybody affected by political persecution or endangered by wars could find shelter in another country.

(*b*) The economic section intends to internalize external effects of migration and to secure an internationally optimal allocation of public goods. Both intentions could be reached through one single instrument, namely a 'migration tax'.

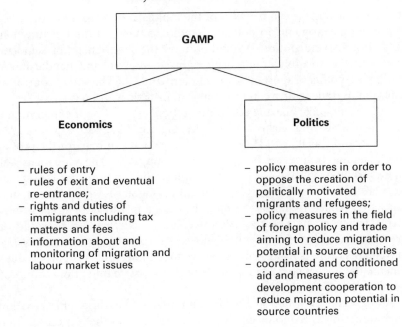

FIG. 5.1. Elements of a General Agreement on Movements of People

The latter (comprising an exit tax and an entrance fee) follows the standard economic suggestion to deal with non-pecuniary externalities of cross-border movements. The exit tax is intended to counterbalance brain drain effects and the entry fee is supposed to compensate non-migrants in the destination area for the congestion or crowding out losses they might have to bear. The migration tax would be a fee rather than a tax. This means that it has no direct fiscal motivation. Its only purpose would be to internalize the non-pecuniary externalities of international migration flows.

The first pillar (i.e. the political section) of the GAMP is intended to lower the non-economically motivated migration potential, including mass migration. Since these mass movements have important political implications, the GAMP should be directed towards policies that promote growth and development in (potential) migrant-sending countries. If expectations about the future development at home improve, the potential for short-term mass migration will decrease. The political section of the GAMP should therefore include both political and economic measures such as improved market access for exports, assistance to improve the working and international integration of financial markets, encouragement of technology diffusion, and last but not least the promotion of 'good governance' in migrant-sending countries. Advantage can be taken of the multilateral influence of the GAMP to prevent governments in potential sending countries from creating politically motivated emigration. It could promote the development of democratic tools and the creation of minority rights to prevent and handle internal conflicts. Another important contribution could be the strict control and abolition of trade in arms and weapons in unstable world regions.

The second pillar (i.e. the economic section) is based on the migration tax idea, proposed and elaborated on by Jagdish Bhagwati (1976a, 1976b; Bhagwati and Dallalfar 1973) years ago (for a good summary of the pros and cons of a migration tax see Bhagwati and Wilson 1989). The main focus—also an important problem—has been (and still is) that some artificial transaction costs are added to the process of migration. Migration would become more expensive. While this increase of mobility costs is intended for all those movements which create negative (non-pecuniary) externalities, it would also lower the incentives for migration flows with positive external effects (e.g. movements from surplus labour areas to region with scarcities). But in general, there is practically no feasible way to separate migration *ex ante* into 'good' and 'bad' flows.

A migration tax would succeed in 'gumming up the works' of international migration. This is economically just as questionable as the suggestions to tax international *capital* movements. The main differences however are the *asymmetries*. Capital is rather homogeneous while labour is extremely heterogeneous. As already noted, according to the 'club strategy', immigration countries should roll out the red carpet and open their golden doors wider— but of course, only to newcomers with knowhow. All the unwanted ones would be taxed or even shut out. In emigration countries, on the other hand, there would exist an incentive to send away all those people who are unskilled, unemployed, politically disliked, or have demands for social support. Highly qualified workers, however, would be induced to stay home.

An international tax regime for migration could be one way to tackle this problem. An efficient solution which would still correspond to the principle of free migration could be a change in the international taxation law. Today, with the exception of the United States, most countries view *citizenship* as irrelevant for tax purposes, only *residency* is the relevant jurisdictional nexus. That is to say, residents are taxable on their worldwide income, but non-residents are not. People leaving their home country are no longer subject to the country's taxation law. A migration tax could add a new principle: the country of origin could levy taxes on its citizens even if they live outside the country. That is to say citizens would become taxable worldwide by their home country as long as they wish to keep their old citizenship. To make this point clear: migrants would be regularly taxed by the host country (like all the other residents living there) and they would be additionally taxed by their home country (of which they keep the nationality). That means that migrants pay an extra fee as compared to the citizens of the receiving country.

Such a migration tax enforces a sort of emigrant loyalty to those left behind. This is justified by the fact that (with very few exceptions) citizens are entitled to return to their home country at any time. Emigrants normally keep their old passports together with a bunch of individual rights. The option to return home at any time can be compared to an insurance against the inclemency of life abroad. Just like for every other risk insurance, it is understandable that for this particular 'citizenship insurance' a financial contribution should be paid as well. Thus, the migration tax could also be seen as an insurance fee to be paid to those left behind since they offer a last shelter or safety net to their more risky compatriots.

The lower the costs of international mobility, due to declining information and transportation costs, the more urgent it is to question the principle of territoriality that guides international tax law today. The standard practice of taxing the gains from foreign direct investment under internationally agreed principles should also apply to labour. The higher the mobility of labour, the more important it will be for the international regime to allow:

(a) a country of emigration to tax their citizens abroad, and
(b) a country of immigration to levy a fee for entry.

At first glance, the migration tax might appear futuristic. However, in everyday life, however, we are already familiar with such practices. As a Swiss citizen living in Germany, for years I was obliged to pay a fee in order to keep my Swiss passport. Or take for example visa fees, naturalization fees, visitor taxes, and user fees for recreation areas, national parks, etc.

Of course many ways are open to design the migration tax more precisely. However, to become politically feasible the GAMP should remain as simple as possible. A fixed lump-sum entrance fee to be paid by every person wishing to immigrate, collected at the country of residence, and shared in equal proportions by sending and destination countries could be a first idea to follow. To keep the GAMP simple it should not address explicitly the question of changes of citizenship, dual or multiple citizenship. As long as migrants are not discriminated against economically this question is not of the highest priority to be regulated on a transnational level. A competition between different national regulations might be more efficient for settling these questions.

The GAMP should start with a stepwise procedure and it might even be a good idea to begin with bilateral agreements within a regional approach. This could also allow sending and receiving countries to agree on a bilateral level to waive the right to levy a migration fee (such as occurred within the European Union or other Common Markets that grant freedom of movement within the integrated area). From such a bilateral beginning it could move on to the regional level and finally to a global agreement.

Some concluding remarks

The daily picture of migration is blurred. We see desperate and hopeless people fleeing from regions of (civil) war, political struggle, and crude repression against minorities. Other people take boats to cross the sea, they swim rivers, climb over border fences, or place their lives into the hands of 'coyotes' just to enter the 'Holy Land' in their search for a better economic future. These emotionally impressive images make us forget the simple fact that most of the world's population does not move.

Consequently in the northern hemisphere, many fears of mass migration flows from the South are quite exaggerated. Nonetheless, the relative immobility of people does not mean that we should disregard the impacts of international movements of people.

As I have shown, there are good reasons to see international migration as an economically positive phenomenon that helps to smooth business cycles and remove imbalances in labour markets, thus serving, in most instances, as an arbitrage process. Like trade in goods and services, international migration leads to an optimal allocation of productive resources and is welfare improving. Under certain conditions, however, international migration might not produce the expected positive outcome. This is because, as already noted, migration involves people and not just goods or inanimate factors of production and as such often provokes diametrically opposed interests in sending and receiving areas.

In view of these diverging national interests, an international framework is needed. In my contribution I have suggested a labour market analogy to the GATT (WTO) and GATS. A GAMP should be directed towards a liberalization of international cross-border movements but should also provide an instrument to internalize the externalities provoked by international migration. To avoid brain drain effects in the sending areas and congestion effects in the receiving areas it might be wise to create a migration fee that makes exit and entry more expensive.

I am fully aware of several potentially severe problems related to the introduction of a migration tax. Probably the most important objection is that it throws sand in the wheels of economically positive migration. However, the GAMP could perhaps provide a consensus-building platform for negotiation between sending and receiving countries in order to lower the tax by stages and eventually abolish it.

As far as 'nations' are or become 'clubs', a migration fee will gain ground and could become more realistic in the future. In sports, transfer fees from the selling to the buying clubs are standard. These transfer fees are transaction costs. They bind players to clubs and prevent a free exit and entry. This gives clubs an incentive to invest in players and to train them. Transfer rules make 'free riding' by other clubs more difficult. Isn't it time we thought about a system of regulations and fees for transfers of people between nations?

REFERENCES

Bauer, T., and Zimmermann, K. F. (1997), 'Network Migration of Ethnic Germans', *International Migration Review,*31: 143–9.

Bhagwati, J. (1976*a*), 'The Brain Drain', *International Social Science Journal,* 28: 691–729.

—— (1976*b*), *The Brain Drain and Taxation: Theory and Empirical Analysis,* vol. ii, Amsterdam: North-Holland.

—— (1985*a*), *Dependence and Interdependence: Essays in Development Economics,* vol. ii, Oxford: Basil Blackwell.

—— (1985*b*), 'The Brain Drain: International Resource Flow Accounting, Compensation, Taxation and Related Policy Proposals', in Bhagwati 1985*a*: 303–46.

—— and Dellalfar, W. (1973), 'The Brain Drain and Income Taxation', *World Development,* 1: 94–101.

—— and Hamada, K. (1974), 'The Brain-Drain, International Integration of Markets for Professionals and Unemployment', *Journal of Development Economics,* 1: 19–42.

—— and Wilson, J. D. (1989), *Income Taxation and International Mobility,* Cambridge: MIT Press.

Buchanan, J. M. (1965), 'An Economic Theory of Clubs', *Economica,* 32: 1–14.

Cornelius, W. A., Martin, P., and Hollifield, J. F., (eds.) (1994), *Controlling Immigration: A Global Perspective,* Stanford, Calif.: Stanford University Press.

Doeringer, P. B. and Piore, M. J. (1971), *Internal Labour Markets and Manpower Analysis,* London: Heath Lexington Books.

Eichengreen, B. (1994), 'Thinking about Migration: Notes on European Migration Pressures at the Dawn of the Next Millenium', in: H. Siebert, (ed.), *Migration: A Challenge for Europe,* Tübingen: Mohr, 3–23.

Fischer, P. A., Holm, E., Malmberg, G., and Straubhaar, T. (1998), *Why Do People Stay?,* CEPR-Discussion Paper No. 1952, London: CEPR.

Ghosh, B. (1997), *Gains from Global Linkages:Trade in Services and Movement of Persons,* London: Macmillan

Grossman, G. M. and Helpman, E. (1994), 'Endogenous Innovations in the Theory of Growth', *Journal of Economic Perspectives,* 8: 23–44.

Hammar, T,. et al. (1997), *International Migration, Immobility and Development: Multidisciplinary Perspectives,* Oxford: Berg.

Hirschman, A. O. (1958), *The Strategy of Economic Development.* New Haven: Yale University Press.

Jahn, A., and Straubhaar T. (1998), 'A Survey of the Economics of Illegal Migration', *South European Society and Politics,* 3: 16–42.

Kindleberger, C. (1967), *Europe's Postwar Growth,* Cambridge, Mass.: Harvard University Press.

Kindleberger, C. (1984), *Multinational Excursions*, Cambridge, Mass: MIT Press.
—— (1986), 'International Public Goods without International Government', *American Economic Review*, 76: 1–13.
Krugman, P. (1991*a*), *Geography and Trade*, Cambridge, Mass.: MIT Press.
—— (1991*b*), 'Increasing Returns and Economic Geography', *Journal of Political Economy*, 99, 483–99.
—— and Smith, A. (1994), *Empirical Studies of Strategic Trade Policy*. Chicago: University of Chicago Press (and NBER).
Kubat, D. (ed.) (1993), *The Politics of Migration Policies*, 2nd edn., New York: Center for Migration Studies.
Markusen, J. R. (1988), 'Production, Trade and Migration with Differentiated, Skilled Workers', *Canadian Journal of Economics*, 21.
Myrdal, G. (1956), *An International Economy*, New York: Harper & Row.
—— (1957), *Rich Lands and Poor*, New York: Harper & Row.
Niehans, J. (1987), 'Transaction Costs', in: J. Eatwell et al. (eds.), *The New Palgrave (A Dictionary of Economics)*, vol. iv (Q to Z),. London: Macmillan, 676–9.
OECD SOPEMI (1997, 1998), *Trends in International Migration* (Annual Reports), Paris: OECD.
Olson, M. (1965), *The Logic of Collective Action*, Cambridge, Mass.: Harvard University Press.
—— (1987), 'Collective Action', in J. Eatwell et al. (eds.), *The New Palgrave (A Dictionary of Economics)*, vol. i (A to D), London: Macmillan, 474–7.
Pack, H. (1994), 'Endogenous Growth Theory', Intellectual Appeal and Empirical Shortcomings, *Journal of Economic Perspectives*, 8: 55–72.
Papademetriou, D. G. (1997), 'Migration: Think Again', *Foreign Policy* 109 (Winter 1997/8).
Romer, P. M. (1994), 'The Origins of Endogenous Growth', *Journal of Economic Perspectives*, 8: 3–22.
Samuelson, P. A. (1954), 'The Pure Theory of Public Expenditure', *Review of Economics and Statistics*, 36: 387–9.
Samuelson, P. A. (1969), 'Pure Theory of Public Expenditure and Taxation', in J. Margolis and H. Guitton (eds.), *Public Economics*, London: Macmillan, 98–123.
Straubhaar, T. (1988), *On the Economics of International Labor Migration*, Bern: Haupt.
—— and Weber, R. (1994), 'On the Economics of Immigration: Some Empirical Evidence for Switzerland', *International Review of Applied Economics*, 8: 107–29.
Walzer, M. (1983), *Spheres of Justice*, New York: Basic Books.
Weiner, M. (1996), 'Nations without Borders', *Foreign Affairs*, 75/2, 128–35.
Williamson, O. E. (1975), *Markets and Hierarchies: Analysis and Antitrust Implications*, New York: The Free Press.
World Bank (1995), *World Development Report 1995*, Washington, DC: World Bank.
—— (1999), *World Development Report 1998/9*, Washington, DC: World Bank.

6

Migration Outcomes of Guest Worker and Free Trade Regimes: The Case of Mexico–US Migration

Philip Martin, B. Lindsay Lowell, Edward J. Taylor

Introduction

Most regional and international regimes—systems in which national governments yield at least some power to a supranational authority that grants member nations rights and impose obligations on them—emerge from crisis, as with security regimes in which nations pledge mutual support, trade regimes in which members agree to lower barriers to the goods from other member nations to promote economic growth,[1] and financial regimes to establish rules for protecting investments and disclosing financial data in order to encourage citizens of one country to invest in another. This chapter is part of a project that aims to think about a global migration regime before a crisis occurs, so that the advantages and disadvantages of various options and structures can be considered without constant reference to the crisis at hand.

To date, all of the various agreements that have been constructed to deal with migration—either directly or indirectly—have worked in ways both desired and undesired. This chapter explores the history of bilateral regimes with the focus on Mexico and the United States. The issues raised in exploring this bilateral relationship in-depth are not unique, each of the regimes discussed here have parallels in other settings around the globe. Issues that arise highlight problems with regimes between less and more developed countries, especially less desirable migration phenomena that emerge from the bilateral regimes themselves.

---

[1] The international trade regime is bolstered by an economic theory that concludes that freer trade means faster economic and job growth, i.e. countries that refuse to participate pay a price in the form of slower economic growth. To prevent national governments from giving in to special interests, the 143-member World Trade Organization sets and enforces rules that seek to promote free trade.

The magnitude of migration and trade between Mexico and the USA makes them one of the more interesting examples of bilateral trade and migration regimes. Somewhere between 1 and 2 million Mexicans move to the USA for more than three months each year. Of course, most of these are temporary seasonal workers. Yet, the numbers of illegal migrants and newly admitted legal immigrants from Mexico far exceeds that from any other nation, comprising about one-third of the total combined flow of about 1 million entrants annually to the USA. Mexico is the source of nearly one-fourth of legal permanent residents in the USA and over 50 per cent of permanent unauthorized residents. In 1998, there were about 7.5 million Mexican- born residents of the USA, including 2 million naturalized US citizens, 3 million legal immigrants, and an estimated 2.5 million unauthorized migrants.

For most of the twentieth century, the major relationship between Mexico and the USA was a migration relationship, and there were many disputes regarding the treatment of Mexicans in the USA. This migration was asymmetric: the United States accepts immigrants from and trades with many nations, but virtually all Mexican emigrants and most Mexican exports come to the United States, leading to the aphorism: 'poor Mexico, so far from God, and so close to the US.' Despite significant advances in recent years in dealing with migration bilaterally, the south–north flow of migrants remains a constant source of tension between the two countries.

The migration policy regime for most of the twentieth century was one of the US government alone, or the US and Mexican governments jointly, permitting US employers to recruit Mexican workers for temporary US employment (*braceros*). However, workers and employers preferred to operate outside the legal temporary worker system, so there were periodic immigration and labour crackdowns by the US government that led to mutual recriminations between the USA and Mexico. The legacy of the Bracero programme has been decades of illegal migration taking place during increasing economic integration of the two countries. In 1994, the prevailing policy regime changed and an effort was made to encourage the trade relationship to replace the dominant migration relationship, as well as to reduce the illegal flow. However, as part of the North American Free Trade Agreement, the US government refused to negotiate a migration side agreement. In 1998 Mexico moved from the United States' third to its second largest trading partner, yet illegal migration from Mexico continues unabated.

Bilateral agreements for temporary workers

There has been significant Mexico–US migration in every decade of the 20th century, but during only two periods, 1917–21 and 1942–64, did formal bilateral agreements regulate the employment of most Mexican workers who were temporarily in the USA. Under a series of labour agreements that are generally referred to as the Bracero programme (Martin 1996; Massey et al.1987), some 4.6 million Mexicans entered the United States on a temporary basis to do farm work between 1942 and 1964. Most of these seasonal Mexican workers shuttled between homes in Mexico and jobs in the USA, but over the course of 22 years, 1 to 2 million Mexicans obtained work experience in the USA as legal guest workers.

This Mexico–US Bracero programme was dogged by controversy from the start. For example, the first 'farm labor supply agreement', signed between the USA and Mexico on 23 July 1942, was bitterly opposed by US farm labour reformers. In 1939 there was an outpouring of writings critical of the treatment of US farm workers by US agribusiness, including John Steinbeck's *The Grapes of Wrath*. Reformers hoped these would lead to farm labour reforms, including the requirement that US farmers pay farm workers at least minimum wages and that farm workers have the right to form unions and bargain collectively with employers under government supervision.[2] US farm labour reformers, in a nutshell, wanted the US government to treat large farms that grew labour-intensive commodities as 'factories in the fields', apply factory labour laws to them, and thereby integrate or make more similar farm and non-farm labour markets.

The Bracero programme, however, helped to keep the farm labour market isolated from other US labour markets. Farm labour reformers complained that calls for braceros were a mere repetition of the age-old obsession of all farmers for a surplus labour supply (Craig 1971: 38–9). The US workers who would have led unions and pushed for reforms found it easier to achieve economic mobility by engaging in geographic and occupational mobility—to get ahead, they quit being farm workers and left rural areas, which they could do in the booming Second World War economy.

The programme was small during the war years—braceros were fewer than 2 per cent of US hired farm workers in 1944. The Mexican government was reportedly doubtful that there was a farm labour shortage, and insisted that the US government guarantee the contracts that farmers provided to Mexican braceros, including round-trip transportation and the payment of wages equal to those of similar American workers (Craig 1971: 41). However, the number of Mexicans and the percentage representing those who arrived illegally, as so-called 'wetbacks', increased in the late 1940s and early 1950s, as both Mexican workers and US farmers learned they could avoid Mexican and US regulatory agencies by making private employment arrangements. The

---

[2] Family members could accompany braceros, but none did. In successive renegotiations of the bracero agreements Mexico got fewer labour protections than they desired, and neither was their administrative involvement increased.

usual practice was for a Mexican worker to enter the US illegally, find a US farm job, and go to work, usually under prevailing wages, but without, for example, government-inspected free housing or other protections specified in the contracts that each bracero worker received. If apprehended inside the USA, the Mexican worker was usually taken to the Mexican border, issued work documents, and returned to his US employer, a process termed, even in official government reports, 'drying out wetbacks'. The fact that there was no enforcement penalty on workers or employers for being outside the programme encouraged illegal immigration, leading one researcher to conclude that 'the Bracero program, instead of diverting the flow of wetbacks into legal channels . . . actually stimulated unlawful emigration' (Scruggs 1961: 151).

The perception that Mexico–US migration was out of control in the early 1950s led to Operation Wetback in 1954, a massive border control and interior enforcement operation that removed from the USA over 1 million Mexicans and relaxed rules for employing Mexicans as legal bracero workers. The number of braceros reached 500,000 in the mid-1950s. The ready availability of braceros permitted California agriculture to expand without raising wages significantly, enabled California and the south-west to gain a comparative advantage over eastern states in the production of labour-intensive fruit and vegetable production, and helped to make US farmers and Mexican workers mutually dependent on each other. US workers, especially Mexican-Americans in the state of California, responded by moving to cities such as Los Angeles and San Jose.[3]

The Bracero programme was ended unilaterally by the USA in 1964 and some ex-braceros became US immigrants. During the 1950s and 1960s, a Mexican could legally immigrate to the USA on the basis of a letter from a US employer asserting that the Mexican being sponsored was the only person capable of filling the job being offered. Most Mexican immigrants to the USA in the 1950s and 1960s were braceros who were sponsored by their US employers in this manner: a 1963 article reported that 80 per cent of the 222,000 immigrants from Mexico between 1957 and 1962 had been braceros (Taylor 1963: 43). Illegal immigration rose after 1964, but only modestly: some 110,000 deportable aliens were located in 1965, 212,000 in 1968, 420,000 in 1971, and 788,000 in 1974.

The number of Mexicans apprehended in the USA first jumped over 1 million in 1983, after Mexico devalued the peso, and then rose to a peak 1.8 million in 1986, when the Immigration Reform and Control Act (IRCA) was enacted. IRCA included the largest-ever amnesty for illegal foreigners, permit-

---

[3] California vegetable production rose 50%, as the state replaced New Jersey, the 'Garden state'. According to the US Department of Agriculture farm worker wages rose 41%, from $0.85 in 1950 to $1.20 in 1960, while factory workers wages rose 63% during the 1950s.

ting about 2.3 million Mexicans who had arrived in the 1980s to become legal immigrants. However, the other part of IRCA's 'Grand Bargain', sanctions on US employers who knowingly hired illegal workers, did not deter illegal immigration because unauthorized workers could purchase and present to employers false documents. One of IRCA's amnesty programmes, the Special Agricultural Worker programme, legalized about 1 million Mexican men who asserted they had done farm work as illegal aliens in the USA. This turned one in six adult men from rural Mexico into US immigrants.

Mexican-born US residents and migrant workers have traditionally come from rural areas of Mexico, because that is where the USA and Mexico authorized the recruitment of Mexican farm workers, and because Mexico was primarily a rural society until recently. Even in 1999, about 25 per cent of Mexico's 97 million residents live on farms and in rural areas. Many Mexicans with homes and families in rural Mexico continue to be sojourners, coming to the USA for six to nine months each year, but the majority of Mexican-born US residents today are settlers who live in US cities and about half are women. They mostly occupy low rungs of the US job ladder. Most Mexican-born persons in the USA have less than eight years of schooling and low US earnings and incomes.

In sum, the Bracero programme turned out to be anything but a managed flow of temporary workers:

- After its cessation there was a growing flow of mostly unskilled illegal (and legal) Mexicans to the USA.
- The flow built upon networks that linked the bottom of the Mexican labour force with the bottom of the US labour market.
- Mexico neglected West Central Mexico, the area from which many migrants came, so that emigration and remittances became core pillars of those local economies.
- The experience often made it hard for the US and Mexican governments to treat each other as equals, as the American experience with Mexicans was often limited to braceros in the USA.

There are parallels in the northern European 'guest worker' programmes of the 1960s and early 1970s. Firms in countries such as Germany, France, and Belgium recruited foreign workers in the late 1950s and 1960s to fill labour shortages to meet the needs of rebuilding in sectors such as construction and light manufacturing. Bilateral agreements between countries, such as between Germany and Turkey, governed working conditions, as well as sending-country obligations. However, soon after the oil shock of 1973–4 there were 'recruitment stops' throughout Northern Europe. In the immediate aftermath, the traditional emigration countries such as Italy, Greece, Yugoslavia, and Turkey asked the ILO and the OECD to assess the benefits of worker emigration. The ensuing studies found that the sending countries reaped little economic returns from the remittances and the skills of those workers who returned (Martin 1990). Workers' monetary remittances might cause inflation in good times and suddenly collapse during economic downturns when they are needed, and often they simply are not spent on productive enterprises. Returning migrants have new skills for which there is no market. In 1976, the ILO argued that migrant worker agreements needed to smooth out fluctuations in migration and remittances.

But Northern European countries have not made a return to the type of guest worker programmes of the past. In the aftermath of those programmes, like the Bracero, was a legacy of permanent settlement of former 'guest workers' in the host countries leading to the well-known phrase 'there is nothing so permanent as a temporary worker program'. While these populations did not generate the same subsequent volume of illegal or legal immigration experienced by the USA, they were nonetheless substantial and the Northern European countries were unprepared to deal with them. If illegal workers in the USA continue to fill low-skilled niches of 'bad jobs', many of the guest workers now in their third generation are likewise often found in the lower segment of the labour market. Further, their integration has been problematic as they occupy a legal status that is often short of full citizenship and has created numerous difficulties for these 'non-immigration' countries (Heisler 1999). Guest workers or braceros—while there are short-term benefits of such temporary working programmes for both the sending and the host country, in the longer term neither party has got quite what they had sought for.

Production sharing agreements and migrant absorption

Following the demise of the Bracero programme, the Mexican border region faced a sudden overflow of farm workers returning from the USA and looking for work. Mexico thought it saw a solution in the production sharing or offshore assembly processing (OAP) regimes between developed countries and developing economies such as Taiwan (China), Singapore, and other East Asian locations. In the 1950s, US companies began to manufacture higher-technology components and shipped them to the Far East for hand assembly by low-cost labour. Aside from tariff relief and tax breaks, the countries involved offered other incentives as an inducement. Yet, already by the mid-1960s, labour costs in the Far East had begun to rise and Mexicans saw an opportunity to create jobs and to reap the 'value-added' in assembly or production sharing arrangements.

In 1965, Mexico adopted a National Programme for Unemployment Abatement in the North, later the Border Industrialization Programme and the Maquiladora Programme. Both the USA and Mexico altered their trade and investment laws so that foreign (US) investors could create jobs in Mexican border areas for the families of braceros who had become dependent on earnings from the US labour market. Under the maquiladora system, components and any machinery needed to assemble them are imported duty free into Mexico and goods are processed or assembled in the maquiladora. As the finished goods enter the United States, the US tariff schedule limits duties on them to the value that was added by Mexican assembly operations—wages and Mexican inputs usually add about 20 per cent to the value of maquiladora products. For example, in the first six months of 1997 maquiladoras exported goods worth \$20 billion, but imported goods worth \$16 billion, so Mexico's value-added was only about \$4 billion.

Maquiladoras have grown steadily over the decades. There were twelve maquiladoras employing 3,000 workers in 1965, almost 600 maquiladoras employing nearly 120,000 workers in 1980, almost 2,000 maquiladoras employing 472,000 workers in 1990, and about 4,000 maquiladoras employing just over 1 million workers in 1998. Foreign direct investment averaged \$11 billion a year between 1994 and 1997, and much of it went into maquiladoras. As a result, maquiladora employment expanded very sharply in the 1990s. Maquiladoras provide almost 10 per cent of the formal sector jobs in Mexico, and about 30 per cent of the manufacturing jobs. Today, maquiladora exports comprise 44 per cent of all Mexican exports and, in 1998, maquiladoras surpassed oil as Mexico's leading source of foreign exchange.

Clearly, the Maquiladora Programme stimulated employment growth, but where did the workers come from? The braceros, almost all of whom were male, and their families were one source of labour, but as we have seen many ultimately settled in the USA, while others returned to their home communities. The assembly plants recruit workers from the interior of Mexico. Most maquiladoras prefer young women workers, a preference that has been ascribed to the willingness of women to work for low wages, their dexterity, and their willingness to perform tedious and repetitive tasks—one manager reportedly asserted that 'we like to recruit people who have never worked, ideally 16 years old, who have finished their primary education . . . they have not yet learned bad habits, and they make the best workers' (quoted in *Free Labor World*, September 1994, p. 4). Young women have remarkably high labour force participation rates in border cities where 60 to 80 per cent of the 20- to 24-year old women may be found in the workforce.

At least most of this labour force is stabilized by assembly employment; although the young women come from the interior of Mexico, it does not appear as if many continue the move northward into the United States. Today, about 60 per cent of the employees in maquiladoras are young women, and most studies of the linkages between maquiladoras and migration conclude that people stay and work in the border areas. The jobs are not always good, but they are better than those available elsewhere. Maquiladoras in Mexican border city labour markets act as local monopsonies facing an elastic supply of labour at the minimum wage—wages and benefits in the maquiladoras averaged about $1.80 per hour in mid-1995, and are projected to remain below $2.50 per hour until the year 2000. So the maquiladora workers tend not to use the assembly plants as stepping stones to the USA. Nevertheless, it has been observed that the young men who often accompany women to border cities may migrate to the USA, although their numbers are not known.

The best example of how maquiladoras can serve as stepping stones for Mexico–US migration occurs in export-oriented vegetable agriculture. Mexico's export-oriented vegetable industry is centred in Sinaloa, about 600 miles south of the US border. Large farms there employ about 170,000 Mexican workers for four to five months. Most of these seasonal workers are migrants: three-fourths migrate to Sinaloa from other parts of Mexico, and seasonal work there ends just as US growers begin to hire farm workers. In 1996, typical wages for tomato picking in Sinaloa were reported to be about $3–5 per day, and children often join their parents in the fields (*Sun-Sentinel*, April 1996). The schools in the camps teach from 5 to 8 p.m., so that children can help their parents in the fields. Most Mexican vegetable exporters provide housing in 125 camps at no charge to their harvest workers, often 150 square feet for each family, which can be 6 to 10. Government doctors visit the camps to dispense basic medicines and to teach methods of birth control.

Mexican migrants in Sinaloa were asked in one survey about their migration intentions, and 27 per cent in 1985 intended to continue migrating north to Baja California or the United States. Continuing migrants tended to be single, young, and landless men: migrant families with small farms were more likely to return to southern Mexico. Once in Baja California, many men continued to migrate to the USA. The ten growers who farm in Baja California's San Quintin Valley use US capital and seeds to produce tomatoes and other vegetables for the US and Mexican markets. Several of these farms have 1,000 to 4,000 acres, making them large operations by US or Mexican standards, with peak migrant workforces of 2,000 or more. Most of the migrant workers they employ are Mixtec Indians from the southern Mexican State of Oaxaca. Surveys of these Mixtec workers in California and Oregon reveal that two-thirds had worked in Baja California and that, while employed there, US foremen, labour contractors, and friends and relatives encouraged them to seek US jobs (Zabin et al. 1993). It can be concluded from the literature on maquiladoras that:

- Maquiladoras did not achieve their original goal, they did not provide jobs for ex-Bracero men who had become dependent on the US labour market in the 1950s. Instead, the plants recruited women from the interior to the border area.
- Maquiladoras stimulated population and economic growth along the

US–Mexican border. About 8 million people live within 50 miles of the US–Mexican border, one of the richest parts of Mexico and one of the poorest parts of the United States.

- Most maquiladoras pay more than the Mexican minimum wage, although critics note labour and environmental practices are sometimes poor. Employee turnover is very high.

Regional concentration of employment, preferential employment of women, high worker turnover, and some tendency to stimulate northward stepwise migration—it is not known how well these features describe production sharing and/or assembly production in developing countries other than Mexico.[4] Unfortunately, there is little systematic research on the relationship between production-sharing plants and internal or external patterns of migration. Although, where smuggling becomes important, which is the case in Mexico and perhaps in China as well, observers note that women working in foreign-owned plants are able to pay the smugglers' fees for accompanying males.

Certainly, production sharing and assembly plants are widespread, involving many developed and developing countries. It is estimated that production sharing is at least 30 per cent of the global trade in manufactured products, or at least $800 billion of world trade (Yeats 1998). This estimate is probably low, since a considerable volume of US imports with selected countries under the Generalized System of Preferences (GSP) or the Caribbean Basin Initiative (CBI) are already exempt from custom duties and so are not reflected in this estimate. The production sharing business involves all member countries of the OECD and there is strong growth in exports from countries in the Caribbean, for example, to the OECD. In 1992, the OECD imported 4.5 billion of Caribbean manufactures with the Dominican Republic having about half the total. Offshore assembly processing (OAP) plants play a key role in this trade.

Perhaps with the fall of the Soviet Union, the most apt case to compare with Mexico and the USA may be Northern Europe and the former socialist countries of Eastern Europe. Due to their proximity and the combined effects of low wages and high literacy rates, the former socialist countries of Eastern Europe have attracted most of the European Union's new assembly processing (OAP) contracts during 1991–4 (Yeats 1998). German hourly wages are 17 to 23 times greater than those of Poland, Czechoslovakia, or Hungary; and per capita GDP differences are between 2.3 and 3.5 times greater. France, in contrast, has wages that range from 11 to 15 times as great as these three countries, although the

---

[4] Today, maquiladoras are hiring more men, moving to interior locations, and producing more sophisticated products with better-educated workers. About two-thirds of maquiladora employment in 1998 is at the border, compared with 90% in 1980 (though border states still retain 80% of the industry's workers). In principle, interior locations could help reduce border growth and stepwise migration to the USA.

per capita GDP spreads are about the same.[5] Here is a region which, except for the high literacy rates of Eastern Europeans, shares with North America many of the same features of proximity between developed and 'developing' nations, as well as significant economic differentials.

Free trade as the ultimate curb on migration

In 1990, Mexico's President Salinas sought additional means of increasing Mexican trade and economic development and approached European nations for trade preferences. He was told that they had their hands full with Eastern Europe and that Mexico should look to its North American neighbours. In a surprise move, Mexico next proposed a free trade agreement with the USA. Canada, which had entered into a free trade agreement with the USA in 1989, felt obliged to join the negotiations for what became the North American Free Trade Agreement (NAFTA), which went into effect on 1 January 1994.[6]

The goal of NAFTA is to lower barriers to trade and investment and thus to spur job and wage growth in all three member countries. Its passage was not a sure thing, however, with strong opposition within the USA by conservatives and union liberals alike during the 1992 presidential campaign. Candidate Ross Perot claimed that NAFTA would create a 'huge sucking sound' as Mexico's cheaper labour attracted US businesses southward at the expense of US workers. The torch for passage was ultimately passed from President Bush to President Clinton who championed NAFTA's 'fast track' passage through Congress. As time to negotiate the agreement closed, NAFTA was argued to be the best means of spurring Mexico's trade and economic development and, thereby, reducing the flow of Mexican labour northward. Although general agreements on migration were explicitly not part of the NAFTA, the idea that NAFTA-led economic development would reduce the significant volume of undesired, illegal migration was a strong selling point at the end. That expectation convinced many who had been undecided.

This raises the question: is the trade liberalization symbolized by NAFTA an effective way to reduce pressures for 'unwanted' South–North migration, as many OECD policy-makers hope?[7] That question was addressed by the US Commission for the Study of International Migration and Cooperative

---

[5] Depending on the base year and methods of calculation, these estimates would vary. They are used here mainly to indicate the wide economic disparities involved.

[6] In 2001, the maquiladora will be incorporated into the Mexican economy and, under NAFTA, restrictions on Mexican sales and temporary imports from the USA and Canada will be no more. New Mexican laws passed in the last decade also stand to stimulate joint ventures and manufacturing employment.

[7] We use 'unwanted' rather than illegal to describe the migration industrial countries

Economic Development that was charged with the mission of learning about and proposing mutually beneficial policies to attack the root causes of migration. The Commission concluded that '*expanded trade* between the sending countries and the United States *is the single most important remedy*' for unwanted migration (INS 1990: xv, emphasis added), i.e. in the long run, trade and migration are substitutes.

However, the Commission warned that 'the economic development process itself tends in the short to medium term to *stimulate* migration,' i.e. the same policies that accelerate economic growth, including privatization, land reform, and freer trade, tend to produce a migration hump, or temporarily more migration, because of the displacement and disruptions that accompany restructuring for faster development. (See Chapter 9 in this connection.) The fact that trade and migration may be complements in the short run creates 'a very real short-term versus long-term dilemma' for a country such as the United States considering a free trade agreement as a means to curb unauthorized immigration from Mexico (INS 1990: xvi, emphasis added).

Near- and long-term development and migration

The Commission embraced the hypothesis that trade and migration can be complements in the short run and substitutes in the long run, i.e. economic integration can produce a 'migration hump'. A more detailed analysis of NAFTA's likely effects on Mexico–US migration reached the same conclusion: as a result of a relatively protectionist Mexico embracing free trade, plus continued opportunities for Mexican immigrants to find US jobs, and due to the existence of strong migration networks that link Mexico and the USA, there is likely to be a migration hump during NAFTA's first decade, 1994–2004 (Martin 1993). A migration hump produces a paradox—the same economic policies that make immigration control less necessary in the long run make it more necessary in the short run. The Commission concluded that a shortrun increase in immigration was a worthwhile price to pay for policies that will reduce unwanted immigration in the long run.

The Commission report and a number of researchers have turned the migration hump into conventional wisdom: it is widely believed that, if there is a pre-existing migration relationship, embracing freer trade as a means of reducing unwanted international migration has a paingain quality. For most researchers, the migration hump is empirical, based on the experiences of

are trying to reduce because much of the migration most amenable to being reduced with trade and other economic development measures involves legal but not necessarily wanted foreigners, such as 'economic refugees' in Western Europe, and Salvadorans with a 'Temporary Protected Status' in the USA. In both cases, the host countries would like to reduce the number of such aliens, but their presence is not unlawful.

countries such as Italy and South Korea or demand-pull, supply-push, and network factors in specific migration relationships, rather than being based on economic theory.[8] However, it does have a theoretical foundation, grounded on the kinds of market imperfections and economies of scale most likely to be present in North–South economic integration.

If trade and migration are substitutes in both the short and long run, the migration hump becomes a migration trough, i.e. trade liberalization immediately and unambiguously reduces migration. This was the implicit assumption of most political leaders and trade negotiators. In the words of Mexican President Salinas, 'more jobs will mean higher wages in Mexico, and this in turn will mean fewer migrants to the United States and Canada. We want to export goods, not people' (quoted in Bush letter to Congress, May 1991, p. 17). At the other extreme, if trade and migration are complements in both the short and long run, the migration hump is a migration plateau: globalization and freer trade permanently increase South–North migration pressures.

When Southern European nations such as Italy and Spain industrialized and were integrated into the European Community (EC, today EU), they too were characterized by significant emigration pressures. However, economic gaps narrowed enough during the six- to ten-year wait for labour mobility that, when Italians and Spaniards were permitted to search freely for jobs throughout the EC, few did (Straubhaar 1988). South Korea experienced one of the world's fastest migration transitions. In 1982, over 200,000 Korean workers emigrated; in 1994, the South Korean government is debating how to deal with 20,000 legal foreign 'trainees' and 50,000 to 100,000 illegal alien workers.

The migration hump is most likely to occur when three conditions are met: (1) continued opportunities abroad pull migrants out of a country; (2) supply-push emigration pressures rise as the economy adjusts to freer trade; and (3) social networks bridge the border. Mexican–US migration satisfies these three conditions and provides a textbook case of how freer trade and investment can accelerate development and affect this migration linkage. The standard comparative static trade model asserts that migration and trade are substitutes in both the short and long run, since adjustments are assumed to occur instantaneously. Thus Heckscher (1949), Ohlin (1933), Mundell (1957), and Stolper and Samuelson (1941) developed models that did not deal with the transition from one equilibrium to another.

An analysis of the assumptions underlying trade theory illustrates how relaxing or abandoning key assumptions can produce a migration hump.

---

[8] Migration humps are not new. The 48 million Europeans who emigrated from Europe between 1850 and 1925 represented about oneeighth of Europe's population in 1900, suggesting that 'large scale emigration was quite common during Europe's period of industrialization' (Massey 1991: 17; Lowell 1987).

Consider two countries: a capital-rich immigration country and a labour-rich emigration country. If the two countries share the same technologies (production functions), and the same two factors of production, capital and labour, are used in each country to produce two goods that are traded freely, then each country exports the good that uses intensively the abundant factor, i.e. capital-rich countries export capital-intensive goods, and capital-poor countries export labour-intensive goods. If these countries free up trade, and exports increase as expected, returns on capital should increase in the rich country (as capital flows from the rich to the poor country), and wages should rise in the poor country, as the new capital employs workers there. There is no need for migration, because the rich country imports the poorer country's labour in the form of labour-intensive goods.

Trade theory and migration

The standard trade model that considers trade and migration to be substitutes rests on five major assumptions. Relaxing these assumptions can turn trade and migration into complements:

- the two countries share identical production technologies;
- the two countries use the same factors of production (factor homogeneity);
- production functions have constant returns to scale (i.e. there are no scale economies);
- adjustment to changes in international market environments is instantaneous, an implicit assumption; and
- there is perfect competition, with full employment and complete markets in each country.

The standard trade model assumes that the two countries share the same technologies (production functions). This means that, if tractors plough fields in the United States and horses pull ploughs in Mexico, the reason is that Mexico has more labour, not that tractor technology is unavailable in Mexico.[9]

If there is no migration, US agriculture is expected to have a higher capital–labour ratio than Mexican agriculture, since higher US wages lead to more use of relatively expensive capital. If there is migration, then we expect more labour-intensive production technologies in US agriculture—the US would still have higher capital–labour ratios, but they would not be as high as they are in the absence of migration. Suppose there is little trade, and the protected good is produced with a labour-intensive technology in Mexico, but with a

---

[9] This is the same thing as saying that differences in the labour and capital intensities of production between the two countries are due solely to differences in their factor endowments.

highly efficient capital intensive technology in the USA, as is the case with corn (maize).

If high-tech US corn production gives the USA a comparative advantage in producing corn, then with free trade the USA may be able to increase corn exports, displacing Mexican corn farmers. The USA produces about ten times as much corn as Mexico; the US state of Iowa alone produces about twice as much corn as Mexico, and the USA can export corn to Mexico for less than Mexican farmers can produce corn with labour-intensive technologies. About half of the man-days worked in Mexican agriculture in the mid-1990s were used to produce corn. Thus, freeing up trade in corn could be expected to eliminate millions of man-days of work for 3 million Mexican farmers and workers. If these workers have no local job alternatives, and if networks link them to US labour markets, this may encourage migration to the USA.

There are policies that can mitigate such migration pressures even with free trade. For example, Mexico changed its farm support policies from buying the corn produced by farmers at about twice the world price, meaning that farmers had to grow corn to get the subsidy, to direct payments to farmers regardless of what they grew. Many of the small farmers most prone to migrate were too far from government corn buying facilities to take advantage of the high government corn prices, but they do receive the direct payments, so they are better off despite a freer trade policy that was expected to hurt them and force more to migrate. If these payments help farm households finance production or consumption, they may increase, rather than decrease, employment and even corn production.

Comparative advantage and thus trade rests on differences in factor productivity, which may be due to a country's endowments of land, labour, and capital, as well as infrastructure—including transportation, communications, markets, and the legal system—which makes the same factor more productive in one country than in the other. If infrastructure has important effects on factor productivity, then a labour-intensive emigration country such as Mexico may not have a comparative advantage even in the production of some labour-intensive goods, especially if migration can permit lower-wage foreign workers to be used with first-class infrastructure. This is what seemed to occur in the shoe industry in the 1980s. The Mexican shoe industry in Leon shrank, in part due to lack of experienced workers, while the shoe industry that employed Mexican workers from Leon in Los Angeles expanded. Shoes produced by Mexican workers in the USA were exported to Mexico.

The standard trade model does not consider cases in which differences in infrastructure and labour quality change the meaning of terms such as labour abundant and capital abundant. If infrastructure increases factor productivity, then a rich country such as the USA may be labour abundant if labour supply is measured in efficiency units rather than in workers. Migration, by converting Mexican workers into US workers, can discourage the production of some labour-intensive goods in Mexico, and thus encourage more migration.

The third critical assumption of standard trade theory is that there are constant returns to scale in both countries, which means that increasing all inputs by 10 per cent will increase output by 10 percent. However, if there are scale economies, if per-unit costs fall as production increases in labour-intensive industries, then freer trade may increase the output of labour-intensive industries in the USA and encourage more migration from Mexico to staff expanding production lines. When the basis for trade is scale economies, migration and trade are complements.

The fourth assumption of the standard trade model is that adjustments to changing prices and wages are instantaneous, and the process of adjustment does not affect the comparative static outcome. However, in many cases, prices drop and workers are displaced in a country such as Mexico as trade barriers fall, but it takes time for foreign and domestic investment to create jobs in sectors in which Mexico has a comparative advantage. This adjustment period offers an intertemporal reason for a migration hump, that can be compounded by factor specificity, e.g. the tendency of older men displaced from Mexican agriculture to be shunned by expanding maquiladora assembly operations that prefer to hire young women.

The final assumption of standard trade theory is perfect markets, including full information, no risk, and zero transactions costs. These conditions are rarely found in emigration countries adjusting to freer trade. The new economics of labour migration (NELM) is based on an analysis of the implications of missing or incomplete markets, imperfect information, and high transaction costs for migration. A number of studies support the NELM theory (Taylor and Martin forthcoming; Massey et al. 1998).

For example, suppose that those wishing to migrate pay smugglers, i.e. there are costs of migration, but the benefits of employment abroad are such that migrants are willing to pay smugglers several thousand dollars. In such a situation, emigration may be slowed by lack of funds to pay smugglers, so that faster economic and income growth due to freer trade may paradoxically increase the money available to finance migration, at least in the short term (Schiff 1996). This is what may have happened in south-western China, as well as in Mexican border cities in which young women migrants got jobs in foreign-owned factories, while the young male migrants who accompanied them got financing to enter the USA illegally. As mentioned above, production sharing arrangements and assembly plants may play a role in facilitating such outcomes.

Differential opportunities by sex and skill may also affect migration patterns as households act to maximize their economic welfare. Families that encourage, for example, a young man to migrate to the USA may not be able to insure against the risk that the youth will be apprehended and fail to obtain a higher wage job. If freer trade creates jobs for young women but not for young men, the family may be more willing to finance the risky unauthorized smuggling attempt for the young man because the young woman's job acts as insurance. The family will be better off if the young man succeeds, but it will not be as badly off if the young man fails and the young woman's wages act as a partial cushion.

Freer trade opens new opportunities for small-scale farmers to switch from corn to fruit and vegetable production for export markets. But many small producers face significant financial, management, and risk constraints, finding it hard to borrow money or acquire the expertise needed to make the move to a higher-income and also higher-risk farming activity. Mexican agriculture in the 1990s was often described as being in crisis, with high input costs and low prices and encouraging some farmers to leave their land fallow, and capital either unavailable or available only at a high cost. Without readily available capital, it will be hard to turn corn and grain farmers into fruit and vegetable growers, which is one reason why former Mexican Undersecretary of Agriculture and architect of the agricultural policy reforms, Luis Tellez, in 1995 predicted an average annual exit of 1 million farmers each year for ten years from Mexican agriculture.

Having a son or daughter employed abroad helps the family to overcome the missing market for loans to change crops and diversify its income sources, perhaps encouraging the risky change that offers more long-run income potential. After families have made the transition to an open economy and social safety nets develop, migration is no longer needed to remedy missing markets. Although migration may have negative short-term impacts on production in rural, migrant-sending economies, there is increasing evidence that the remittances migrants send home promote development by financing rural farm and non-farm activities (Taylor and Martin forthcoming; Rozelle et al. 1999).

The NAFTA migration experience

Those arguing for NAFTA were well aware of the theoretical trade models and the migration hump. But numerous economic models showed that (1) the greatest adjustments, as well as (2) the greatest benefits would accrue to Mexico. No one knew how quickly migration would be affected, it was simply assumed that reductions in migration would be forthcoming after a relatively short period of adjustment. How well have the forecasts matched the early years of NAFTA?

A number of computable general equilibrium (CGE) models were developed to try to estimate just how much restructuring there would be in the economies and labour markets of Canada, Mexico, and the United States due to NAFTA (Hinojosa-Ojeda and Robinson 1991). Virtually all of the models projected that Mexico's economy would grow faster, creating more jobs at higher wages than would exist in Mexico without NAFTA. The US International Trade Commission summarized the models' results, noting that, because of NAFTA, Mexico's real GDP was projected to rise by 0.1 to 11.4 per cent, its employment was expected to be 7 per cent higher, and real wages would be 0.7 to 16.2 per cent higher. The primary mechanism by which these results would be achieved was through foreign investment—foreign capital would flow to Mexico, the argument ran, bringing new technology and new management and creating jobs and hope. As a Latin American tiger, Mexico could run a trade deficit for years as foreign investors built up its productive capacity and infrastructure, much as South Korea did during a similar phase of development in the 1960s and 1970s.[10]

In reality, NAFTA got off to a rocky start, with the emphasis on the cost of adjustment rather than the benefits of increased trade and investment. Foreign capital had flowed into Mexico in anticipation of NAFTA turning Mexico into a Latin American tiger economy. There was an influx of foreign capital in 1993–4, but Mexico permitted the peso to become overvalued, making imports of both capital and consumer goods cheap. US and other foreign investors lent billions of dollars to Mexico, and Mexicans used many of these foreign savings to buy US and other foreign goods, not to build factories and create jobs. Migration pressures remained at their historically high levels, but there is disagreement over whether they were affected appreciably by changes in Mexico's policies (Taylor et al. forthcoming).

In 1994 a series of events transpired that began to temper investor enthusiasm: Zapatista rebels launched an armed campaign in the state of Chiapas on 1 January 1994; the leading presidential candidate was assassinated in March 1994; and the Mexican money supply was increased sharply in summer 1994 in support of the ruling party's presidential candidate. President Salinas resisted an 'orderly' devaluation of the peso in the autumn of 1994, but in December 1994, just after Salinas left office, Mexican and foreign investors began converting pesos into dollars at the fixed, 3.45 to $1 rate, and Mexico ran out of reserves to support the peso. The peso was sharply devalued in December 1994.

Although most migration experts had predicted that the closer economic integration symbolized by NAFTA would at least temporarily increase migration, none predicted the 1994–5 devaluation and severe recession. Mexico, a country with almost 100 million residents and about 10 million formal sector private jobs for a paid labour force of 30 million, experienced almost 1 million layoffs from formal sector jobs in 1995. In the villages from which many migrants come, economic models projected a migration elasticity with respect

---

[10] However, aggregate models predicted that, in the mean time, agricultural liberalization policies in Mexico, including the removal of price supports for corn, would stimulate migration from rural areas, with many migrants heading to the USA.

to peso devaluations of 0.7 per cent—that is, a 7 per cent increase in emigration for every 10 per cent devaluation of the Mexican peso, which was down almost 60 per cent between November 1994 and November 1995. Instead of job and wage growth with NAFTA, Mexico in 1995 suffered its worst recession in decades. Many Mexicans responded to the 1994–5 crisis by migrating to the USA despite stepped-up border controls. The USA apprehended 1.1 million foreigners, over 95 per cent Mexicans, in 1994; 1.4 million in 1995; 1.6 million in 1996; 1.5 million in 1997; and 1.7 million in 1998.

Nevertheless, since those events there has been remarkable economic growth in Mexico and there may be, once again, reason to forecast a migration hump of the sort originally envisioned. GDP growth has exceeded 6 per cent in recent years and long-term foreign investment has returned to Mexico. Between 1994 and 1998, foreigners invested $57 billion for long-term projects, making Mexico second only to China in the receipt of foreign investment dollars. The number of Mexican workers in formal private-sector jobs rose by 400,000 in 1998.[11] Mexican exports have surged leading strong year-to-year GDP growth and Mexico has moved from the United States' third to its second largest trading partner. A team of Mexican and US scholars under joint-government aegis, the Binational Study on Migration, released a report in 1997 noting that the same demographic and economic factors that in the mid-1990s produced high levels of Mexico–US migration may soon ebb. Mexico in 1997 had 970,000 labour force entrants, but birth rates fell sharply in the 1980s and 1990s, so that the number of new job seekers will be 500,000 to 550,000 per year by 2010. Second, each 1.35 per cent increment to economic growth was associated with 1 per cent job growth in Mexico between 1988 and 1995. If this ratio persists, then 5 per cent economic growth can generate 3.7 per cent job growth, or 1.1 million new jobs each year, enough to employ new job seekers and begin to reduce un- and underemployment.

These more favourable demographic and economic growth trends would suggest that pressures for emigration will begin to lessen early in the next century. Further, NAFTA, the Binational Study on Migration group, and other developments symbolize a new era of US–Mexican cooperation on difficult issues, including migration. Other notable steps that have increased US–Mexican cooperation on migration issues include the Regional Consultation Group on Migration (Puebla process), which brings together ten North and Central American countries each year to discuss migration issues, and often quiet Mexico–US cooperation to reduce the entry through Mexico of non-Mexicans, to prevent border violence, and to avoid deaths and injuries to migrants attempting unauthorized entry through remote areas of the border (see chapter 3 in this volume).

---

[11] There were 10,216,940 permanently insured workers in IMSS, the Mexican social security system, in October 1998, up 380,000 or 4% from the year before.

Policy implications

Globally, international migration has great potential for disrupting orderly relations between nations, despite the fact that the number of migrants is small relative to the population of those who do not move. The world's population reached 6 billion in 1999. The number of international migrants—persons living outside their country of birth or citizenship—was estimated at more than 130 million, meaning that about 2.5 per cent of the world's residents were legal or unauthorized immigrants, non-immigrant guest workers, students, business people, or refugees or asylum seekers.[12] Most of these migrants have been or intend to stay outside their country of birth or citizenship for twelve months or more.

In relative terms, most foreign-born residents are found in developed nations—in 1990, by UN definitions, there were 54 million foreigners among the 1.2 billion residents in developed nations, and 66 million foreigners among the 3.6 billion residents of developing nations. There were 28 countries with 1 million or more foreign-born persons in 1990—they collectively included 77 per cent of all foreigners—led by the USA with 19.6 million; followed by India with 8.6 million; Pakistan with 7.3 million; France with 5.9 million; Germany with 5 million; Canada with 4.3 million; Saudi Arabia with 4 million; and Australia, with 3.9 million.

The number and type of migrants has increased faster than the capacity of national governments, regional bodies, or international organizations and agreements to deal with international migration.[13] (See Chapter 1 in this volume.) In response, many national governments have dramatically increased their expenditures on immigration control, new regional forums have developed to discuss migration issues, and there is a growing call to expand from one global migration regime—that dealing with refugees—to at least one additional migration regime to deal with the types of non-refugee migration that seem bound to increase in a globalizing world economy.

[12] These UN data do not distinguish foreign-born persons by their reason for migration, by their date of arrival, or by their duration of stay. The UN data also do not distinguish between people moving across borders as, for example, immigration into the USA and Canada and borders moving over people, as occurred, for example, with the break-up of Yugoslavia and the USSR. The UN defines developed countries to include Europe, the ex-USSR, the USA, Canada, Japan, Australia, and New Zealand.

[13] Still, most of the world's residents will never be migrants. Most people will live and die within the borders of one of the world's 190-odd countries without ever spending an extended period of time abroad.

Guest worker regimes

Guest worker regimes based upon bilateral agreements between developed and developing countries have not worked all that well. Their benefits to the sending country have been muted because remittances have not been productively spent, and because there is little market for the newly acquired skills of returning migrants. From the host countries' side, the greatest problem has been that in filling labour shortages the assumption that foreign workers do not settle has not held. Temporary workers become permanent settlers.

The simple implications for guest worker policies are that functioning regimes should create incentives for both countries to fulfil their part in agreements: (1) that special trade rights, investments, and other preferred treatments be extended to the sending country; this would help to secure (2) their active involvement in complying with a policy of return of the temporary workers from the receiving country, as well as steps taken against irregular movement. In other words, specific reciprocity is called for, the involvement of both parties in accomplishing the major objectives of the other (Hollifield 1999).

The new guest worker programmes for agriculture being entertained by the US Congress remain primarily unilateral in their approach. A limited role for the Mexican government is envisioned and no incentives are extended. Instead, it is proposed that a fairly large number of Mexican workers should be available for US agriculture, and that their return be ensured by withdrawing funds from their pay packets payable only upon their return to Mexico. This has been attempted in other countries and in Mexico, with little success, and it is certain that many Mexican workers will choose to forfeit the withholdings for a chance to remain in the USA.

At the same time, the predominant view in Mexico remains that, while they would welcome an active role in administering a temporary worker programme in coordination with the USA, there is little inclination to actively curb illegal entry over the border. The Mexican constitution is read as countering the possibility of restricting the right of their citizens' movement. At the same time, renewed interest in Mexico in another guest worker programme has thus far not come to grips with the fact that the idea in the USA is for reduced labour protections (in comparison with the little used 'H-2A' agricultural workers programme). This was the greatest source of contention in the Bracero programme of the 1950s and 1960s and, without bilateral agreement addressing labour conditions, would surely become a new flash point in an otherwise improving relationship.

In contrast, 'strategic interactions' between the states of Western and Eastern Europe have explored bilateral accords. The reunited halves of the German government have made deals with east and central European states that lay out joint efforts against irregular migration. In particular, Germany has extended investment and debt relief to Poland, as well as greater freedom of movement for Polish nationals within Germany (Hollifield 1999).

Trade agreements

Freer trade and investment regimes accelerate economic growth in both emigration and immigration countries, and thus they are desirable for their own sake. However, the transition to freer trade in relatively closed emigration economies such as Mexico's is disruptive, altering relative prices and thus wages, incomes, and job opportunities. If migration networks link those adversely affected by restructuring to the international labour market, and if the labour markets in which migrants seek jobs abroad are not hurt or are stimulated by freer trade, then trade and migration are likely to be shortrun complements—that is, increased trade is likely to be accompanied by increased migration.

Over time, freer trade and investment should increase the rate of income and job growth in the emigration country, thus diminishing migration pressures. When viewed over a decade or two, the number of migrants first increases and then decreases, producing a migration hump, which can be relatively small and short. When wage differences decrease to 4 or 5 to 1 and economic and wage growth seems assured in the emigration country, economically motivated migration often drops dramatically. This offers a powerful reduce-unwanted-migration argument for freer trade and investment regimes.

The possibility of a migration hump accompanying freer trade regimes has three major policy implications. First, freer trade and investment should be advocated as the best longrun policies to promote what has been called 'stay-at-home' development. However, free trade should not be sold as a short-term cure for unwanted migration. The US debate over NAFTA, the narrow margin by which NAFTA was approved, and the approval one year after NAFTA of Proposition 187 in California indicate the dangers of trying to use trade agreements as short-term solutions for unwanted migration.

Second, a better understanding of adjustment costs and migration networks and other factors that motivate migration could help to prevent some of the unwanted migration associated with freer trade. The obvious example in the case of NAFTA was how to deal with the 3 million Mexican farmers growing corn, particularly in the light of market imperfections characterizing the rural Mexican economy.

Third, the emigration countries that benefit from freer trade and investment should be expected to help immigration countries manage migration, especially the unwanted or unauthorized migration that freer trade is expected eventually to reduce. Given the resistance to free trade in many ageing industrial democracies worried about unwanted immigration, it seems

naive to suggest that migration can continue to be excluded from trade negotiations.

It is important to emphasize, as Ghosh (1997) does, that the industrial
democracies seeking to reduce unwanted migration must also look inside
their own back yards. Restricting imports of agricultural commodities and
textiles, for example, reduces employment in emigration countries and
increases employment for migrant workers in industrial countries.
Furthermore, the 1994 liberalization of trade in services under the General
Agreement on Trade in Services that benefits banks, insurance companies, and
other firms in industrial countries can benefit both developing and industrial
countries, but only if GATS is accompanied 'by an internationally harmonized
visa regime for trade-related movements as distinct from migration for
employment or permanent settlement' (Ghosh 1997).

REFERENCES

Craig, R. B. (1971), *The Bracero Program: Interest Groups and Foreign Policy*, Austin:
University of Texas Press.
Ghosh, B. (1997), *Gains from Global Linkages: Trade in Services and Movement of
Persons*, London: Macmillan Press.
Heckscher, E. F. (1949), 'The Effects of Foreign Trade on the Distribution of Income',
in Ellis and Metzler (eds.),   *Readings in the Theory of International Trade*,
Philadelphia: Blakiston.
Heisler, M. (1999), 'Contextualizing Global Migration: Sketching the Socio-Political
Landscape in Europe', in C. Rudolph (ed.), *Reconsidering Immigration in an
Integrating World*, UCLA Journal of International Law and Foreign Affairs, 3(2):
557–94.
Hinojosa-Ojeda, R., and Robinson, S. (1991), *Alternative Scenarios of U.S.-Mexico
Integration: A Computable General Equilibrium Approach*. Working Paper No. 609,
Dept. of Agricultural and Resource Economics, Univ. of California, Berkeley.
Hollifield, J. F. (1999), 'Migration, Trade, and the Nation-State: The Myth of
Globalization', in C. Rudolph (ed.), *Reconsidering Immigration in an Integrating
World*, UCLA Journal of International Law and Foreign Affairs, 3/2: 595–636.
Immigration and Naturalization Service (INS) (1990), *INS Statistical Yearbook, 1990*,
Washington, DC: Immigration and Naturalization Service.
Krauss, M. B. (1976), 'The Economics of the "Guest Worker" Problem: A Neo-
Heckscher-Ohlin Approach', *Scandinavian Journal of Economics*, 78: 470–6.
Lowell, B. L. (1987), *Scandinavian Exodus: Demography and Social Development of
19th-Century Rural Communities*, Boulder, Colo.: Westview Press.
Martin, P. L. (1990), 'Labor Migration and Economic Development', in Commission
for the Study of International Migration and Cooperative Economic Development,
Unauthorized Migration: Addressing Root Causes. Research Addendum, vol. ii.
Washington DC, 647–64.

—— (1993), *Trade and Migration: NAFTA and Agriculture*, Washington, DC: Institute for International Economics.

—— (1996), *Promises to Keep: Collective Bargaining in California Agriculture*, Ames, Ia.: Iowa State University Press.

—— and Taylor, J. E., (1996), 'The Anatomy of a Migration Hump', in J. E. Taylor (ed.), *Development Strategy, Employment and Migration: Insights from Models*, Paris: Organization for Economic Cooperation and Development.

——, Hönekopp, E., and Ulmann, H. (1990), 'Europe 1992: Effects on Labor Migration', *International Migration Review*, 24/91, (Fall), 591–603.

Massey, D.S. (1991), 'Economic Development and International Migration in Comparative Perspective', in S. Diaz-Briquets and S. Weintraub (eds.), *Determinants of Emigration from Mexico, Central America and the Caribbean 1.* Boulder, Colo.: Westview Press.

—— et al. (1998), *Worlds in Motion: Understanding International Migration at the End of the Millennium*, Oxford: Oxford University Press.

—— et al. (1987), *Return to Aztlan: The Social Process of International Migration from Western Mexico*, Berkeley and Los Angeles: University of California Press.

Mundell, R. A. (1957), 'International Trade and Factor Mobility', *American Economic Review*, 47: 321–35.

Ohlin, B. (1933), *Interregional and International Trade*, Cambridge, Mass.: Harvard University Press.

Rozelle, S., Taylor, J. E. and deBrauw, A. (forthcoming), 'Migration, Remittances, and Agricultural Productivity in China', *American Economic Review*.

Schiff, M. (1996), 'Trade Policy and International Migration: Substitutes or Complements?', in J. E. Taylor (ed.), *Development Strategy, Employment and Migration: Insights from Models*, Paris: OECD Development Centre.

Scruggs, O. (1961), 'The United States, Mexico, and the Wetbacks: 1942–1947', *Pacific Historical Review*, 30 (May).

Stark, O. (1991), *The Migration of Labor*, Oxford: Basil Blackwell.

Stolper, W. F., and Samuelson, P. A. (1941), 'Protection and Real Wages', *Review of Economic Studies*, 9 (Nove.), 58–73.

Straubhaar, T. (1988), *On the Economics of International Labor Migration*, Bern/Stuttgart: Paul Haupt.

Taylor, D. (1963), 'How Mexico Feels about the Bracero Program', *California Farmer* (20 Apr.).

Taylor, J. E. and Martin P. L. (forthcoming), 'Human Capital: Migration and Rural Population Change', in B. Gardener and G. Rausser (eds.), *Handbook of Agricultural Economics*, vol. i, Amsterdam: Elsevier.

—— Yunez-Naude, A., and Dyer-Leal, G. (forthcoming), 'Agricultural Price Policy, Employment, and Migration in a Diversified Rural Economy: A Village-Town CGE Analysis from Mexico', *American Journal of Agricultural Economics*.

Yeats, A. J. (1998), 'Just How Big is Global Production Sharing?' Development Research Group, World Bank, Washington, DC.

Zabin, C., et al. (1993), 'A New Cycle of Rural Poverty: Mixed Migrants in California Agriculture', Davis: California Institute for Rural Studies.

7

Migration: International Law and Human Rights

Guy S. Goodwin-Gill

Introduction[1]

International human rights law has developed with little direct regard either for migrants or refugees, yet it is clearly and necessarily related to both groups of human beings, who often remain on the periphery of effective protection. In part, this is due to still potent notions of state sovereignty, and non-nationals, simply because of their lack of citizenship and regardless of the fact of physical presence, are seen as standing outside the community and the substantive and procedural entitlements normally accorded to members.

In fact, most provisions of most human rights instruments draw few distinctions between nationals and non-nationals; the right to life, for example, or the right to integrity of the person and to human dignity, are guaranteed to everyone without distinction. But the principle of non-discrimination as it applies to certain other human rights and procedural guarantees is less well founded, as was evident during the 1980s debate in the United Nations General Assembly on the Declaration on the Rights of Non-Citizens, and again on the 1990 UN Migrant Workers Convention. The perceptions of labour-exporting and labour-importing states diverged on important rights-related issues, and the gap seems as wide today as it ever was.

Similar lacunae are evident in national responses to refugee flows, especially those from developing to industrialized countries. Gaps in both formal and informal systems of refugee protection exist in areas such as refugee definition, admission, standards of treatment, and solutions. International human rights law offers an additional, sometimes parallel system of protection, but its

---

[1] The present chapter draws in some respects, and intentionally, on an article, 'International Law and Human Rights: Trends concerning International Migrants and Refugees', published ten years ago in Tomasi 1989); though the times have changed, the overall situation of the migrant and the refugee has not greatly improved, even if there is perhaps a great consciousness of the need, and the obligation, to protect his or her human rights.

extension into the migrant and refugee field is not yet fully effective, and must now meet the challenges of national security, the HIV/AIDS pandemic, and the inexorable drive toward economic betterment. Nonetheless, both the elective migrant and the forced migrant are located squarely within the human rights context. Migrants and refugees alike have a particular interest in liberty and personal integrity rights, whether they relate to movement, admission, due process, family, employment, personal and social security, freedom of expression, culture, and language. At the same time, any such rights, and the rules behind them, operate in a context of ever-changing national priorities and sensitivities. As the twentieth century draws to a close, however, it ought to be clear that the very nature of the migration phenomenon demands a significant measure of agreement, between sending and receiving states, on common standards, including the protection of human rights; only with a consensus in this domain, can the international community look forward to better, more efficient and effective management.

Community, citizenship, and non-discrimination

Arguably, the true end of government—dispensing justice and deciding rights by promulgated laws rather than absolute, arbitrary power, together with the promotion of the good of the people (Locke 1690: 132–42)—is a sufficient reason for ignoring the narrow badge of citizenship when it comes to fundamentals. The narrow, contrary claim that only those committed to and depend-ent on a social collective have rights 'against' that group leaves begging essential, perhaps unanswerable questions about community, membership, commitment, and dependency, none of which is self-applying. Bills of rights, indeed, tend to work more from the particular to the general, founding themselves upon the inalienability of certain individual rights. At the international level, article 1 of the 1948 Universal Declaration of Human Rights (UDHR48) opens with the affirmative, 'All human beings are born *free and equal* in dignity and rights.' The Preamble to the Charter of the United Nations proclaims the determination 'to reaffirm faith in fundamental human rights, in the *dignity and worth* of the human person'. The Annex to the ILO Constitution affirms that 'all human beings, irrespective of race, creed or sex, have the right to pursue both their material wellbeing and their spiritual development in conditions of freedom and dignity, of economic security and equal opportunity' (Brownlie 1990).

Independent of citizenship, fundamental rights in the strong sense have the anti-utilitarian consequence that they may not be denied by governments, even in the general interest (Dworkin 1977). Yet the doctrine of inalienable rights, inherent in the individual, has frequently had to give way to 'sovereignty', considered in its high positivist sense, as an absolute assertion of right and power in a society of competing nation states. Non-nationals suffer from the classification of alienage, as examples of mass and arbitrary expulsion show only too often.[2] States today are even more vocal in demanding controls, less so in acknowledging their obligations towards non-nationals within their territory, who have contributed and continue to contribute to their economic well-being.

Nevertheless, fundamental human rights represent a critical point of departure in international discourse. They stress individual security and autonomy, and are founded upon assumptions regarding human dignity, upon the inhering principle that justice depends on an equal right to equal concern and respect (Dworkin 1977: 180–3, 272–8; Rawls 1972: 29, 51) and upon pragmatic recognition that the effective protection of rights commonly requires that judicial intervention resolve conflicts of interest, or set limits to the scope of discretionary power, in accordance with the rule of law.

The factual situation within which rules operate, change, and develop, must still be taken into account, however, together with the interests and entitlements of national or host communities and the frequently conditional or qualified nature of many human rights. States have long practised discrimination in immigration,[3] and have attempted to relate their policies and choices to rational or defensible bases, such as social and economic grounds. In the past and even into the present, states have weighted the balance in favour of those who, as near as can be, reflect the ethnic and cultural origins of the majority of the populace, or who are sponsored by relatives, or who will contribute to population growth, stability, and economic development. Membership in the community remains a fundamental question, but so too are the equities which arise from long residence, family links, and situations of distress or humanitarian necessity. The challenge for international law, today as in the past, is to provide principled guidance to states in the exercise of sovereign powers, and to international organizations in the promotion of policies and practices oriented towards human welfare.

Migration and human rights

Once thought to be readily distinguishable, migratory and refugee flows are now interwoven, perhaps inextricably, and are assisted by the booming business in the traffic of human beings. Many developed states, particularly in Western Europe, have attempted to stifle the flow, for the numbers arriving, including refugees, asylum seekers, and those merely seeking to gain admission, for

---

[2] For examples and analysis of applicable international law standards, see Henckaerts 1995.

[3] And it still continues; see comments by the representative of Mexico in Report of the working group of intergovernmental experts on the human rights of migrants. (Mar. 1998)

whatever reason, have indeed increased.[4] Responses have undoubtedly been influenced by the fact that between two-thirds and three-quarters of new arrivals have come from non-European countries, but they have also been characterized by their frequently unilateral and uncoordinated nature. In the case of refugee movements and forced migration, many states have attempted to contain or 'regionalize' the movement of persons, that is, to keep those in need of protection and solutions within their regions of origin, beyond the developed world. This objective is pursued through visa and transit visa requirements; sanctions against airlines; socio-economic measures of deterrence; accelerated refugee status procedures, even to the point of determining applications prior to disembarkation; and procedural devices designed to avoid the necessity for decisions on the merits in favour of rapid removal to some other country deemed or imagined to be responsible or secure. Within the European Union, the possibility of developing comprehensive schemes is increasingly discussed, with the primary objectives including both the suppression of extra-regional arrivals and the prompt and summary return to regions of origin of any who slip the net.

So far, neither dissuasive nor preventive measures appear to have had any lasting impact on the movements of people, whether driven by the need for protection or economic betterment; nor have international obligations been well served in the process. Migrants and asylum seekers still arrive, and refugees are still sent back to where they may be persecuted. During the protracted wait for decisions, they may also be bound by restrictions on work, education, freedom of movement, and family reunion, which have serious social implications for both individuals and host communities.

Nevertheless, the rights of those who move are increasingly a matter of concern to the international community,[5] irrespective of their status in

---

[4] For statistics, particularly on refugees and asylum seekers, see www.igc.org; also chapters 1 and 3 in this volume.

[5] See Report of the working group of intergovernmental experts on the human rights of migrants (Mar. 1998), paras. 45–8 (Commission on Human Rights, 54th session). The Working Group paid particular attention to migrants' vulnerability relative to states of origin and states of destination; the role of internal legislation; problems linked to the integration of migrants into the host society (cultural, linguistic, and religious differences), the relationship between state sovereignty and irregular migration; and problems relating to the trafficking of migrants. It was noted that migrants often were powerless, and that while 'powerlessness' was an essential element in understanding vulnerability, it was not an inherent condition, but rather one imposed on migrants within the confines of a specific country. See further Draft Elements for an international legal instrument against illegal trafficking and transport of migrants (Proposal submitted by Austria and Italy): UN Document (Dec. 1998) (Ad Hoc Committee on the Elaboration of a Convention against Transnational Organized Crime, 1st Sess., Vienna, 19–29 Jan. 1999. Draft art. B(2): 'Any person whose illegal entry is procured or intended by such trafficking and transport shall not become punishable on account of such trafficking and transport.' Also, A. Kirchner and L. & Schiano di Pepe, 'International Attempts to Conclude a Convention to Combat Illegal Migration', 10 *IJRL* 662 (1998).

municipal law and even as some states attempt to reduce the opportunities for legal challenge to migration-related decisions, such as detention or summary removal. As sending states have continued to advocate for better protection of their constituency of migrant citizens abroad, support is beginning to strengthen in human rights institutions at both regional and international levels. The United Nations Commission on Human Rights, for example, now regularly focuses on the situation of migrants, refugees, and the displaced, and on thematic issues, such as violence against migrant women.[6] Treaty-monitoring bodies and individual complaints procedures are also developing a coherent mass of jurisprudence impacting on the 'sovereign' rights of states to regulate admission to their territory.

The movement of persons between states is self-evidently an area in which competing and conflicting interests arise, engaging communities, individuals, and states. While it may be debatable how much can be achieved in the long-term through a purely adversarial and confrontational approach to the human rights of migrants and refugees, experience suggests that much may be gained by ensuring that this dimension is effectively integrated into the development and implementation of policy and legislation. There clearly *are* human rights aspects to traditionally sovereign questions about the admission, treatment, and removal of non-nationals, and the failure so far to manage these disparate elements argues strongly for more highly developed institutional arrangements competent to pursue strategic goals on behalf of the international community, in cooperation with states and in furtherance of the promotion and protection of the human rights of migrants and refugees.

This chapter, which reviews the situation of both migrant and refugee,[7] therefore aims to identify more clearly the human rights dimensions involved, while remaining aware of the context of state and community interest. It is based on the conviction, in turn borne out by the empirical experience recounted throughout this volume, that states can only hope to 'manage' aspects of the migration phenomenon if they collaborate and coordinate their

---

[6] See, for example, Commission on Human Rights resolutions 1997/13, 1997/14, 1997/15, 1998/15, 1998/16, 1998/17, on violence against women migrants, the 1990 Convention on the Protection of All Migrants Workers and Members of their Families, and Migrants and Human Rights, respectively.

[7] A limited definition of the term 'migrant' may be appropriate in some circumstances; for example, the Intergovernmental Working Group of Experts established by the Commission on Human Rights (resolution 1997/15) decided to use the term 'migrant' to cover 'all cases where the decision to migrate is taken freely by the individual concerned, for reasons of "personal convenience" and without intervention of an external compelling factor': Report of the Working Group: UN doc. Mar. 1998, para. 44. This was considered broad enough also to cover irregular or undocumented migrants, but not 'refugees, exiles or others compelled to leave their homes'; some of the human rights dimensions to the latter categories of displacement are dealt with here, if only briefly.

actions, but that such endeavours will be ultimately ineffective (and frequently indefensible) unless they are firmly premissed on human rights principles.

States, sovereignty, and human rights

Human rights: the general obligation

Each state is responsible for promoting universal respect for, and observance and protection of, all human rights and fundamental freedoms; the protection and promotion of human rights, moreover, are the first responsibility of governments.[8] The state, of course, has responsibilities towards its population, not the least of which relate to development, welfare, health, and security. The state also has special duties with respect to membership of the community, including the acquisition of citizenship, and international law recognizes its sovereign power to control the entry of non-nationals into the territory. In a variety of declarations and in the drafting of conventions on the question of non-nationals or migrant workers, states have therefore been careful to avoid being seen as abandoning their general powers, even if their daily application is limited by pragmatic considerations, such as the necessity to maintain a certain level of inter-state travel for reasons of international trade, or in the interests of regional and good neighbourly relations (Nafziger 1983). Nonetheless, the majority of receiving countries today, particularly in the developed world, are already linked by family and community ties to a host of sending countries; these links raise natural expectations on both sides, while specific *legal* constraints may also benefit migrant workers, resident non-nationals, and children, particularly when separated from their parents. Wide, general powers of control must therefore be balanced against the fact that claims to enter will often have a basis in international law, or in community expectations, or in both. The human rights dimensions may also require close attention to individual aspects, beginning even with the question of freedom of movement and the right to leave a country.

The nature and limits of human rights

The modern sources of human rights include major declarations and inter-national agreements, such as the 1948 Universal Declaration of Human Rights (UDHR48), the 1965 Convention on the Elimination of All Forms of Racial Discrimination, the 1966 Covenants on Civil and Political Rights (ICCPR66), and Economic, Social and Cultural Rights (ICESCR66), the 1979 Convention on the Elimination of All Forms of Discrimination against Women, the 1984 Convention against Torture and Other Cruel, Inhuman, or Degrading

---

[8]   Vienna Declaration and Programme of Action (1993), para. 1.

Treatment or Punishment (CAT84), and the 1989 Convention on the Rights of the Child (CRC89). Other treaties that focus on specific human rights-related issues include the 1951 Convention (CSR51) and 1967 Protocol relating to the Status of Refugees (CSRP67), the standard-setting treaties promoted by the International Labour Organization, and the various protection schemes established under regional arrangements, such as the 1950 European Convention on Human Rights (ECHR50), the 1969 American Convention on Human Rights (ACHR69), and the 1981 African Convention on Peoples' and Human Rights. In addition to treaty-based obligations, states also have human rights duties deriving from customary international law.[9] The basic obligation, referred to above, is illustrated by article 2(1) of the Covenant on Civil and Political Rights, requiring every state party to respect and to ensure human rights to 'all individuals within its territory and subject to its jurisdiction'.

Human rights are inalienable and fundamental, but this does not mean that they are 'absolute'. Rights generally must be exercised with due regard to the rights of others; in certain circumstances and within the limits prescribed by international law, governments may thus restrict their exercise in favour of other community interests. For example, a typical limitation, recognized in similar language in many different treaties, provides with respect to the protected right that, 'No restrictions may be placed on the exercise of this right other than those which are prescribed by law and which are necessary in a democratic society in the interests of national security or public safety, public order (*ordre public*), the protection of public health or morals or the protection of the rights and freedoms of others . . .'[10] States have a margin of appreciation, or discretion, in determining whether and what restrictions may be called for in the light of local circumstances, but the standard of compliance remains an international one, involving elements of necessity and proportionality.[11] Some rights, however, are 'non-derogable'; no derogation or exceptions are permitted, even in exceptional circumstances; they benefit everyone, nationals, foreigners, migrants and refugees, whether lawfully or unlawfully in thestate, and regardless of any situation of emergency.[12]

---

[9] For recognition of the fundamental importance (obligations *erga omnes*) of the principles and rules concerning the basic human rights of the human person, see the views of the International Court of Justice in *Barcelona Traction Case*, ICJ Reports, 1970, 3, at 32.

[10] See for example art. 22(1) ICCPR66.

[11] For the jurisprudence of the European Court of Human Rights, to the effect that restrictive measures must be in accordance with law, adopted in pursuit of a legitimate aim, and necessary in a democratic society, that is, 'justified by a pressing social need and . . . proportionate to the legitimate aim pursued', see *Moustaquim* v. *Belgium* (1991), para. 43; *Beldjoudi* v. *France* (1992); *Kokkinakis* v. *Greece* (1993); *Otto-Preminger-Institut* v. *Austria* (1994); *Berrehab* (1988).

[12] Such non-derogable rights traditionally include the prohibitions on genocide, slav-

The principle of non-discrimination

The major human rights treaties acknowledge the inherent dignity and equal and inalienable rights of all.[13] In respect of fundamental rights, they recognize no distinction between the national and the non-national,[14] but do acknowledge the continuing authority of the state to maintain distinctions between citizens and non-citizens in certain areas of activity. At one end of the spectrum, all persons shall be free from torture, and cruel and unusual treatment or punishment, whether directly, within state territory, or indirectly, in another state, as a consequence of removal or refusal of admission. At the other end, there is no obvious reason to differentiate between citizen and non-citizen in the availability of legal remedies, such as habeas corpus, in the provision of a fair trial, or generally in regard to due process.[15] Rights such as the right to life, liberty, and security of the person and the right to equality before and to the equal protection of the law clearly allow for no distinction between nationals and aliens. The principle of non-discrimination, originally limited to distinctions drawn on the basis of race alone, has much wider scope today. By unlawful discrimination is meant some exclusion or restriction, privilege or preference, which has the effect of nullifying a particular right. The general principle of equality imposes on those who wish to treat individuals differently the duty of showing valid reasons for such differential treatment.[16] The question is whether the bases advanced for distinction are *relevant*, and thereafter whether the measures adopted are reasonable and proportional.[17] The

---

ery, and racial discrimination, the right to life, so far as the individual is guaranteed against arbitrary deprivation; freedom from torture or inhuman treatment; the right not to be convicted or punished under retroactive laws; the right to recognition as a person before the law; and the right to freedom of conscience, thought, and religion.

[13] See Preamble and art.1 UDHR48; Preamble ICESCR66; Preamble ICCPR66; Preamble, 1965 Convention on the Elimination of All Forms of Racial Discrimination.

[14] Art. 1(2) ACHR69 declares that 'For the purposes of this convention, "person" means every human being'.

[15] Art. 10 UDHR48 declares that 'Everyone is entitled in full equality to a fair and public hearing by an independent and impartial tribunal, in the determination of his rights and obligations and of any criminal charge against him.' These principles are reiterated in art. 14(1) ICCPR66 and art. 6 ECHR50.

[16] See generally, Goodwin-Gill 1978: 58–87. Note also the interpretation of 'arbitrary interference' adopted by the Human Rights Committee: 'The introduction of the concept of arbitrariness is intended to guarantee that even interference provided for by law should be in accordance with the provisions, aims and objectives of the Covenant and should be, in any event, *reasonable in the particular circumstances*': Human Rights Committee, General Comments (May 1989) (emphasis supplied). This interpretation is supported in the Commission on Human Rights study on the right of everyone to be free from arbitrary arrest, detention, and exile; see UN doc. E/CN.4/826/Rev.1, paras. 23–30.

[17] As Judge Tanaka said in his dissenting judgment in the *South West Africa Cases* (Second Phase), ICJ Reports, 1966, 6, 305 f., 313: 'If individuals differ one from another

international legal concept of discrimination thus connotes distinctions
which are unfair, unjustifiable, or arbitrary.

Nevertheless, one question remaining in regard to the principle of non-
discrimination is where it begins and where it ends. Article 2 of the Universal
Declaration of Human Rights provides that 'Everyone is entitled to all the
rights and freedoms *set forth in this Declaration*, without distinction of any
kind, such as race, colour, sex, language, religion, political or other opinion,
national or social origin, property, birth or other status' (emphasis supplied).
Article 7 in turn provides that, 'All are equal before the law and are entitled
without any discrimination to equal protection of the law. All are entitled to
equal protection against any discrimination in violation of this Declaration
...' Article 26 of the 1966 Covenant on Civil and Political Rights seems to
provide in similar fashion:

All persons are equal before the law and are entitled without any discrimination to the
equal protection of the law. *In this respect,* the law shall prohibit any discrimination
and guarantee to all persons equal and effective protection against discrimination on
any ground such as race, colour, sex, language, religion, political or other opinion,
national or social origin, property, birth or other status.[18]

The uncertain meaning of the phrase 'equal protection of the law' has
attracted comment, and one interpretation of article 26, based on the *travaux
préparatoires*, holds that the words 'In this respect' were added precisely to
limit the scope of this provision, so that articles 7 and 26 even together do not
give rise to a 'general norm of non-discrimination', that might be invoked in
contexts other than those involving the rights set forth in the instrument in
question (Lillich 1984: 132–3; Brownlie 1999: 602–5). The Human Rights
Committee, however, has rejected this position, taking the view that article 26
constitutes an independent principle of equal protection, not merely prohibiting discrimination in the enjoyment of the rights and freedoms set out elsewhere in the Covenant:

[A]rticle 26 provides that all persons are equal before the law and are entitled to equal
protection of the law without discrimination, and that the law shall guarantee to all
persons equal and effective protection against discrimination on any of the enumer-
ated grounds. In the view of the Committee, article 26 ... provides in itself an
autonomous right. It prohibits discrimination in law or in fact in any field regulated
and protected by public authorities. Article 26 is therefore concerned with the obligations imposed on States parties in regard to their legislation and the application

..., their needs will be different, and accordingly, the content of law may not be identical.
Hence is derived the relativity of law to individual circumstances ... A different treatment
comes into question only when and to the extent that it corresponds to the nature of the
difference ... The issue is whether the difference exists ... Different treatment must not be
given arbitrarily; it requires reasonableness, or must be in conformity with justice.'

[18] Emphases supplied; see also art. 24 ACHR69.

thereof. Thus, when legislation is adopted by a State party, it must comply with the requirement of article 26 that its content should not be discriminatory. In other words, the application of the principle of nondiscrimination contained in article 26 is not limited to those rights which are provided for in the Covenant. (Human Rights Committee Nov. 1989)

In regulating entry to, residence in, and removal from its territory, therefore, the state ought also to ensure that its laws and policies comply with these international legal requirements. If international law does not recognize the right to enter or remain in a state other than the state of one's nationality, still an otherwise permissible restriction or limitation must not be imposed in a discriminatory manner. Even though a state may not be obliged to provide a benefit or entitlement, where it does so then it ought not to introduce discriminatory measures in its implementation.

Freedom of movement and the right to leave one's country

The right to leave any country, including one's own, features in most international human rights instruments, beginning with the 1948 Universal Declaration of Human Rights. Article 13(2) declares the right, immediately after the right to freedom of movement and residence within the borders of each state, set out in the first paragraph.

Together with its universal and regional treaty counterparts, article 13 UDHR48 proclaims a general right to freedom of movement for everyone, including the right to leave any country, including their own, and to return to their country.[19] So far as the *right to leave* any country, including one's own, may be relatively well accepted, the right to enter or to return to a particular country, as a matter of law, generally depends on possessing its nationality.[20] However, even if there is thus no right of entry to a foreign state as such, the denial or restriction of admission through the application of discriminatory practices does not signal an end to the matter, for other rights, interests, and expectations may be involved.

Article 5 of the 1965 Convention on the Elimination of all Forms of Racial Discrimination, for example, requires equality and no impermissible distinctions in the enjoyment of the right in question. Article 12(2) of the 1966 Covenant on Civil and Political Rights provides similarly, as does article 10(2) of the 1989 Convention on the Rights of the Child, which speaks both to

---

[19] See also art. 12 ICCPR66; art. 2, Protocol 4, ECHR50; art. 12 ACHR69. Freedom of movement, of course, has both internal and external aspects; human rights treaties also speak to the right of everyone to move freely *within* the territory of the state of which they are citizens or residents, which in turn will have an impact on treatment policies, including detention or compulsory quarantining.

[20] See arts. 12(2), 15 UDHR48; art. 12(4) ICCPR66; art. 3, Protocol 4, ECHR50; art. 12(5) ACHR69; Hannum, H., (1987).

family reunion and to the right of the child and his or her parents to leave any country, including their own. Regional instruments recognize the right almost without exception: article 12(2) of the 1981 African Charter of Human and People's Rights, article 22(2) of the 1969 American Convention on Human Rights, and article 2(2) of the Fourth Protocol to the European Convention on Human Rights. Treaties and instruments with more specific purposes also support the basic principle, for example, article 5(2) of the 1985 UN Declaration on the Rights of Non-Nationals (UN General Assembly 1985), article 8 of the 1990 UN Convention on the Protection of the Rights of All Migrant Workers and Members of their Families (UN General Assembly 1990), and article 4(1) of the 1977 European Convention on the Status of Migrant Workers,[21] which requires each Contracting State to guarantee to migrant workers the right to leave the state party of which they are nationals.

Scope and limits

The right to leave one's country clearly shares in the greater or more general *value* attributed to freedom of movement,[22] but precisely how much value is placed on it is likely to reflect a very personal scale, as well as the intensity of 'push' factors, such as conflict, persecution, and underdevelopment. Moreover, the conditional and limited nature of freedom of movement has long been recognized, so far as the state is recognized as having the right to limit its exercise. For the 'right to leave' has never been considered an absolute right. Common sense says that it does not apply to convicted criminals, that it should be restricted in the case of some minor children, and those seeking to evade prosecution or certain civil obligations. Examples of state practice go further still, extending to those in possession of military secrets, who have attained or are about to attain military age, whose education has been paid for or subsidized by the state, who do not possess a visa for entry to another state, or who are intending to travel to restricted territories.[23] Not all these examples of the 'national interest' are necessarily accepted by even a majority of states, but the

---

[21] ETS No. 93; see also art. 18(4), 1961 European Social Charter: 529 UNTS No. 89; ETS No. 35.

[22] Sieghart identifies six aspects to freedom of movement: freedom to choose a residence within the territory of a state; freedom to move about within the borders of a state; freedom to leave a state; freedom to enter/return to a state; freedom from expulsion from a state; and freedom from exile: Sieghart 1983: 178–9.

[23] For a recent example of restrictions, see UN doc. E/CN.4/1993/43 (Report on human rights in Albania), para. 43: `Albanian law guarantees freedom of movement. Any Albanian national, irrespective of race, national origin, colour, sex, language, social status and so on, enjoys the right to travel abroad, whether for official, health or personal reasons. This right does not apply to persons who have not yet reached the age of 16 (except when they are accompanied by their parents), persons physically unable to travel, persons convicted of a criminal offence or against whom proceedings have been instituted, persons with financial obligations towards the State or towards other individuals, or persons who

very breadth of actual practice is strong evidence against the emergence of an unrestricted principle of free movement.

Indeed, the Covenant on Civil and Political Rights, Protocol 4 to the European Convention on Human Rights, the American Convention on Human Rights, and the African Charter of Human and People's Rights all allow limits on the right to leave a state. The terminology varies slightly. The restriction must be provided by or according to law and, in the case of the American and European Conventions, also be 'necessary in a democratic society'. The permissible objectives of such restrictions nevertheless include national security and public order, the rights and freedoms of others, public health, public safety, and public morals.

Notwithstanding almost universal formal support for the principle of freedom of movement, including the right to leave one's country, the scope of permissible restrictions and the nature and extent of state practice show clearly why the right in question has scarcely emerged from the context of domestic, constitutional norms (Goodwin-Gill 1978, cf. on the 'right to passport', 29) to the level of one that is internationally 'enforceable'. Many commentators see freedom of movement as an essential part of personal liberty, arguing that it is fundamental to the integrity and development of individual personality.[24] However, although freedom to leave any country may be a good in itself, it is still not considered to impose either obligations or expectations on other states. In 1948, article 13(2) of the Universal Declaration made a statement, but neither then nor as a result of later developments can it be considered to require any international 'implementation' or any correlative obligations beyond the particular nation state.[25]

State practice today offers no convincing support for any alternative conclusion. During the 1970s and early 1980s, the United States attempted to use trade sanctions and political pressure to secure compliance by other states with the 'right to leave', but with little overall success.[26] The work in the late

---

have not done military service. To travel abroad, persons must have a passport and a visa for the country they are visiting . . .'

[24] See, for example, Dowty 1987 (linking the 'right to personal self-determination' to the right to freedom of movement); Lillich 1984: 115.

[25] The International Organization for Migration (IOM), set up in 1951 outside the United Nations but in the same political context, is founded on one human right in particular—freedom of movement. The organization's Constitution, however, recognizes that 'control of standards of admission and the number of immigrants to be admitted are matters within the domestic jurisdiction of States': art. 1(3), IOM Constitution. Text in 1 International Journal of Refugee Law 597 (1989).

[26] See Lillich 1984: 115, 151–2. So far as the USSR did allow more of its citizens to leave, this may reflect more the results of a bilateral, contractual engagement than recognition of any universal principle. In that context, the right to leave one's country, in the absence of another state's formal undertaking to admit, was meaningless; and in the presence of such undertaking, it was redundant.

1980s on a draft declaration on freedom and non-discrimination with respect to the right to leave and return was remarkable more for its confusion and lack of focus, than for any concrete results.[27] With the end of the Cold War and the democratization of many formerly totalitarian states, *domestic* recognition of the 'right to travel' arrived in many countries, but with the usual national controls and in a form leaving relatively unscathed the sovereign rights of other states to maintain control over entry. Free or 'freer' movement of persons between states seems likely to be best realized at the juridical level within regional, political, and economic arrangements, such as the European Union, where national concerns are met by reciprocal reassurances and mutual confidence. Nonetheless, a *better*, more efficient and more human regime would certainly follow if there were agreement on the basic principles governing the movements of people between states.

Emergent rights: to enter, to leave, to remain

Although the right of entry to a state other than one's state of nationality may not be protected *as such* by general international law or by the basic human rights treaties, the individual's interest in admission will often be protected indirectly. In its General Comment No. 15 on the position of aliens under the 1966 Covenant relating to Civil and Political Rights, for example, the Human Rights Committee observed:

> 5. The Covenant does not recognize the right of aliens to enter or reside in the territory of a State party. It is in principle a matter for the State to decide who it will admit to its territory. However, *in certain circumstances an alien may enjoy the protection of the Covenant even in relation to entry or residence, for example, when considerations of non-discrimination, prohibition of inhuman treatment and respect for family life arise.* . . .
>
> 7. . . . Aliens shall be equal before the courts and tribunals, and shall be entitled to a fair and public hearing by a competent, independent and impartial tribunal established by law in the determination of any criminal charge or of rights and obligations in a suit at law. *Aliens . . . are entitled to recognition before the law. They may not be subjected to arbitrary or unlawful interference with their privacy, family, home or correspondence . . . may marry when at marriageable age . . . are entitled to equal protection by the law . . .* (Human Rights Committee May 1989, emphasis supplied)

In a case involving the refusal of admission to the United Kingdom, precisely in a context in which the applicants were not able to invoke a right of entry as such, the European Commission on Human Rights concluded, 'discrimina-

---

[27] See, among others, UN docs. E/CN.4/Sub.2/1989/44 (with a draft declaration by Special Rapporteur Mubanga-Chipoya annexed at 20), E/CN.4/Sub.2/1989/47 (containing a summary of general observations and specific comments and alternative drafts and suggestions on the proposed declaration), and E/CN.4/Sub.2/1989/54 (working paper prepared by Mr Diaconu). See also the 1986 and 1989 Declarations adopted by the International Institute of Human Rights, Strasbourg; Hannum 1987.

tion based on race could, in certain circumstances, of itself amount to degrading treatment within the meaning of Article 3 . . . It is generally recognized that a special importance should be attached to discrimination based on race and that publicly to single out a group of persons for differential treatment on the basis of race might . . . constitute a special form of affront to human dignity.'[28] The European Commission declared several of the applications admissible on the ground that the action of refusing entry was capable of constituting an interference with the right to respect for family life under article 8 of the Convention, or of raising a related issue of discrimination.[29]

In regard to entry and removal, a protected right will thus be involved, for example, if the applicant falls within the international law provisions on children, the family, and refugees. Thus, for example, no state may return a refugee in any manner whatsoever to a country in which he or she may be persecuted, and this prohibition extends also to measures such as rejection at the frontier, where the effect is to compel the individual to return to or remain in a territory where his or her life, physical integrity, or liberty would be threatened for relevant reasons.[30] Moreover, the 1989 Convention on the Rights of the Child endorses the standard of the 'best interests' of the child which, in principle and in appropriate circumstances, is capable of prevailing over other considerations, including the legally recognized but competing interests of the state. In a wide range of other universal and regional instruments, states have also recognized that the family should receive 'protection by society and the State', and that 'special measures of protection and assistance should be taken on behalf of all children and young persons'.[31] Together with the principle of the best interests of the child as a primary consideration,[32] this puts in question any state action with respect to children that might either 'officially' remove the child from the family environment, or have the effect of leaving the child without care and support.

It might also be argued that the right to leave one's country is in fact completed in one context in particular, namely, as 'the right to seek' asylum from persecution; here the correlative duty of states combines the principle of

[28] *S. M. L. Patel (Application No. 4403/70) and others* v. *U.K.*, Decision of the European Commission of Human Rights, Oct. 1970, 36 Collection of Decisions 92.

[29] Later decisions by the European Court of Human Rights have confirmed the protection due to the family and, among others, to 'second generation migrants' threatened with removal. On the extent of the family relationship, see, for example, *Berrehab* (1988); *Keegan* v. *Ireland* (1994); on expulsion of second generation migrants, see *Djeroud* v. *France* (1991); *Lamguindaz* v. *United Kingdom*, (1993); *Beldjoudi* v. *France* (1992).

[30] Art. II(4), 1969 OAU Convention; art. 3, 1966 AALCC Principles Concerning Treatment of Refugees.

[31] Art. 23(1) ICCPR66; art. 10(3) ICESCR66.

[32] Art 3(1) CRC89; see also art. 4, 1990 African Charter on the Rights and Welfare of the Child.

non-refoulement with a duty not to impede exercise of the right where it would leave individuals exposed to persecution, torture, or other serious violations of human rights. Certainly, the effort expended by states on 'containment' and alternatives to movement (so-called safe havens, for example) suggests there is some weight to this argument.[33]

Removals from state territory

Many of the human rights aspects of state powers over the entry and residence of non-citizens bear generally on the question of removal. In principle, the state retains competence to terminate the lawful residence or the irregular physical presence of non-citizens within its territory, and to require them to depart; in the event of non-departure, the state may enforce its decision through measures of expulsion or deportation. State practice over many decades has established a number of limitations on this sovereign power, for example, to the effect that it should not be exercised arbitrarily, that it should respect acquired rights, be implemented in accordance with due process, and carried out with full regard for the dignity and integrity of the individual (Goodwin-Gill 1978: 202–5, 228, 262, 280–1, 307–8). The collective or mass expulsion of non-citizens has also been condemned, in particular, for its necessarily arbitrary and discriminatory character.[34]

As is the case with other manifestations of state power in regard to non-citizens, the power of expulsion has also attracted both comment and rulings from treaty supervisory bodies. Article 3 CAT84, article 13 ICCPR66, and articles 32 and 33 CSR51 all mention expulsion specifically when laying down protection standards for non-citizens generally, in favour of refugees, or against return to torture. The Human Rights Committee has considered the lawfulness of expulsion against the requirements of article 13 ICCPR66 (entitlement to a remedy for the purpose of challenging an order of removal) in a number of cases,[35] while the European Court and European Commission of Human Rights have reviewed the exercise of the competence to expel non-citizens more broadly, against a range of ECHR50 rights including article 3, article 8 (freedom from interference with private or family life), and article 14 (non-discrimination).[36]

In practice, actually removing people often proves difficult, for example, in

---

[33] For tentative suggestions in this regard, see Goodwin-Gill 1995.

[34] See Henckaerts 1995: 8–49, on the prohibition of mass expulsion; 50–77 on mass expulsion of migrant workers. See also ECHR50, Protocol No. 4, art. 4.

[35] See, for example, *Mafroufidou* v. *Sweden*, No. 58/1979: *Selected Decisions of the Human Rights Committee,* vol. i: UN doc. ICCPR/C/CP/1, 80; *Hammel* v. *Madagascar,* No. 155/1983: ibid., vol. ii, 11; *M.F.* v. *The Netherlands,* No. 173/1984: ibid., vol. ii, 179, cited in Andrysek 1997.

[36] See below, n. 41; also *Abdulaziz, Cabales and Balkandali* (1985).

instances of no documentation, contested citizenship, or constituency pressure. The Comprehensive Plan of Action for refugees in South-East Asia 'institutionalized', among others, a programme of 'monitored returns' in the case of rejected Vietnamese asylum seekers, and a similar programme was proposed, though with little success at the time, for Central Americans denied asylum in the USA in the 1980s. Early 1999, however, witnessed the beginning of a collaborative arrangement between governments and NGOs for the reception of migrants deported from the USA,[37] and similar possibilities are under consideration in other regions. European countries, for example, have already developed a considerable network of 'readmission agreements', intended to facilitate the removal, on a bilateral basis, of both nationals and citizens of third countries.[38]

Rights and status: migrants, non-citizens, refugees, and asylum seekers

During the seventeenth, eighteenth, and nineteenth centuries, bilateral treaties of friendship, commerce, and establishment promoted the interests of the individual merchant. Treaties concluded after the Second World War concentrated on securing certain minimum rights for foreign nationals engaged in trade and for entrepreneurs, including the right to a hearing in the case of refusal of a residence permit, the right to counsel, to an interpreter, to communicate with one's consul, and for restrictions on the expulsion of long-term residents. The earlier bilateral treaties of establishment were frequently as vague on requisite standards of treatment, as they were limited in their personal scope. Historically, however, they came increasingly to reflect matters of common interest, even if the interests themselves remained unevenly balanced.

Migrant workers

Defence of the interests of workers employed abroad is expressly included, in the Preamble to its Constitution, among the objectives of the International Labour Organization (ILO). The position of migrant workers, that is, those who migrate from one country to another for the purpose of being employed there other than on their own account, remains especially weak. They face

---

[37] Regional Conference on Migration (the 'Puebla Group'), 4th Annual Vice-Ministerial Meeting, San Salvador, 25–9 Jan. 1999, reported in Mexico–US Advocates, *Network News,* 1999: www.msn.com.

[38] See, among others, Achermann and Gattiker 1995; Noll 1997 and 2000; Abell 1999.

hostility and exploitation, as well as problems in balancing pressures, both internal and external, to assimilate or integrate while preserving their national, ethnic, and linguistic identity.

The ILO's standard-setting activities have produced a variety of conventions and recommendations on behalf of migrant workers, the most important of which are: the Migration for Employment Convention (Revised) 1949 (No. 97); the Migration for Employment Recommendation (Revised) 1949 (No. 86); the Migrant Workers (Supplementary Provisions) Convention 1975 (No. 143); and the Migrant Workers Recommendation 1975 (No. 151). These conventions rely on the principle of choice of methods by states, and on the principle of progressive implementation, an approach intended to encourage greater readiness on the part of states with different legal and administrative systems, and at different levels of development, to adopt the standards in question.[39] However, the standards themselves seem often to fall short of those required by international human rights, even though article 1 of the 1975 Convention (No. 143) proclaims that 'Each Member for which this Convention is in force undertakes to respect the basic human rights of all migrant workers.'[40] For example, while ILO standards recognize the principle of family reunification, what counts at the point of implementation is the type of migration involved, whether permanent or temporary and, if the latter, for what duration. Surprisingly, no ILO provision contemplates any obligation to permit reunion.[41]

Recognizing the precariousness of a status tied to employment, and there-

---

[39] See also Social Security (Minimum Standards) Convention 1952 (No. 102); Discrimination (Employment and Occupation) Convention 1958 (No. 111); Social Policy (Basic Aims and Standards) Convention 1962 (No. 118); Employment Policy Convention 1964 (No. 122). To a varying degree, each proposes, in the context of its subject matter, the objective of non-discrimination between nationals and migrant workers. Certain exceptions are retained, however, and the 1958 Convention (No. 111), for example, does not include 'nationality' amongst the prohibited grounds of discrimination, though this may be added by states parties after consultation with employers' and workers' organizations and other appropriate bodies. The 1964 Convention (No. 122), which had full employment as its objective, may be applied to non-nationals at the discretion of states parties. In contrast to the instruments which allow flexibility when it comes to discrimination on grounds of nationality, the Convention on Freedom of Association 1948 (No. 87), applies 'without distinction'. See further the Report of the Committee of Experts, International Labour Conference, *Migrant Workers*, (1980), 66th Session, 44 f., n. 49.

[40] The Report of the Committee of Experts, International Labour Conference, above n. 39, 68–9, proposed for inclusion within this category of rights the right to life, to protection against torture, cruel, inhuman, or degrading treatment or punishment, liberty and security of the person, protection against arbitrary arrest and detention, and the right to a fair trial.

[41] Paras. 17, 18 of the 1975 Recommendation (No. 151) encourage 'family visits', but even if accepted by receiving states, their positive contribution to maintaining family life may be doubtful.

fore subject to market forces, article 8 of the 1949 Convention (No. 97) expressly provides that a migrant worker admitted on a permanent basis should not generally be required to return home in the event of incapacity arising from illness or injury subsequent to entry. Article 8 of the 1975 Convention (No. 143) goes further, to provide that lawfully resident migrant workers shall not be regarded as in an illegal or irregular situation merely by reason of loss of employment. Likewise, provision should be made for appeal against termination of employment and for equality of treatment in matters such as reinstatement and compensation.[42] However, these standards have not been noticeably followed in many of the labour-importing countries in Western Europe, where the unemployment of the migrant labour force has often been viewed as a social and economic burden that is best re-exported to the home state. Studies have also confirmed, for example, that ethnic minorities in Western Europe, which is what the migrant labour force has become, remain vulnerable to dismissal during recession, and generally have high rates of unemployment (Castles, Booth, and Wallace 1984; Böhning 1986).

Although the principal ILO standard-setting conventions are in force, the number of ratifications is low and their efficacy correspondingly limited, particularly in a relationship of labour-importing and labour-exporting states. Why this should be so merits attention, and understanding the weaknesses of present arrangements is essential to forging a new regime. A detailed analysis is beyond the scope of the present chapter, but one deficiency in particular may be that the ILO-type regime is incomplete, being insufficiently reciprocal and paying little regard to the practicalities of migration management which so concern states today. This is perhaps not surprising, given the ILO's constitutional mandate in favour of the rights of migrant workers, but experience now suggests that other 'operational' factors will need to be integrated into a new regime.

The United Nations and the protection of non-citizens

In December 1985, the United Nations General Assembly adopted the Declaration on the Human Rights of Individuals who are not Nationals of the Country in which they live.[43] In the *Study* that ultimately led to this Declaration, the Special Rapporteur of the Sub-Commission on Prevention of Discrimination and Protection of Minorities noted the potential for protection—by the international community, international organizations, under

---

[42] Ibid., paras. 30–3. In the event of threatened expulsion, the migrant worker should enjoy the right of appeal, and the appeal itself should stay execution of the order of expulsion, 'subject to the duly substantiated requirements of national security or public order': ibid., para. 33. Cf. art. 13 ICCPR66.

[43] UNGA res. 40/144, Annex.

international instruments, and by regional organizations.[44] Even though, as a resolution adopted by the General Assembly, it does not impose international legal obligations, throughout its drafting history states were divided on the scope of the Declaration, and on whether it should apply to every non-national or only to those lawfully residing in state territory. As finally adopted, article 1 provides that 'For the purposes of this Declaration, the term "alien" shall apply, with due regard to qualifications made in subsequent articles, to any individual who is not a national of the State in which he or she is present. Article 2 affirms that nothing in the Declaration shall be taken as 'legitimizing' illegal entry or presence, or as restricting a state's right to govern entry and stay, 'or to establish differences between nationals and aliens'; general savings clauses attempt to preserve the entitlement of all non-nationals to human rights.[45] In the course of debate leading to the final compromise, the United States of America and the United Kingdom successfully proposed a modification of article 5.1(c); while all should be equal before the courts, the right to equal access to courts and tribunals 'could not be accorded to everybody and in particular to unlawful aliens'. The right to equal treatment before the courts was dropped in favour of an alternative, 'the right to be equal before the courts' (UN Open Ended Working Group 1985, paras. 103, 113), which the United States' representative explained 'as referring to the general principle of equal justice, and not as prohibiting appropriate distinctions in law and procedure based on alien status or on the terms and lawfulness of entry and stay'.[46]

On family reunion, article 5(4) of the Declaration provides that 'subject to national legislation and due authorization, the spouse and minor or dependent

[44] International Provisions protecting Human Rights of Non-Citizens: UN doc. E/CN.4/Sub.2/392/Rev.1 (1980), 5–12.

[45] Art. 2 provides that laws and regulations 'shall not be incompatible with the international legal obligations of (the) State, including those in the field of human rights. (2) This Declaration shall not prejudice the enjoyment of the rights accorded by domestic law and of the rights which under international law a State is obliged to accord to aliens, even where the present Declaration does not recognize such rights or recognizes them to a lesser extent'. See also art. 5. For the different views on entitlement to protection by reference to presence or 'lawful' residence, see Report of the Open-Ended Working Group (Nov. 1980): UN doc. A/C.3/35/14, para. 2; Annex I, CRP.2 (Mexico); CRP.4 (United Kingdom); ibid., Dec.1982: UN doc. A/C.3/37/8, paras. 12, 13, 19, 24, 32, 49, 53 (views of the USA, in particular); ibid., Nov. 1983: UN doc. A/C.3/38/11, paras. 28, 30, 40, 67; 70–1; ibid., Nov. 1984: UN doc. A/C.3/39/9; Report of the Secretary-General, Replies of Governments, Sept. 1985: UN doc. A/40/638, 34 (Federal Republic of Germany, Netherlands), Add. 13; Report of the Open-Ended Working Group, Dec. 1985: UN doc. A/C.3/40/12, paras. 825, 6188.

[46] Summary records of the Third Committee: UN doc. A/C.3/40/SR.72, para. 17. The object and purpose of this observation and the intent behind it may have been unclear at the time, although legislation introduced in 1996 effectively reduced the protection due in the United States even to established, resident non-citizens; see the 1996 Illegal Immigration Reform and Immigrant Responsibility Act.

children of an alien lawfully residing in the territory of a State shall be admitted to accompany, join and stay with the alien'. This was favoured over an earlier formulation proposed by Mexico, which would have referred simply to the non-national's right 'to be joined by his or her family'.[47]

Similar arguments emerged again when the draft United Nations convention on migrant workers came up for debate. In 1985, the United States sought to limit the Convention to 'documented migrant workers', invoking sovereign rights, insisting that it was 'essential that the rights of non-documented migrant workers be limited to basic human rights',[48] and that those with temporary and those with permanent resident status should be clearly distinguished. The United States and the Netherlands expressed further reservations regarding draft article 18, concerning the right to equality with citizens as regards access to, and treatment by, courts and tribunals. The proposed text could imply legal recognition or regularization of status (UN Open Ended Working Group 1981, paras. 56–7, 73), and in regard to expulsion, said the United States, the distinction between legal and illegal migrants must be maintained.[49]

Although the UN Convention on the Protection of the Rights of All Migrant Workers and Members of their Families was finally adopted by the United Nations General Assembly in December 1990 (UN General Assembly 1990), by 31 August 1999, it had attracted only twelve ratifications.[50] Many

---

[47] UN doc. A/C.3/36/11, paras. 16, 17. In later discussion, the United States of America noted that textual references to domestic law 'did not necessarily impose an obligation to legislate and the right of reunification of families existed but was subject to the right of sovereign states to enact laws' on entry and immigration: UN doc. A/C.3/39/9, paras. 827 at 41; cf. Sweden's contrasting pro-reunion stand at para. 24. In the meantime, CRC89 has introduced an important new dimension; see further above, text to nn. 43–4.

[48] Report of the Open-Ended Working Group (June 1985): UN doc. A/C.3/40/1, paras. 61–2, 198; Report (Oct. 1985): UN doc. A/C.3/40/6, paras. 212. The Federal Republic of Germany was yet more outspoken, referring to its own non-ratification of ILO Convention No. 143, and observing that it was hardly likely to ratify a convention the provisions of which 'would be less favourable to the States of employment'; those in an irregular situation should be categorically excluded from the convention: UN doc. A/C.3/40/1, paras. 201, 178.

[49] Ibid., paras. 62, 67. But cf. US concerns regarding the possibility of state pressure to encourage 'voluntary exit': ibid., para. 70; and its views on non-retroactivity of criminal legislation.

[50] States parties were Azerbaijan, Bosnia and Herzegovina, Cape Verde, Colombia, Egypt, Mexico, Morocco, Philippines, Senegal, Seychelles, Sri Lanka, and Uganda and it had been signed by Bangladesh, Chile, and Turkey. In accordance with art. 87, the Convention will enter into force following twenty ratifications or accession: 'Multilateral Treaties deposited with the Secretary-General', United Nations, New York (ST/LEG/SER.E), available on www.un.org/Depts/Treaty at 31 Aug. 1999. See also Reports of the Secretary-General on the Status of the International Convention on the Protection of the Rights of All Migrant Workers and Members of their Families: UN doc. E/CN.4/1997/65; UN doc. E/CN.4/1998/75; Commission on Human Rights resolutions 1997/14, 2 Apr. 1997; 1998/15, 9 Apr. 1998.

states continue to be reluctant formally to acknowledge that the protection of international human rights law now attaches to the migrant, whether regular or irregular. Once again, the gap between the positions and expectations of labour-exporting and labour-importing states is clear; a new regime will need to redress that balance, for example, by way of practical measures that will not only guarantee protection, but also ensure that migration is ultimately a manageable, two-way or reciprocal process.

The protection of refugees and asylum seekers

Refugees are a class known to and enjoying the protection of general international law (Goodwin-Gill 1996). The principle of asylum has been consistently endorsed by the United Nations, both in the resolutions adopted by the General Assembly and in the practice of member states individually and at the regional level. Article 14 of the 1948 Universal Declaration of Human Rights, for example, provides that 'Everyone has the right to seek and to enjoy in other countries asylum from persecution.' The main international instruments, such as the 1951 Convention and 1967 Protocol relating to the Status of Refugees, have been widely ratified. By 31 August 1999, 137 states had agreed to be bound, among others, by the definition of a refugee in article 1 and by the fundamental principle of *non-refoulement* in article 33.[51] This rule, which requires that states parties not return a refugee to a country in which he or she may face persecution on grounds of race, religion, nationality, membership of a particular group, or political opinion, now also extends to the protection of those who, if returned to a particular country, would face a substantial risk of torture.[52] Lawfully resident refugees are also protected against expulsion, save on the most serious grounds and subject to lawful procedures and the opportunity for challenge.[53]

At the regional level, in the 1969 Organization of African Unity Convention on the Specific Aspects of Refugee Problems in Africa[54] and in the 1984 Cartagena Declaration on the problems of refugees and the displaced in Central America,[55] states have also developed the content of refugee protection, either directly, by way of treaty obligations, or indirectly, through statements of principle backed by concerted practice.

However, the precise meaning and scope of international obligations towards refugees is by no means free from doubt. While there is no legal

---

[51] 1951 Convention (CSR51): 189 UNTS 150; 1967 Protocol (CSRP67): 606 UNTS 267. For details of ratifications, see *RefWorld:* www.unhcr.ch/refworld

[52] Art. 3, 1984 Convention against Torture and Other Cruel, Inhuman or Degrading Treatment or Punishment (CAT84): 1465 UNTS 85 (No. 24841)–114 States parties at 31 Aug. 1999.   [53] Art. 32 CSR51.   [54] 1000 UNTS 46.

[55] OAS/Ser.L/V/II.66, doc. 10, rev. 1; text in Goodwin-Gill, 1996: 444.

obligation to accord to refugees asylum in the sense of a lasting solution, recognition as a refugee has often been accepted by states as both the necessary and the sufficient condition for the grant of residence and related rights, including access to the labour market. In fact, asylum has never been defined in any international instrument, and practice varies among states. The general notion remains governed largely by municipal law and practice, although the core content—protection of the individual against the exercise of jurisdiction by another state or against the consequences of a failure by that state to protect its citizens—is reasonably clear. The precise meaning of the right to *seek* asylum, on the other hand, is more uncertain, at least from a practical perspective, and in the light of recent state practice in regard to interdiction or interception at sea, visa controls, carrier sanctions, and the development of so-called safe havens in arenas of conflict (Goodwin-Gill 1995). The tendency to institutionalize 'temporary protection', as reflected in Western European policies on refugees from the former Yugoslavia, can also be seen as a step away from the simplified, reactive practices of the past, which tended, almost automatically, to link flight to one or other permanent solution in exile. While state policies certainly call for re-evaluation in the aftermath of the end of the Cold War, it is by no means evident that the alternatives currently being developed are compatible with obligations in regard to human rights (Mertus 1998; Rudge 1998; see also Ghosh 2000).

Similarly, even though many states acknowledge as a matter of fact that international protection is often due to individuals or groups falling outside or not immediately covered by article 1 of the 1951 Convention/1967 Protocol, such as those having reasonable fear of prejudice or discrimination in the exercise of fundamental rights, or who flee conflict or serious disturbances of public order, there is little consistency in the treatment accorded to such refugees, who may be granted time-limited residence, with or without social rights, or be formally or informally tolerated, or simply left, undocumented, to fend for themselves.

On the other hand, it has long been recognized that the right to seek asylum, and indeed, the right to benefit from the principle of *non-refoulement,* is largely meaningless unless an applicant is able to present his or her case for determination by an independent, impartial authority. Minimum standards for asylum procedures were recommended by the Executive Committee of the Programme of the United Nations High Commissioner for Refugees in 1977 (UNHCR 1979), to include the provision of advice to asylum seekers and the opportunity to present a claim before the responsible authority, with the assistance of an interpreter, and the availability of appeal or review of negative decisions.[56]

---

[56] In *Amuur* v. *France* (1994), para. 50, the European Court of Human Rights ruled that detention or confinement 'must not deprive the asylum seekers of the right to gain

That refugee protection also engages a human rights responsibility has been recognized by a number of treaty supervisory bodies. The Human Rights Committee, for example, considers that the principle of *non-refoulement* is effectively included within article 7 ICCPR66:

In the view of the Committee, States parties must not expose individuals to the danger of torture or cruel, inhuman or degrading treatment or punishment upon return to another country by way of their extradition, expulsion or refoulement . . . (Human Rights Committee 1992, para. 9)

While the 1966 Covenant does not recognize the right of non-citizens to enter or reside in the territory of a state party, 'in certain circumstances an alien may enjoy the protection of the Covenant even in [such matters], for example, when considerations of nondiscrimination, [or] prohibition of inhuman treatment . . . arise' (Human Rights Committee 1986). The Committee against Torture also has indicated that 'non-admission to a country engages the responsibility of the State Party [to CAT84] under article 3 if returning a person would result in exposure to torture.' In several 'Views', the Committee has confirmed the protection due to the non-citizen at risk on expulsion or return.[57]

In particularly striking fashion, the European Court of Human Rights has ruled that there are no exceptions to the protection required under article 3 ECHR50. The case of *Chahal,* for example, involved an individual whom the United Kingdom wished to expel on grounds of national security. The Court noted that, whereas the state had disputed the principle of non-expulsion if the person concerned would face a real risk of treatment contrary to article 3 in the country to which he or she was returned, it had accepted it before the Court. However, the government had further argued that the protection due under article 3 was not absolute in national security cases, but was subject to an implied limitation, or alternatively that the threat posed by the individual should be weighed in the balance against the interest of the state. The Court disagreed, finding that,

the Convention prohibits in absolute terms torture or inhuman or degrading treatment or punishment, irrespective of the victim's conduct.. Article 3 makes no provision for exceptions and no derogation from it is permissible . . . even in the event of a public emergency threatening the life of the nation . . . The prohibition . . . against ill-

effective access to the procedure for determining refugee status . . .', and that there is a need, 'to reconcile the protection of fundamental rights with the requirements of States' immigration policies'.

[57] *Mutombo* v. *Switzerland,* Communication No. 13/1993, Committee against Torture, 27 Apr. 1994: 7 IJRL 322 (1995); *Alan* v. *Switzerland,* Communication No. 21/1995, Committee against Torture, 8 May 1996: 8 IJRL 440 (1996); *Kisoki* v. *Sweden,* Communication No. 41/1996, Committee against Torture, 8 May 1996: 8 IJRL 651 (1996). See also Andrysek 1997.

treatment is equally absolute in expulsion cases. Thus, whenever substantial grounds have been shown for believing that an individual would face a real risk of being subjected to treatment contrary to Article 3 if removed to another State, the responsibility of the Contracting State to safeguard him or her against such treatment is engaged in the event of expulsion . . . In these circumstances, the activities of the individual in question, however undesirable or dangerous, cannot be a material consideration. The protection afforded by Article 3 is thus wider than that provided by Articles 32 and 33 of the United Nations 1951 Convention on the Status of Refugees.[58]

The Court further criticized the then existing procedures in the United Kingdom for dealing with expulsion or removal on national security grounds, insisting that the authorities cannot avoid 'effective control by the domestic courts whenever they choose to assert that national security and terrorism are involved . . .'[59] An effective remedy within the meaning of article 13 ECHR50 is therefore required.[60]

Conclusions

From the above, it can be seen that international legal standards of treatment for migrants and refugees are not new, that they extend even into such areas of 'sovereign competence' as control over admission and expulsion, but that they are all well founded in treaty and general international law. Whether they will remain effective, however, depends very much on how states will react in the face of current and imminent flows, and how they will treat existing non-citizen populations. Neither migration pressures nor refugee movements from the developing world have shown any propensity to decrease, at least so long as the developed world maintains its emphasis largely on reactive policies, rather than seeking a more proactive approach to what drives people to move.

The existing international systems of legal guarantees for migrants, refugees, and minorities are far from complete, however. One question raised or implicit throughout the above review is that of compliance; even where the principles seem clear, their effective implementation depends upon levels of official action that are not always forthcoming. The decade of the 1990s has once again

---

[58] *Chahal* v. *United Kingdom*, No. 70/1995/576/662, Judgment of 15 Nov. 1996, paras. 79, 80.

[59] Ibid., para. 131. In *Ahmed* v. *Austria*, No. 71/1995/577/663, Judgment of 17 Dec. 1996, the Court also emphasized the irrelevance of the personal conduct of the individual, in that instance, conviction for attempted robbery, to the state's obligations under art. 3.

[60] *Chahal* v. *United Kingdom*, Judgment, paras. 145–51. Following this judgment, the United Kingdom not only terminated removal proceedings against Mr Chahal, but it also enacted the Special Immigration Appeal Commission Act 1997 to meet the remedies requirement.

seen mass expulsions, the forced repatriation of refugees, and xenophobic and violent attacks upon established 'migrant' minorities and asylum seekers. Apart from those countries still committed to immigration, such as Australia, Canada, and the United States, many other states with long-resident non-citizen populations continued to deny their membership in the community or to facilitate their final acceptance by way of naturalization. While much rhetoric was expended on the necessity to reduce the need to migrate and to avert the compulsion to flee, few resources overall were invested either in realistically negotiating a framework for management, or in the processes of democratization and development which are likely to have a long-term impact. At the receiving end also, and despite some considerable experience now with the human dimensions of migration and flight, states still lack the operational techniques essential to the credible and effective implementation of policy.

Neither international law at large nor human rights law in particular contains all the answers. On the contrary, law is a tool in the service of society, and a dynamic institution. If it is to be fully effective, and to evolve, it must respond to the problems which are the reality of its existence; and if new or changing rules are to achieve 'legitimacy', they must meet criteria of coherence and integrity. Today's issues include questions of state responsibility to communities both inside and outside territory and jurisdiction; cooperation and agreement are still needed on the question of refugee definition (who should be protected), protection standards (the contours of asylum and refuge), and institutional mandates and coordination. The growing problem of irregular migration, and the business that trafficking of human beings has become, pose an especially probing challenge to the concept of civil rights and obligations, to the overarching demands for procedural fairness, and generally to the validity of the concept of alienage as a basis for discrimination in the protection of human rights.

Compliance with international human rights obligations in the migration field is patchy at best, and the reasons for this failing call for serious attention. States are disinclined to legislate on family reunion, for example, or to incorporate international standards into policy guidelines or best practice statements. The traditional conception of sovereign state rights to control entry, removal and membership still carries weight, but in this writer's view, it is rather the incompleteness and lack of balance in the present regime that militates against effectiveness.

The movement of persons between states is a matter of international relations and raises international human rights issues, while also bringing state responsibilities clearly into the picture. At a certain level of generality, states are responsible not only for protecting the human rights of all those within territory and jurisdiction, but also between themselves, for 'operationalizing' the duties which attach to the fact of nationality, and for making the migration bridge a truly two-way, reciprocal process.

A new framework for the better management of migration must therefore be premissed on the foundations of international human rights law, the essentials of which are obligations *erga omnes* and much of which draws its authority from peremptory rules of international law (*jus cogens*). But it must also promote effective cooperation to these ends by institutionalizing mechanisms whereby states are able to fulfil their responsibilities, such as that of sending states or states of origin towards their citizens; this is a matter both of individual rights, and of responsibility in and towards the international community. While some attention has been given to the right of the refugee to return, and to the obligation of the state to readmit, far too little has been paid to those responsibilities in the everyday, unexceptional context of migration.

State interests, such as economic and demographic development or more general responsibilities to the community, including security, are a recognized basis for exercising control over entry and residence. It is hard to see, however, that this justifies the separation of spouses or of children from their parents, let alone the return of individuals or groups to situations of imminent danger. Equally, the state has no legal basis for denying responsibility for those, its citizens, linked by birth or other social fact of attachment to the territory over which it exercises jurisdiction and which is the source of its authority in the society of nations. The sovereignty of the state exists within a community of principle; given the manifestly international dimensions to migratory and refugee movements, a significantly higher degree of cooperation among states is now called for if these are to be effectively dealt with.

The 'collective' duty with respect to the protection of persons moving across borders and the obligation to cooperate derive, in part at least, from the character *erga omnes* of human rights obligations, considered within the cooperative framework established by the United Nations Charter and general international law. They extend through the general structure of international organization to cover measures to prevent the necessity for flight, to regulate and humanize the natural phenomenon of migration, in 'both directions', and to protect the common interest of the international community in the protection of individual human rights and the preservation of international public order—a challenging agenda for decades to come.

REFERENCES

Books, chapters, and articles

Abell, N. A. (1999), 'The Compatibility of Readmission Agreements with the 1951 Convention relating to the Status of Refugees', 11 *International Journal of Refugee Law* 000.
Achermann, A., and Gattiker, M. (1995), 'Safe Third Countries: European Developments', 7 *International Journal of Refugee Law* 19.

Andrysek, O. (1997), 'Gaps in International Protection and the Potential for Redress through Individual Complaints Procedures', 9 *International Journal of Refugee Law* 392.

Böhning, W. R. (1986), 'Basic Rights of "Temporary" Migrant Workers: Law vs. Power', in L. F. Tomasi (ed.), *In Defense of the Alien*, vol. viii, New York: Center for Migration Studies, 108.

Brownlie, I. (1990), *Basic Documents in International Law*, Oxford: Clarendon Press, 4th edn.

—— (1999), *Principles of Public International Law*, Oxford: Clarendon Press, 5th edn.

Castles, S. (1986), 'The Guestworker in Western Europe: An Obituary', 22 *International Migration Review* 761.

——, Booth, H., and Wallace, T. (1984), *Here for Good: Western Europe's New Ethnic Minorities*, London: Pluto Press.

Dowty, A. (1987), *Closed Borders: The Contemporary Assault on Freedom of Movement*, New Haven: Yale University Press.

Dworkin, R. (1977), *Taking Rights Seriously*, London: Duckworth.

Goodwin-Gill, G. S. (1978), *International Law and the Movement of Persons between States*, Oxford: Clarendon Press.

—— (1989), 'International Law and Human Rights: Trends concerning International Migrants and Refugees', in L. F. Tomasi (ed.), *International Migration: An Assessment for the '90s*, Special Silver Anniversary Issue, 23 *International Migration Review*, 526–46.

—— (1995), 'The Right to Leave, the Right to Return and the Question of a Right to Remain', in V. Gowlland-Debbas (ed.), *The Problem of Refugees in the Light of Contemporary International Law Issues*, The Hague: Martinus Nijhoff, 95–106.

—— (1996), *The Refugee in International Law*, Oxford: Clarendon Press, 2nd edn.

Hannum, H. (1987), *The Right to Leave and Return in International Law and Practice*, The Hague: Martinus Nijhoff.

Henckaerts, Jean-Marie (1995), *Mass Expulsion in Modern International Law and Practice*, The Hague: Martinus Nijhoff.

Kirchner, A., and Schiano di Pepe, L. (1998), 'International Attempts to Conclude a Convention to Combat Illegal Migration', 10 *International Journal of Refugee Law* 662.

Lillich, R. B. (1984), 'Civil Rights', in T. Meron (ed.), *Human Rights in International Law*, Oxford: Clarendon Press, 115.

Mertus, J. (1998), 'The State and the Post-Cold War Refugee Regime: New Models, New Questions', 10 *International Journal of Refugee Law* 321.

Nafziger, J. A. (1983), 'The General Admission of Aliens under International Law', 77 *American Journal of International Law* 804.

Noll, G. (1997), 'The Non-Admission and Return of Protection Seekers in Germany', 9 *International Journal of Refugee Law* 415.

Rawls, J. (1972), *A Theory of Justice*, Oxford: Oxford University Press.

Rudge, P. (1998), 'Challenges to Refugee Protection in the 21st Century. Reconciling State Interests with International Responsibilities: Asylum in North America and Western Europe', 10 *International Journal of Refugee Law* 7

Sieghart, P. (1983), *The International Law of Human Rights*, Oxford: Clarendon Press.

Tomasi, L. F. (ed.) (1989), *International Migration: An Assessment for the '90s*, Special

Silver Anniversary Issue, 23 *International Migration Review*, Staten Ireland, NY: Center for Migration Studies.

United Nations Documents

Draft Elements for an international legal instrument against illegal trafficking and transport of migrants. Proposal submitted by Austria and Italy. Ad Hoc Committee on the Elaboration of a Convention against Transnational Organized Crime, 1st Sess., Vienna, 19–29 January 1999: UN doc. A/AC.254/4/Add.1, 15 Dec. 1998

Human Rights Committee, General Comment 15, 'The position of aliens under the Covenant', 11 Apr. 1986.

—— General Comment on article 26 (non-discrimination), 21 Nov. 1989.

—— General Comment 20, 'Replaces General Comment 7 concerning prohibition of torture or cruel treatment or punishment (Article 7)', 10 Apr. 1992.

International Provisions protecting Human Rights of Non-Citizens: UN doc. E/CN.4/Sub.2/392/Rev.1 (1980).

Multilateral Treaties deposited with the Secretary-General, United Nations, New York (ST/LEG/SER.E), available on www.un.org/Depts/Treaty

Report of the working group of intergovernmental experts on the human rights of migrants submitted in accordance with Commission on Human Rights resolution 1997/15: UN doc. E/CN.4/1998/76, 10 Mar. 1998.

Report of the Intergovernmental Working Group of Experts: UN doc. E/CN.4/1998/76, 10 Mar. 1998.

Report of the Secretary-General on the Status of the International Convention on the Protection of the Rights of All Migrant Workers and Members of their Families (1997): UN doc. E/CN.4/1997/65.

Report of the Secretary-General on the Status of the International Convention on the Protection of the Rights of All Migrant Workers and Members of their Families (1998): UN doc. E/CN.4/1998/75.

UNHCR, *RefWorld:* www.unhcr.ch/refworld

—— *Handbook on Procedures and Criteria for Determining Refugee Status,* Geneva, 1979.

Vienna Declaration and Programme of Action on Human Rightsw (1993): UN doc. A/CONF.157/23.

Treaties and other international instruments

1948 Universal Declaration of Human Rights (UDHR48)
1948 ILO Convention on Freedom of Association (No.87)
1950 European Convention on Human Rights (ECHR50)
1951 Convention relating to the Status of Refugees (CSR51)
1952 ILO Social Security (Minimum Standards) Convention (No. 102)
1958 ILO Discrimination (Employment and Occupation) Convention (No. 111)
1960 American Convention on Human Rights

1961 European Social Charter
1962 ILO Social Policy (Basic Aims and Standards) Convention (No. 118)
1964 ILO Employment Policy Convention (No. 122)
1965 Convention on the Elimination of All Forms of Racial Discrimination
1966 International Covenant on Civil and Political Rights (ICCPR66)
1966 International Covenant on Economic, Social, and Cultural Rights (ICESCR66)
1967 Protocol relating to the Status of Refugees (CSRP67)
1969 American Convention on Human Rights (ACHR69)
1969 Convention relating to Specific Aspects of the Refugee Problem in Africa
1984 Convention against Torture and Other Cruel, Inhuman, or Degrading Treatment
   or Punishment (CAT84)
1989 Constitution of the International Organization for Migration
1989 Convention on the Rights of the Child (CRC89)
1990 Convention on the Protection of All Migrants Workers and Members of their
   Families, and Migrants and Human Rights
1990 African Charter on the Rights and Welfare of the Child

Decisions of the International Court of Justice

Barcelona Traction Case, ICJ Reports, 1970, 3.
South West Africa Cases (Second Phase), ICJ Reports, 1966, 6.

Decisions of the European Court and European Commission of Human Rights

Abdulaziz, Cabales and Balkandali (15/1983/71/107–9), 28 May 1985.
Ahmed v. Austria (71/1995/577/663), 17 Dec. 1996.
Amuur v. France (17/1995/523/609), 20 Jan. 1994.
Beldjoudi v. France (55/1990/246/317), 26 Mar. 1992.
Berrehab v. France (3/1987/126/177), 21 June 1988.
Chahal v. United Kingdom (70/1995/576/662), 15 Nov. 1996.
Djeroud v. France (34/1990/225/289), 23 Jan. 1991.
Keegan v. Ireland (16/1993/411/490), 26 May 1994.
Kokkinakis v. Greece (3/1992/348/421), 25 May 1993.
Lamguindaz v. United Kingdom (48/1992/393/471), 28 June 1993.
Moustaquim v. Belgium (31/1989/191/291), 18 Feb. 1991.
Otto-Preminger-Institut v. Austria (11/1993/406/485), 20 Sept. 1994.
S.M.L. Patel (Application No. 4403/70) and others v. U.K., Oct. 1970.

Views of the Committee against Torture

Alan v. Switzerland, Communication No. 21/1995, Committee against Torture, 8 May
   1996.

Kisoki v. *Sweden,* Communication No. 41/1996, Committee against Torture, 8 May 1996.

Mutombo v. *Switzerland,* Communication No. 13/1993, Committee against Torture, 27 Apr. 1994.

Decisions of the Human Rights Committee

Hammel v. *Madagascar,* No. 155/1983: Selected Decisions of the Human Rights Committee, vol. ii, 11.

M.F. v. *The Netherlands,* No. 173/1984: Selected Decisions of the Human Rights Committee, vol. ii, 179.

Mafroufidou v. *Sweden,* No. 58/1979: Selected Decisions of the Human Rights Committee, vol. i, 80

8

Forced Migration in the Post-Cold War Era: The Need for a Comprehensive Approach

Gil Loescher

Introduction

The post-Cold War era has confronted the international refugee regime with ever-increasing numbers of forcibly displaced people. In recent years, the problem of forced displacement has become larger, more complex, and geographically more widespread. Forcibly displaced people include *refugees* in the legal sense of the word, namely people who have fled from and are unable to return to their own country because of persecution and violence as well as *internally displaced* people, namely people who have been uprooted because of persecution or violence but who remain in their own countries and do not or cannot seek refuge across borders.

During the past two decades, the overall number of refugees and internally displaced persons has been growing.[1] In 1980, there were about 6 million refugees from 38 countries and 2 million internally displaced from 10 countries. Between 1980 and 1990, the number of refugees tripled to about 17 million from 50 countries and the number of internally displaced rose rapidly to over 22 million in 23 countries. Although the number of refugee-sending countries kept increasing from 50 in 1990 to 63 in 1994, the actual number of refugees started to decline after 1994. According to UNHCR, there were some 11.4 million refugees at the end of 1998 (UNHCR 1999). Unlike refugees, internal displacement did not decline in the 1990s and totalled an estimated 23 million in 1998 (Hampton 1998).

These figures do not tell the whole story, however, as many victims of forced displacement, do not feature in these statistics. For example, in responding to the needs of displaced populations caught up in intra-state

---

[1] The following statistics are provided in Schmeidl 1998 and the United Nations High Commissioner for Refugees and the US Committee for Refugees, both of which have tried to systematically report annual refugee estimates over the past three decade.

wars, UNHCR has extended its services to a much wider range of people who are in need of assistance including returnees, internally displaced people, war-affected populations, the victims of mass expulsions, and unsuccessful asylum seekers as well as refugees. For example, 'war affected populations', that is people who had not been uprooted but needed humanitarian assistance and protection, comprised a substantial proportion of UNHCR's beneficiary population during the height of the Bosnian conflict. In addition to the 11.4 million refugees at the end of 1998, other 'people of concern' to UNHCR included 900,000 asylum seekers, 1.7 million returnees, 5.4 million internally displaced people, 500,000 returnee internally displaced, 1.4 million displaced in the CIS, and over 2 million others of concern (UNHCR 1999).

Millions of others who are outside UNHCR concern include migrants who have been expelled en masse from their countries of residence and people who have been uprooted by development projects, among others. While it is difficult to provide accurate figures, there are probably more than 50 million people around the world who might be legitimately described as 'displaced'. This figure means that one out of every 130 people on earth has been forced into flight.

While refugees and other migrants differ considerably with regard to their specific circumstances and legal status, these groups cannot always be easily disentangled. The worldwide increase in migration occurs because of wide-spread unemployment and poverty, growing disparities in income and economic opportunities both within and between countries, as well as due to flagrant violation of human rights, increasingly violent civil conflicts, and serious environmental degradation. Migration is often the result of an inter-play of these economic, political, and environmental factors. Equally, most migration is the result of some form of compulsion. Migrants often flee both because of poverty and economic survival and in order to escape from an oppressive regime or violence. Frequently, these factors are interrelated and cannot be clearly separated. Similarly, people sometimes choose to become asylum seekers or illegal entrants because official avenues for legal migration or family reunification are often closed, as in Western Europe. It is also the case that almost all migration involves some choice. Even in the worst of circumstances, such as in Kosovo, people frequently enjoy some latitude to decide when or, indeed, whether to flee their homes at all. Even in the largest and most tragic displacements, some people will decide to stay in their country, rather than to flee, despite grave personal risk to themselves and their families. Since refugee flight often requires resources and family or social networks abroad, those who manage to escape across borders normally represent just a small minority of those whose lives are at risk. Thus, the protection and assistance provided to refugees and asylum seekers must be combined with similar if not greater efforts on behalf of those people who are unable or unwilling to leave their own country (UNHCR 1997: 35). A sound and effective international regime to protect and assist forced migrants must, therefore, be comprehensive enough to deal with a broad range of refugee flows or groups of migrants.

The globalization of transportation, communication, and news dissemination transform these population displacements and flows into international events. Over the past decade, the international community, and the public at large, have come to recognize some of the implications of such trends. The refugee crisis is no longer a national or regional problem, but a global one requiring unparalleled regional and global cooperation. No continent is now immune from the problem of mass displacement. Regarded for many years as essentially a phenomenon occurring in the developing world, significant movements of refugees and asylum seekers have recently taken place in the Balkans, the Caribbean, the Caucasus, and other parts of the former Soviet Union. Refugee populations in excess of 10,000 can now be found in more than seventy different countries across the world (UNHCR 1995, 20).

The traditional cause of refugee movements—persecution—is now just one factor amongst an array of forces that cause people to flee their homelands. The majority of mass movements are caused by war, ethnic strife, and sharp socio-economic inequalities. The difficulty of building durable state structures in the context of deep ethnic divisions and economic underdevelopment has resulted in much of the domestic conflict and political instability that the developing countries have experienced.[2] These conditions not only generate refugee flows, but also make the resolution of refugee problems in the developing world especially problematic. Compounding the internal difficulties involved with nation building and social transformation, the proliferation of internal conflicts characterized by strong ethnic and communal hostilities, independent warlords, and the easy availability of small arms, land mines, and other instruments of violence constitute a massive stimulus to militarization and conflict in the third world and in parts of the former communist bloc. A by-product of this deterioration in regional and international security has been the proliferation of so-called complex emergencies, combining internal conflicts with large-scale displacements of people, mass famine, and fragile or failing economic, political, and social institutions (US Mission to the UN, 1995).

As the problem of forced displacement has become a much broader and more complex phenomenon, it is evident that future policy must involve a comprehensive approach addressing factors such as unbalanced global development, environmental degradation, the collapse of civil society and new forms of violence and warfare. The international refugee regime which originated in the inter-war period and evolved further in response to the problems

---

[2] For general background see Sayigh 1990.

of the Cold War is proving inadequate to deal with the challenges posed by these new and increasingly large movements of people in the post-Cold War era. Humanitarian action alone cannot resolve situations of forced displacement. Furthermore, as noted above, the close interrelationship between refugee flows and other types of migratory movements necessitates concerted political and economic action on the part of governments through the establishment of an internationally harmonized regime. Because forcible movements of people are determined by a complex number of factors, it is also necessary for governments to address not only migration policies and practices but also policies in other areas that influence the movements of people, such as human rights, civil society, trade and development policies, as well as conflict prevention and management. These developments necessitate a realistic assessment of the challenges posed by forced migrants today as well as the capacity of the international community to respond.

This chapter will (1) briefly describe the scope, dimensions, problems, and trends of contemporary refugee movements by analysing some of the forces which shape these flows; (2) assess the approaches and constraints of the refugee regime and evolving efforts to deal with the current crisis; (3) point to possible future refugee movements of great concern to the international community; and (4) underscore some of the refugee issues that governments and international institutions will have to confront in the future as well as identify possible future solutions, policies, partners, and funding strategies to deal with forced migration.

Scope and dimensions of contemporary refugee movements

First, one of the most significant recent developments has been the growing number of refugees and internally displaced peoples caused no longer by ideological conflict but by ethnic, communal, and religious violence. Very few modern states are ethnically homogeneous as approximately 5,000 ethnic groups and over 8,000 languages exist in the world today. Ethnic antagonisms between Hutus and Tutsis, Armenians and Azeris, Tamils and Sinhalese, and Serbs, Croats, Muslims, and Kosovar Albanians illustrate the local roots of many refugee exoduses. Virtually all of the refugee-producing conflicts taking place today are within states rather than between them.[3]

---

[3] As the Stockholm International Peace Research Institute noted in its 1996 Yearbook, all 30 major conflicts currently under way are primarily internal. The distinction between inter-state and intra-state war is never simple, however. For example, the conflict between Hutus and Tutsis in Rwanda and Burundi spilled over into Zaire and Tanzania and threatened to destabilize those countries.

It is also the case that mass population movements are now assuming a larger scale and occurring in a shorter time frame than in previous years. Recent conflicts in Northern Iraq, Liberia, former Yugoslavia, Rwanda, and Kosovo, for example, have each resulted in the displacement of more than a million people. A number of trends have contributed to the growing scale and speed of forced displacement in these and other locations. In many situations, extreme nationalist leaders use the media to exacerbate conflict, promote violence among ethnic groups, and induce people to flee. New forms of violence and warfare have emerged particularly in collapsing states where competing warlords destroy entire social, economic, and political systems in their fight for a share of resources. The growth in the worldwide market in small arms and land mines has made internal wars more violent. Consequently, conflicts today displace more people than in the past. One study, for example, cites the fact that the numbers of forcibly displaced have risen from 400,000 per conflict in 1969 to 857,000 per conflict in 1992 (Weiner 1996: 5–42).

Most significantly, mass expulsions are now regularly used as a weapon of war. Governments and their opponents use population displacements for a variety of political and military purposes. Such strategies help armed groups gain or maintain control over people, territory, and other resources. They can be used to establish culturally or ethnically homogeneous societies, to perpetuate the dominance of one group over another, to provide a means of removing groups of people whose loyalty to the state is questioned, or as human shields to protect military forces from air attack. Thus, in many situations, population displacement has become the very objective of wars.

Second, present refugee crises are complex emergencies, combining political instability, ethnic tensions, armed conflict, economic collapse, environmental degradation, and the disintegration of civil society. Refugee movements frequently spill over borders and aggravate existing problems, such as environmental damage or severe food shortages. Refugee emergencies are seldom confined to single countries but often affect entire regions, such as the Great Lakes region, the Horn of Africa, the Caucasus, or the Balkans. In recent years, few of these refugee crises have been fully resolved. Consequently, resources from one crisis often have not been made available for use in the next.

Today's wars are also lasting longer than before as new power structures and parallel economies are created within war societies, making the settlement of conflicts extremely difficult (Duffield 1994). With the absence of formal military authority in many war societies, combatants have tended to mobilize around loyalties and allegiances which have as much to do with personal survival and enrichment as with any political or ideological agenda. Those possessing power are almost invariably opposed to the settlement of crises as such initiatives endanger and erode their power base and access to resources.

Consequently, it is not surprising that the average humanitarian relief operation today lasts for three to five years and is extremely costly for the international community (Walker 1996).

During the first half of the 1990s, the resources devoted to humanitarian assistance soared while development aid to the least developed countries fell (*The Reality of Aid* 1996). Among official aid agencies, spending on emergencies increased fivefold from 1985 to 1994 (OECD 1994). Annual aggregate funding levels peaked at around $7 billion in 1994, and have since leveled off at $3 to 4 billion per year (Forman and Parhard 1997). In the late 1990s, the UN departments and intergovernmental agencies most active in humanitarian relief often struggle to obtain funds from governments who are more concerned with identifying national and security interests for their response. The political and security considerations guiding government decisions seriously compromise the equitable distribution of humanitarian assistance, making it insufficient in many cases. For example, in mid-1999, while donor governments spent hundreds of millions of dollars on both international emergency and reconstruction assistance to Kosovo, the UN and its specialized agencies, including UNHCR, received less than half of the assistance requested for emergencies in Africa.[4]

Many donor governments are now channelling their humanitarian assistance through non-governmental organizations (NGOs). This, in turn, has encouraged a proliferation of humanitarian NGOs which now openly compete with each other for funds (Weiss and Gordenker 1996). As a consequence, NGOs and intergovernmental organizations have felt forced to shift their focus to emergency relief. Many NGOs, such as Oxfam or CARE, now devote a substantial proportion of their resources to emergency assistance, despite the fact that preventive intervention and longer-term development assistance are widely believed to be more cost effective. The World Food Programme now devotes about 80 per cent of its resources to emergency food relief, and UNICEF directs about 25 per cent of its expenditure towards emergencies (Weiss and Gordenker 1996).

Third, refugee movements have also assumed a new degree of political importance in the discourse about global and regional security and are the subject of increasing discussion in political and military fora such as the UN

---

[4] By August 1999, the UN had received less than half the $796 million it appealed for that year to give urgent help to 12 million people in Africa. See Victoria Brittain, 'UN Begs World Not to Spurn Africa', *Guardian*, 14 Aug. 1999, 15. At the same time, UNHCR had received only 25% of its requests, totalling $165 million, for aid to confront refugee crises in sub-Saharan Africa. In addition, only 60% of UNHCR's $137 million annual budget for Africa had been funded. At the same time, by contrast, the UNHCR had received commitments of $265 million for its emergency programme in Kosovo. See Colum Lynch, 'UN Refugee Chief Warns West of a Double Standard on Africa', *International Herald Tribune*, 28 July 1999, 4.

Security Council and the North Atlantic Treaty Organization. Fundamental changes have also occurred in the international refugee regime, especially the way in which the UNHCR operates.

During the Cold War, in-country, cross-border assistance and protection was taboo for UN agencies because this involved violation of sovereignty. In the post-Cold War period, by contrast, states have come to view refugee movements as potential threats to international and regional security and have been willing in selective instances to invoke an expanded interpretation of the phrase 'threat to peace' in the UN Charter to intervene in internal conflicts involving humanitarian concerns.[5] The UN Security Council has increasingly defined not only refugee flows but also domestic disorder more generally as a threat to peace and security, thus opening the door to enforcement action under Chapter VII of the UN Charter. Certain internal acts—especially those creating massive unrest—are increasingly regarded as threats to others, particularly by their neighbours. From this perspective, grievous human rights abuses are not an internal matter when neighbouring states must bear the cost of repression. Thus, after invoking Chapter VII enforcement powers in only two cases (South Africa and Rhodesia) during the first forty-five years of existence of the UN, the Security Council has invoked them frequently since 1990, and most of these cases involved civil disorder or refugee flows rather than classic international aggression of one state against another.[6]

In these situations, states have increasingly called upon UN agencies to operate on both sides of borders where there is conflict, to ease tensions, and to assist and protect civilians during fighting and immediately afterwards. While facile assumptions about the capacities of outside humanitarian agencies and military forces to relieve suffering and help sustain civilians trapped in war zones have been replaced by more realistic estimates about the limits of such operations (Weiss 1999), humanitarian interventions and the involvement of UNHCR in countries of origin are much more commonplace today than in the past. Consequently, an increasing proportion of UNHCR's operations now occur within countries of origin, in zones of active conflict, and often in close association with UN mandated peacekeeping forces. In terms of sheer numbers and operational difficulties, those fleeing civil wars, ethnic conflicts, and generalized violence in the developing countries and in the

---

[5] For further development of this argument see Dowty and Loescher 1996: 43–71 and 1999: 199–222.

[6] These cases include: Iraq 1991 (UN Doc. S/RES/688 [5 Apr. 1991]), Somalia 1992 (UN Doc. S/RES/733 [23 Jan. 1993] and UN Doc. S/RES/814 [26 Mar. 1993]), Bosnia 1992 (UN Doc. S/RES/757 [30 May 1992]), Croatia 1993 (UN Doc. S/RES/807 [19 Feb. 1993] and UN Doc. S/RES/1093 [14 Jan. 1997]), Liberia 1993 (UN Doc. S/RES/813 [26 Mar. 1993]), Haiti 1993 (UN Doc. S/RES/841 [16 June 1993]), Rwanda 1994 (UN Doc. S/RES/929 [22 June, 1994]), Zaire 1996 (UN Doc. S/RES/1080 [15 Nov. 1996]), Albania 1997 (UN Doc. S/RES/1101 [28 Mar. 1997]), and Kosovo 1998 (UN Doc. S/RES/1160 [31 Mar. 1998]).

former Soviet Union and Eastern Europe are a bigger problem for the inter-national community than refugees who meet the narrow definition contained in the 1951 UN Refugee Convention. As a result, the numbers of displaced people and war-affected populations receiving UNHCR protection and assistance increased from some 17 million in 1991 to 21.1 million at the end of 1998 (UNHCR 1999). Of this total, refugees now constitute less than 50 per cent of UNHCR's beneficiaries. Consequently, UNHCR has in many senses expanded from a refugee organization into a more broadly-based humanitarian agency.

This expansion of the UNHCR into a fully-fledged operational agency has raised widespread concern both within and outside the Office that the agency has downgraded its special responsibility to provide international protection to refugees (Goodwin-Gill 1996; Hathaway 1995). The transformation of the UNHCR into a more general humanitarian emergency organization has compromised its capacity and willingness to provide protection and has put the agency at the mercy of a much broader set of political and strategic calculations. Because UNHCR needs to raise more and more voluntary funds for its operations, obtain access to increasingly volatile internal situations, win the confidence of competing actors, and promote compromise solutions, the agency is not well placed to stand up for protection principles regarding refugees. To fully promote protection would threaten funding, access to conflict situations, and the ability to be operational (Alston 1995). It is not surprising, therefore, that UNHCR has come under increasing criticism from many quarters for failing to adequately fulfil its protection mandate in places like the former Zaire, Tanzania, Bosnia, Kosovo, Western Europe, and the United States.

Fourth, while there is a new international emphasis placed upon humanitarian action, post-Cold War humanitarianism has focused primarily on assistance—the delivery of food, shelter, and medicine—to refugees and war-affected populations. What has easily become neglected is the central importance of human rights protection of displaced and threatened populations. Recent high-level relief efforts in Iraqi Kurdistan, Bosnia, Rwanda, Democratic Congo, and Kosovo underline dramatically the detachment of assistance and protection and the inadequacy of providing protection in traditional humanitarian relief programmes. In each of these operations, the international community was largely reactive to events and failed to address the direct links between violence, human rights abuses, and humanitarian emergencies.

These operations also demonstrate that as long as the underlying causes of conflict are not addressed, relief risks serving as a mere palliative to human suffering, or even worse, prolonging it. In Bosnia, for example, the provision of humanitarian assistance was the foundation upon which the multilateral response to the Balkans crises was built and remained virtually the sole substitute for an overall approach to the political problem there. Even the establishment of 'safe areas' in Bosnia at the height of that conflict in the spring of 1993 were in practice more focused on humanitarian assistance than on protection of those within these enclaves. In Rwanda, the critical issue of genocide was not adequately addressed, and no substantive measures were taken by the international community to provide protection. The relief effort for Rwandan refugees in the former Zaire was plagued from the beginning by the manipulation and diversion of aid to the very soldiers who had engineered the genocide and fuelled the exodus. Nothing was done in the former Zaire to separate the criminals from the main body of refugees or to isolate the suspects, thus causing huge protection problems for the refugees trapped in the camps.

The militarization of refugee camps is not a new phenomenon.[7] When combatants are present in refugee camps, these settlements are viewed by antagonistic forces as sources of assistance and protection to their enemies and therefore as legitimate military targets. The presence of 'refugee warriors' in camps also undermines civilian and international authority and can lead to camps falling under the control of military forces. In addition, camps contain undefended resources, such as food, vehicles, and relief supplies, and people who can constitute new soldiers or can be taken as hostages.

During the 1980s, 'refugee warriors' used refugee camps in Pakistan, along the Thai-Cambodian border, in Central America, and in the Horn of Africa to provide themselves with food and medicines, to forcibly recruit new soldiers, and, in some instances, to tax refugee workers to purchase arms. As in eastern Zaire (now Democratic Republic of Congo) since mid-1994, armed militias also prevented refugees from returning home, in effect keeping them hostage to their struggles. In almost every refugee crisis in recent years, camps have been subject to some sort of military pressure, ranging from bombardment by the Turkish air force of Kurdish camps in northern Iraq, raids by rebel forces of Sudanese camps in northern Uganda, and forced recruitment by the Kosovo Liberation Army of refugees out of camps in Albania and Macedonia. Despite greater attention to this issue by UNHCR in recent years (McNamara 1998), the main focus of the international humanitarian response to refugee crises continues to be material assistance at the expense of the human rights protection of refugees.

Fifth, increasing humanitarian action to respond to refugee crises has coincided with a weakening of traditional protection and asylum mechanisms in most states. More and more governments are becoming less enthusiastic about receiving refugees and asylum seekers especially when the newcomers are of a markedly different cultural or racial background. In industrialized societies the rise in crime and violence has routinely been associated with the

---

[7] For a background to these developments at the international level during the 1980s see Mtango 1989: 87–121.

increase in asylum seekers, refugees, and migrants. Thus, in recent years, states have tried to curtail the entry of asylum seekers by erecting barriers to those seeking refuge from war and persecution.

During the period 1983 to 1992, there was a rapid increase in the number of asylum applicants in industrialized countries.[8] In 1983, less than 100,000 people requested asylum in Europe, North America, Australia, and Japan. By 1992, the number had risen to over 841,000. In total, approximately 3.7 million asylum applicants were recorded in the Western industrial countries during the decade 1983–92. Germany was the most seriously affected by the sharp increase, with the number of asylum seekers rising from 121,000 in 1989 to 438,000 in 1992. As a result, huge backlogs of asylum cases and rising costs exceeding $7 billion per year put heavy strains on the asylum systems in industrialized states.

This rapid growth in asylum applications combined with high structural unemployment in most West European states led to increased xenophobia and anti-refugee sentiments throughout Europe. In response to these growing asylum pressures, the advanced industrialized states became increasingly reluctant to let people enter their countries to apply for political asylum. Most industrial states concluded that preventing entry of asylum seekers by imposing visa requirements on the nationals of refugee-producing states, fining airlines for bringing refugees into their countries, and forcibly interdicting refugees at frontiers and in international waters was the best way to reduce both the numbers and the costs of asylum applications.

Pressures to control entry into Europe were also dictated by the pace of European integration. The 1986 Single European Act mandated the abolition of internal borders and hence the parallel need to tighten control over the common external frontier. In a climate of national restrictionism, EU states started a process of harmonization which by the late 1990s has led to a regional regime of exclusionary controls and agreements.

The European Union has the most advanced regional regime to deal with refugees, asylum seekers and migrants. EU states have created a plethora of fora in which to discuss common concerns and plan strategies. For example, West European states have drafted several agreements to formalize intensified cooperation on asylum seekers and related issues, the central pillars of which are the Schengen Agreement of 1985 and the Schengen and Dublin Conventions of 1990. Together these European instruments constitute a framework for policy which permits asylum seekers to lodge an application only in one state and allow information about applicants to be extensively shared among member states. In addition, EU states adopted the principle of

---

[8] The following are figures provided by the Inter-Governmental Consultations on Migration cited in Loescher 1993. More recent figures come from UNHCR 1998. See also Table 3.3 in this volume.

'manifestly unfounded' claim, permitting applicants who make spurious asylum claims to be screened out through fast-track mechanisms. These regional policies, however, were established outside the framework of the European Union. The development and implementation of the Schengen and Dublin Conventions mostly took place in the EU's Ad Hoc Group on Immigration, which met regularly and made recommendations to the Ministers of Immigration for final approval by the Council of Ministers. The fact that the European Parliament, the European Commission, and the European Court of Justice were largely bypassed in this process has resulted in the evolution of a regional approach which is essentially restrictionist.

In the early 1990s, the Ad Hoc Group and the Council formulated two concepts of 'safe country' designed to permit states to return asylum seekers without strictly violating the *non-refoulement* provision in international refugee law. According to this procedure, nationals of a state judged to be a 'safe country of origin' *ipso facto* had 'manifestly unfounded' claims to asylum and could be excluded from the asylum process in EU states. The criteria for defining 'safe' were at best uncertain and mostly controversial. Germany after 1993 defined a 'safe state of origin' as a country 'where it was safe to assume that neither political persecution nor inhumane or degrading practices take place'. Britain put Sri Lanka and Nigeria on its list of 'safe countries of origin' in late 1995.

Potential refugees could also be excluded from the EU states' asylum procedures if on their journey to Europe they transited a so-called 'safe third country'. Under this procedure governments assume the right to refuse admission to an asylum seeker if he or she has arrived via a country where their claim to refugee status might have been submitted. Thus, because Germany has declared all of its neighbours to the east to be either 'safe countries of origin' or 'safe third countries', it has effectively renounced responsibility for considering the asylum request of any person arriving in the country by land without a valid visa. Critics argue that the 'safe third country' concept fundamentally compromises refugee protection because it withholds due process and lacks other basic safeguards to ensure that refugees will in fact have access to a comprehensive and fair asylum procedure somewhere. Moreover, the 'safe third country' procedure fails to distinguish bona fide refugees from those with spurious claims. A person's travel route into exile, rather than the reasons behind his or her flight, becomes the overriding factor in deciding whether protection will be granted. Finally, many of the countries considered 'safe' either implement safe third country laws of their own, or routinely deport asylum seekers to fourth countries without reviewing their cases. Thus, the ultimate danger for refugees is that 'safe country' policies may cause 'chain deportations', whereby no country assumes responsibility for examining a specific asylum request and an asylum seeker is bounced from one country to the next; either to countries with no means to protect them adequately, or worse, to the countries where they were persecuted. Such cases of 'refugees in orbit' have been well documented by European NGOs in recent years.

The cumulative effect of all these measures undertaken by EU states during the past decade has been to drastically limit—and in many cases to reduce— the numbers of asylum seekers arriving on their territory and applying for refugee status. Starting in 1993, asylum applications in many industrialized states fell considerably. In Germany, for example, the number of asylum applications declined from 438,000 in 1992 to 99,000 in 1998, while in the United States, the number fell from 150,700 in 1992 to 51,000 in 1998 (UNHCR 1999). Overall, the numbers of asylum applicants in the industrialized countries fell from a high of 841,000 in 1992 to 389,000 in 1997, the lowest number since 1989 (see Chapter 3, Table 3.3). This is viewed as a successful reform effort by states. However, it remains unknown the extent to which the new border control measures have in fact acted as a deterrent for fraudulent asylum seekers, or whether these measures have deterred bona fide asylum seekers, merely shifted refugee flows to other countries, or resulted in an expansion of migrant trafficking, illegal immigration, and organized crime in the industrialized states.

There is some evidence that, far from resolving the asylum problem, these measures have merely diverted the problem elsewhere. Initially, such diversions tended to take place from one of these countries to another. For example, in 1994, when the introduction of new asylum regulations in Germany caused a 60 per cent drop in the number of applications submitted there, the number of asylum applications in the neighbouring Netherlands increased by 50 per cent. In 1998, when asylum applications in Germany dropped by a third from 1997, asylum applications in neighbouring Luxembourg increased from 400 per annum in 1997 to 1600 in 1998, they almost doubled in Belgium during 1998 and increased by over 70 per cent in Switzerland (UNHCR 1999). Now that all EU states have introduced stricter policies, the countries on the periphery of Western Europe are experiencing a substantial increase in the number of asylum seekers arriving from other continents. According to some estimates, there are now around 700,000 illegal and transit migrants in the Commonwealth of Independent States (CIS), of whom 500,000 are to be found in the Russian Federation alone (Ghosh 1998).

Some experts believe that greater controls have meant that more people have simply 'gone underground' and are entering the country illegally. In other words, the restrictive asylum practices introduced by EU states have converted what was a visible flow of asylum seekers into a covert movement of irregular migrants that is even more difficult for states to count and control. Irregular migration now represents one-quarter of the total yearly inflow into the United States and as much as one-half of that in Europe. At the global level some $7 billion is channelled every year into human trafficking (Ghosh 1998).

It is also the case that the entry of these migrants and asylum seekers is increasingly arranged and organized by professional traffickers. The covert nature of migrant trafficking almost inevitably means that international criminal syndicates are involved, making huge profits on the stealing and forging of travel documents, passports, and work and residence permits. The migrants themselves are subject to constant physical insecurity and financial exploitation. Many have drowned in unseaworthy boats or died suffocating in containers or hidden compartments in trucks. In some situations, immigration officers, police, and local government officials are bribed to look the other way as illegal migrants are smuggled across their borders. Migrants who manage to reach their destinations often find that they have to turn to crime to pay off their debts to traffickers. Increasingly, illegal migrants are forced to transport or sell drugs for criminal organizations or engage in prostitution or other criminal activities. Thus, an unintended consequence of the restrictive measures of EU states has been to further expand the marginalized, excluded, and criminalized underclass in West European societies. The association with organized crime also makes it more difficult for some refugee groups to seek asylum in EU member states. It seems clear that in Europe, the most advanced regional system, the deterrent and control policies now in operation are proving increasingly inadequate to deal with the problem of asylum seekers.

It is also significant that the trend towards excluding asylum seekers is spreading to governments in the South as well as the North. Alarmed by the economic, environmental, social, and security costs of hosting mass influxes of refugees, a number of governments across the world have taken steps to exclude asylum seekers from their territory and to ensure the rapid—and in some cases involuntary—repatriation of refugees.

Most of the world's refugees are presently confined to their region of origin in the less developed countries. Faced with mass influxes and a greater share of the world's refugee burden, many governments in the South which in the past had generally responded humanely to the needs of millions who were forced from their homelands are now closing their doors to new arrivals. In many countries, refugees are perceived as a threat to the physical environment or security of the host state, especially when they include persons who are determined to use the asylum country as a base for political and military activities. Receiving countries perceive sudden and massive refugee movements as a cause for economic dislocation, social and political instability, and cultural conflict. Diminishing donor government support for long-term refugee assistance, coupled with declining levels of official development assistance and the imposition of structural adjustment programmes on many poorer and less stable states, has reinforced this attitude and contributed to the hostility towards refugees. Indeed, as some developing countries improve their administrative and military capacities, we can anticipate a hardening of borders and more restrictive policies both towards the admission of refugees and their early repatriation. Consequently, there exist parallel asylum crises in both the North and South.

Sixth, even as new refugee crises emerge, the easing of East–West tensions and the consequent resolution of several long-standing regional conflicts made it possible for more than 9 million refugees to return to their homes during the first five years of the last decade compared to only 1.2 million from 1985 to 1990. Consequently, there is much greater attention today on repatriation and returns to areas characterized by human rights abuses and widespread conflict. Under state pressure to promote repatriation, UNHCR has been forced to undercut its own protection mandate in certain key instances. Though not explicit, the principle of voluntary return has been abandoned in favour of 'managed' repatriation often to unsafe areas. In former Zaire, for instance, UNHCR was left with having to choose between two uncomfortable options: either attempt to rescue and repatriate refugees to some unsafe areas of western Rwanda, or leave them to their fate in the forests of Zaire. This particular crisis highlighted the changing geo-political climate and the unwillingness of UN member states to strengthen UNHCR's capacity to protect displaced people. At the UNHCR 48th Executive Committee meeting in October 1997, governments were criticized for their failure to give guidance on issues of protection, and their increasing tendency to 'tip the balance towards state interests to the point where protection . . . is seriously marginalized' (McNamara 1998). (See Chapter 1 in this volume.)

If large numbers of refugees continue to repatriate in the coming years, the focus of international concern must inevitably shift from repatriation to more long-standing reintegration and development. It is becoming increasingly evident that in most war-torn countries one of the preconditions for successful returns is development aid and reintegration assistance aimed both at alleviating poverty and building local institutions and civil society in countries of origin. Without sustained reintegration and reconciliation, returning refugees will compete for scarce developmental resources which, in turn, may well result in fierce political and economic competition with local populations which did not flee (Ghosh 2000).

Finally, the refugee problem is a part of the emerging global crisis of mass migration which is generated by structural economic, political, environmental, and social changes in the world, particularly in large parts of the developing world and in Eastern Europe and the former Soviet Union. The growing interdependence of national economies, the transnational impacts of the global communications, information, and transportation systems, and the expanding gap between poor and rich countries have led millions of people from the developing countries to seek jobs and security in the wealthier countries of the world. Increasing numbers of people are seeking entry not only to the industrialized states of North America and Western Europe, but also to the newly industrialized states of Asia and the oil-producing states of the Middle East.

Underdevelopment and poverty also exacerbate the political and social instability that generates refugee movements and thus serve to further globalize the refugee problem. Recent years have witnessed a widening in economic disparities both within and between states.[9] During the past three decades, the income differential between the richest and poorest fifth of the world's population has doubled from 30 : 1 to 61 : 1. In the less developed regions, no fewer than eighty-nine countries now have lower per capita incomes than they had ten years ago. While refugees flee mainly persecution and political violence and not economic hardship, poverty often exacerbates existing conflicts and struggles over scarce resources, destabilizes social and civil institutions, undermines human rights, and can therefore act as an accelerating factor in the creation of refugee flows. It is no coincidence that the overwhelming majority of complex emergencies officially recognized by the UN are to be found within the most economically marginalized regions of the world.

Likely sources of refugee movements in the future

Refugee movements are not produced by random upheavals and conflicts, but are the result of identifiable, patterned international processes which vary from region to region. Most refugee movements in the next two decades will occur either as a result of demands for democratization in many parts of the developing and post-communist worlds or as a result of the communal violence and the fragmentation, implosion, or restructuring of existing states caused by nationality disputes and ethnic conflicts and shaped by demographic pressures, environmental degradation, and poverty. Political upheavals in unstable regions will be exacerbated by the diffusion of weapons via the arms trade from the advanced to the developing world. A failure by the international community to promote better observance of human rights, to manage national minority and ethnic conflict issues, and to curb the global small arms trade could result in a reccurrence of major refugee flows.

Democratization and refugee movements

As we enter the 21st century, more people than ever before are living in relatively pluralistic political systems. But recent political events have also illustrated that the transition to democracy can have a destabilizing impact on

---

[9] This data is drawn from UNDP 1996 and United Nations 1997.

society, leading to conflict and the forced displacement of people. In recent years, popular demands for political openness and liberalization in many parts of Africa and Latin America have gained ground. However, the movement towards democratization in both regions is likely to prove increasingly difficult in the years ahead as social and economic conditions continue to deteriorate.

Most of Africa, which already hosts a large proportion of the world's refugees, is in a severe economic crisis, manifested in a drastic decline of per capita income, low or negative rates of economic growth, a collapsing social and physical infrastructure, high rates of population increase and urbanization growth, declining terms of trade of primary commodities, and problems of indebtedness. The entire continent of Africa currently accounts for less than 5 per cent of global trading activity (UNDP 1996; UN 1997). Without strong political and civil institutions, many African states will be unable to contain and channel the inevitable political tensions which will result from the problems of poverty and economic readjustment. These weaknesses will, in turn, lead to breakdowns of law and order, to secessionist movements, and to civil wars. The situation will be exacerbated by chronic problems of deforestation and soil degradation that will inevitably increase the numbers of people who uproot themselves in search of viable livelihoods.

Even if democratization succeeds in Africa, it does not mean that there will be an end to ethnic conflicts and refugee movements. Indeed, democratization may in fact be destabilizing—especially if the process of liberalization gives free rein to demands from national minorities for greater autonomy or secession. Thus, it is likely that with the end or weakening of authoritarian regimes across Africa, long repressed factional grievances and antagonisms will result in increased conflicts as groups contend for control of the political systems.

Rwanda, Burundi, Liberia, Sierra Leone, Angola, Sudan, and Somalia are among the most tragic examples of this resurgence of long-standing ethnic grievances and protracted refugee situations. Already one-third, or sixteen African countries are involved in one form or another of civil conflict. There are some 3.5 million refugees on the continent in areas beyond their own borders. An additional 8 to 9 million of the world's internally displaced are in Africa. Unfortunately, this trend is likely to continue well into the next century.

In Latin America, despite the election of constitutional governments and the reduction of ideological polarities and tensions during the 1980s and early 1990s, democratization in the region will continue to be fragile. The majority of people live in poverty and on the margins of the democratic process, and the growing inequalities of wealth, the lack of public facilities in housing, health care, and education, the lack of strong civil institutions, unions, and peasant associations to counterbalance strong administrations, the continuing mistrust and hatred between former enemies after years of civil strife in

Central America and the Andean region, and the underlying ethnic divisions
between Indians and people of Spanish origin could produce violent
confrontations and refugee exoduses. Conflicts between government forces
and guerrilla opposition groups and drug cartels have already displaced well
over a million people in Peru and Colombia, and prolonged power struggles
and the resumption of armed conflict between old foes in Nicaragua threaten
to create new refugee movements.

National minorities and refugee movements

Nationality and minority rights issues will undoubtedly be a major source of
conflicts and refugee movements in future years. Refugee movements will be
the result of ethnic and communal conflicts, fuelled by the increasing availability of modern weaponry and socio-economic inequalities. The underlying
dynamic of many third world conflicts will be competition for political power
among fiercely rival ethnic groups. Not only will massive population displacement be the direct consequence of such conflicts but, as we have seen in the
former Yugoslavia and the Caucasus, the forced relocation of ethnic groups
will often be the very objective of these conflicts.

Currently more than one-half of the world's refugees flee communally based
violence, and this trend is likely to continue. As already noted, ethnic warfare
will flare up repeatedly not only in the former Soviet Union where imperial and
political structures have collapsed but also in places like Kosovo and Macedonia
and in parts of Africa and Asia where old ethnic conflicts have begun to re-
emerge. Because of cheap, accessible modern weaponry, civil wars devastate
physical infrastructure and will displace huge numbers of people, particularly in
densely populated countries. Since 1947, some 35 to 40 million people (some
economic migrants but mostly refugees) have moved across national boundaries in the Indian subcontinent. As ethnic, communal, and religious communities seek to assert their own identity across South Asia, unwanted flows of
people will continue to cross borders. In Africa, the combination of pressures
for political change and the resurgence of political violence in that continent's
most populous states of Nigeria and Democratic Congo create great potential
for future instability and refugee movements. In South-East Asia, economic and
political crises could lead to domestic instability and racial and ethnic pogroms
resulting in mass displacements. For example, the Chinese community in
Indonesia is likely to be targeted as a scapegoat in the event of economic collapse
and civil conflict. In addition, sudden and unanticipated political upheavals,
such as the collapse of communist regimes, the outbreak of civil wars, and the
breakdown of border controls in North Korea, the Peoples Republic of China or
in Cuba, could create huge refugee movements.

Future policy actions to deal with refugee movements

National and international policy-makers are not prepared for large-scale forced migration movements. To date, the majority of international action has been characterized by domestic and unilateral responses on the part of governments that focus on controls and enforcement measures. If the international community is to deal effectively with the global refugee problem, policy-makers must turn their attention to the more difficult task of concerted bi- and multilateral responses that address the root causes of refugee flows. This requires, on the one hand, greater North–South and East–West cooperation in trade liberalization and development assistance and more effective curbs on small arms sales, and, on the other hand, stricter observance of human rights conditions in a number of countries, particularly with respect to the treatment of national minorities. These tasks will inevitably involve greater government support not only for the traditional international refugee and relief organizations but also political and financial backing for more active involvement of international development agencies, human rights networks, and peacekeeping and conflict resolution mechanisms in global and regional refugee matters.

Despite the need for a multifaceted approach to future refugee problems, the overall response of the international community remains compartmentalized with political, development, security, and humanitarian issues mostly being discussed in different fora, each with their own institutional arrangements and independent policy approaches. There exist little or no strategic integration of approaches and little effective coordination in the field. Moreover, there is a serious disjuncture between expectations of international refugee and human rights agencies to work in this new global environment and the institutional capacity of these organizations to respond to massive human rights abuses and refugee flows. The absence of an autonomous resource base and the limited mandates and competencies of international humanitarian agencies will continue to constrain the international community in its response to future refugee crises just as they have done for the past fifty years.

It is increasingly evident that if the international refugee regime is to achieve its basic objectives and resolve future refugee problems, it must be comprehensive enough in scope to assist and protect refugees but also to extend beyond humanitarian action into broader policy realms that address the problems that generate forced migrants. In the future, responses to forced migration cannot proceed solely within the mandate of international humanitarian organizations and cannot be separated from other areas of international concern, in particular, human rights, economic development, and peace and security issues.

Addressing the growing problem of internal displacement

In future years, the problem of internal displacement and the plight of war-affected populations will acquire increasing humanitarian and strategic importance for the international community. Internally displaced generally find themselves in more difficult and dangerous circumstances than refugees, primarily because they remain under the jurisdiction of the state which is unable or unwilling to protect them (Cohen and Deng 1998*a*, 1998*b*). At the same time, given the continuing intra-state violence in many parts of the world, coupled with the growing readiness of states in both North and South to avert or obstruct mass refugee outflows from such situations by closing their doors to asylum seekers and insisting on the early repatriation of refugee populations, the number of people forcibly displaced and trapped within their own country can be expected to increase. Moreover, despite the new degree of caution that exists concerning humanitarian intervention, there is growing recognition amongst both governments and the public that the domestic affairs of states can also be a subject of legitimate international concern (Dowty and Loescher 1999). Thus, in addition to the problem of refugees, more attention will have to be given to the question of how to provide in-country protection and assistance to internally displaced people (IDPs).

A critical weakness of the international humanitarian system is that at present there is no special international organization to protect and assist the world's estimated 23 million IDPs. While there is a clear mandate for the protection and the provision of humanitarian assistance to refugees, there is a lack of clarity within existing international instruments regarding the allocation of responsibilities and mechanisms for addressing the immediate needs of IDPs. One of the major gaps in the international response system for the internally displaced is the lack of predictability. No UN agency can be counted upon to respond automatically when there is a crisis involving massive internal displacement. Agencies choose the situations in which they will become involved in the light of their mandates, resources, and interests. The selectivity and conditionality of the response often result in limited and inconsistent coverage for the internally displaced, leaving large numbers with little or no protection and assistance. The 1999 Kosovo emergency was a case in point. UNHCR and other international agencies were heavily involved in assisting refugees who fled the country whereas practically no international attention was directed towards the victims of ethnic cleansing and the internally displaced within the country.[10]

---

[10] For a critique of UNHCR's operation in Kosovo, including its neglect of internally displaced there during the conflict, see United Kingdom, House of Commons, International Development Committee, 1999.

In the absence of a single organization within the UN system for the internally displaced, reliance has been placed since 1991 on a system-wide approach, coordinated by the Department of Humanitarian Affairs from 1991 to 1998, and by the Office for the Coordination of Humanitarian Affairs (OCHA) since 1998. This collaborative approach has often been constrained by delays, duplication of effort and programmes, neglect of protection issues, and insufficient support for reintegration and post-conflict development efforts. Resident coordinators who have been assigned to manage assistance to internally displaced populations frequently have had no operational capacity, little experience in dealing with the internally displaced, and minimal understanding of protection concerns. In his programme for reform of the UN in July 1997, the UN Secretary-General, Kofi Annan, recognized the challenge of providing protection, assistance and reintegration, and development support for internally displaced and cited this area as an example of a humanitarian issue that falls between the gaps of existing mandates of the different agencies (UN Secretary-General 1997).

There is also no adequate body of international law to regulate their treatment by governments and international organizations. The 1949 Geneva Conventions and their Additional Protocols of 1977 make allowance for protection of civilians in internal conflicts, but they were formulated when conventional war was the norm and when the task of disseminating the rules was easier. When the UN Secretary-General's Special Representative for Internally Displaced Persons made a compilation of legal norms applicable to the internally displaced in 1996, he found a significant number of gaps in existing human rights and humanitarian law. Two years later, Francis Deng submitted a set of thirty Guiding Principles which addressed the specific needs of the internally displaced by identifying rights and guarantees relevant to their protection.[11] The Guiding Principles address all phases of displacement including protection from arbitrary displacement, protection during displacement, principles relating to humanitarian assistance, and protection during resettlement and reintegration.[12] Governments at the UN Human Rights Commission unanimously adopted a resolution acknowledging the Principles and encouraged Deng to utilize them in future efforts, including his dialogue with governments.

In discussing the Guiding Principles, the UN Human Rights Commission also noted the need to develop an institutional framework for the internally displaced. Governments signalled their clear preference for inter-agency coordination rather than the establishment of a new agency for addressing the assistance and protection needs of the internally displaced. UN Resolution

---

[11] The 30 Guiding Principles are reproduced in the *International Journal of Refugee Law*, 10/ 3 (1998) 563–72.

[12] For an analysis, see Bagshaw 1998: 548–56.

1998/50[13] encouraged the UN High Commissioner for Human Rights, UNHCR, the Emergency Relief Coordinator, Office for the Coordination of Humanitarian Affairs, UNDP, Unicef, WFP, WHO, IOM, ICRC and others to develop 'frameworks of cooperation' to promote protection, assistance and development for internally displaced persons, by appointing focal points within their organizations for these matters. It is still the case that there exists only a weak and incoherent arrangement at the international level for internally displaced. A new comprehensive international regime for forced migrants will necessarily have to place internally displaced persons at the centre of its concerns.

Empowerment of the international human rights regime

One of the greatest challenges confronting international organizations in the years to come will be to link the task of refugee protection to the broader defence of human rights. If the international community hopes to respond more effectively to the global problem of refugees and internal displacement, it must strengthen its capacity to monitor developments in human rights issues and to intercede on behalf of forced migrants. Governments must guarantee a meaningful funding base to the specialized human rights bodies and withdraw the financial and political constraints on human rights action.

The creation of the Office of the UN High Commissioner for Human Rights in 1993 brought a higher profile to human rights within the UN system and stepped up the monitoring of protection concerns in major crises. As part of a UN-wide effort to give a higher priority to the integration of human rights into the various activities and programmes of the UN, the High Commissioner has participated actively in dialogue with other UN agencies. Mary Robinson is a member of each of the four Executive Committees through which the UN system's work in humanitarian affairs, peace and security, economic and social affairs, and development is orchestrated. Despite considerable improvements, however, inter-agency coordination and the institutional division of labour regarding human rights within the UN remain problematic.

In recent years, there has also been an increase in the presence of the UN Human Rights Office staff in the field, especially as part of UN peacekeeping and peace enforcement missions, and increased activities by special rapporteurs appointed by the UN Human Rights Commission to document human rights violations in certain countries and to report back to the Commission.

---

[13] UN Doc. E/CN/1998/50, 1998.

Nevertheless, as in the past, major weaknesses continue to exist in the UN human rights system. UN human rights work depends on the cooperation of countries which can refuse entry to human rights officials and special rapporteurs and can often stonewall any new initiatives.

A key to strengthening UN capacity to monitor human rights in the future is enhancing its capacity to undertake a protection role in the field which involves a radical change of focus for the UN High Commissioner for Human Rights. To be effective, human rights monitoring requires good planning, specialized professional expertise, clear lines of authority, and significant financial resources. At the same time, UN human rights machinery and UN agencies should continue to expand their advisory services and technical assistance programmes by offering services such as training judges, strengthening electoral commissions, establishing ombudsmen, training prison staff, and advising governments on constitutions and legislation regarding national minorities and human rights.

UN member states should also support the newly created permanent international criminal tribunal. Such a mechanism is potentially an extremely important and effective innovation towards achieving the objectives of both justice and peace in situations where there have been intra-state conflict, genocide, human rights abuses, and forcible displacement. Institutions and individuals that are responsible for the human rights abuses which provoke forced population displacements must know they cannot act with impunity. An international tribunal can create consistent expectations of accountability for violations of human rights. As such, it would serve as a deterrent as well as a vehicle of truth-telling, reconciliation, and inter-ethnic healing in societies torn by violent conflict and mass killings.

Until the time when the capacity of the UN human rights regime is fully developed, non-governmental organizations (NGOs), especially human rights NGOs, will have to assume a larger share of responsibility for ensuring the protection of forcibly displaced people. Protection of refugees and other displaced people requires a readiness on the part of human rights agencies to act on observed human rights abuses. In order to accomplish this, human rights NGOs need to establish a continuous presence in regions experiencing conflict. NGOs provide a basis for consciousness-raising regarding humanitarian norms and democratic principles within regions, and they could enable local organizations to assume responsibility for monitoring, intervening, and managing humanitarian programmes without major external involvement or infringements of concepts of national sovereignty. UN agencies can contribute to this development through programmes aimed at strengthening the capacity of NGOs to work in the human rights field.

Relief NGOs, likewise, have an essential protection role to play. Many NGOs today are far more willing and able to address protection issues than they have been in the past. Their presence in most civil war situations makes them important sources of information on human rights abuses, refugee movements, and emergency food needs. This information is crucial for human rights monitoring, early warning of conflicts and refugee crises, and preventive diplomacy. Humanitarian organizations that operate in conflict situations should institutionalize procedures to manage and report information on human rights abuses using their own personnel in the field. Efforts should also be made to improve both the channels of communication and the readiness to act on human rights information at high political levels. At a minimum, NGOs, with the assistance of UN agencies, should train their staff regarding human rights principles and protection techniques to be used in the field—both as concerted human rights efforts and as part of normal relief efforts.

Moreover, because NGOs also have a central role in securing humanitarian access to the civilian victims of conflicts and are often in close contact with both governments and opposition movements, they can play a significant role in conflict resolution, mediation, and reconciliation. As a result of working with disenfranchised populations, NGOs are also often able to gain an understanding of the culture and underlying tensions which comprise the conflict. Such information is crucial to the potential for conflict resolution processes, even more so in societies where ongoing human rights violations have become part of the spectrum of issues to resolve in any comprehensive settlement. NGOs' presence within communities at war and their ability to move among civilian populations and armed forces are characteristics not shared by UN agencies and donor governments. Thus, NGOs are well placed to engage in a new comprehensive form of humanitarian action, encompassing assistance and protection, mediation and conflict resolution.

Reintegration of refugees and rebuilding war-torn societies

The former UN Secretary-General, Boutros-Ghali called attention in his *Agenda for Development* to the need to assist 'countries emerging from crisis situations in the rehabilitation phase' and to the widely accepted conclusion that without reconstruction and development following conflict, 'there can be little expectation that peace will endure' (Boutros-Ghali 1994). Indeed, rebuilding war-torn societies is one of the most urgent tasks currently facing the international community. Over half of the low-income countries in the world today have been at war during the past decade. As I have argued above, these trends are likely to continue in the future.

Despite a virtually universal consensus that peace agreements must be consolidated by investments which improve the security and economic well-being of the former adversaries and the victims of conflict, too little funding has been invested in post-conflict rebuilding. International funding invariably declines soon after ceasefires are in place and elections are held. Moreover, the assistance given to countries emerging from war is conditioned in ways that emergency relief funds are not, with major impacts on humanitarian and social initiatives. In the future, greater resources must be devoted over longer periods of time to catalyse sustainable forms of development and to create conditions which will prevent refugee movements from reoccurring (Weiss-Fagen 1996).

In countries where central government itself is weak or non-existent and therefore unable to protect its citizens, the key issue will be not only how to bring together contending groups but how to build institutions of governance. In such situations, economic development and social stability are inseparable. Rehabilitative relief and development activities must be accompanied by support for civil society[14] in order to be effective. Sustainable progress can only be achieved if built on a strong civil foundation that allows the gains made to be consolidated throughout society. Without this foundation, relief and development activities will constitute a one-time consumption of resources which will result in little long-term change. The development of civil society is also related to the avoidance of violence. Violent political conflict can generally be avoided only in a context in which the citizenry (1) is able to participate meaningfully in the political decisions that affect their lives, (2) can hold the persons and institutions that exercise power over them accountable for their actions, and (3) is equipped to negotiate a change in a peaceful and effective manner (Hippler 1995; Ross 1993).

International organizations need to adopt programmes and policies to strengthen civil society and local institutions. With the growth and strengthening of institutions, citizens and citizens' groups will be able to influence the behaviour of their leaders through pressure group activities, elections, and other democratic mechanisms. Advocacy programmes that promote the cause of refugees and asylum seekers at the local level and mobilize public support for these groups can have a very immediate impact on the world's displaced. The strengthening of democratic institutions and civil society are among the major preventive actions against future conflict and refugee migration.

Achieving peace and security through multilateral action

In the future, there will have to be a growing focus on international cooperation, particularly in achieving peace and security, without which there will be

---

[14] 'Civil Society' refers to non-state community-based groups, such as religious associations, advocacy groups focusing on human rights, democracy or the environment, civic associations, business and professional associations, labour unions, women's groups, cooperatives, academic institutions, and student groups.

no end to refugee movements. Future threats to national and regional stability will essentially be transnational in nature and will not be countered solely by unilateral action.

In future years the supply of small arms and antipersonnel mines to all sides in intra-state conflicts will continue to play a major role in the formation of refugee migration. As long as small arms are widely available, conflicts will continue to be violent and protracted and cause mass displacement. International attention needs to focus on reducing the level of violence associated with future conflicts by the imposition of limits on the amount and kinds of weapons that can be used. While total global spending on arms has dropped in recent years, cuts have been most significant in the richer countries and have been channelled to domestic priorities. Many developing countries, however, continue to divert limited resources from development to buy arms. This is stimulating an increase in the $20 billion plus arms trade, particularly in small arms and other light weapons (Klare 1995). It will be difficult to control small weapons trade because of the surplus stocks of such weapons dating from the Cold War, the large numbers of producers of small arms, the existence and growth of black market channels, and the difficulties of monitoring and controlling the transport and sales of these goods. Nevertheless, the international community should try to control future arms trade. It should also explore other possibilities to control the transfer of small weaponry, such as supporting regional organizations in efforts to enforce embargoes on weapons trade in conflict areas.

In the years to come, the international community will call upon the UN to deal more actively with the consequences of many future conflicts, including refugee movements. It is increasingly obvious that the UN will also need to address the causes of displacement before people are forced to flee to another country—not as a substitute for asylum, but as a way of enabling people to remain in their own countries in safety. Yet, significant remaining obstacles will have to be overcome before the UN can mobilize an active anticipatory strategy for refugee movements.

Many UN member states continue to resist a more assertive international organization, fearing that any Security Council-sanctioned intervention would simply be a cover for more powerful governments to use in pursuing their own interests and in wielding their international influence. Moreover, the Security Council is reluctant to support structural reforms that would give the Secretary-General real power to engage in effective preventive action. Finally, the ability of the UN to play a major role in peacekeeping and peacemaking is sharply limited by financial constraints.

Notwithstanding these constraints, the upsurge of UN peacekeeping and enforcement activities in recent years has demonstrated the indispensability of international organizations for future international peace and security. But in order for the UN to realize its full potential and to become more proactive in future years, a number of vital changes need to take place.

The key to future UN effectiveness in preventive action depends on the UN's capacity to move at the very earliest stage of a crisis. Some UN member states have proposed the establishment of a UN rapid reaction force, incorporating military, humanitarian, civil affairs, and human rights components. Such a force could be employed to protect minorities and refugees threatened by communal violence, oversee disengagement agreements in civil wars, protect and deliver humanitarian relief, monitor human rights violations, help build civil and legal institutions, and enforce sanctions, among other activities. A permanent force is also needed to demilitarize refugee camps, to separate military from civilian populations in camps in the future, and to control the distribution of aid in these situations. At present, the mandates of the UN agencies carrying out these tasks are often unclear, and their activities are usually uncoordinated. In the future, the UN should rationalize and clarify responsibilities, improve inter-agency coordination, and establish guidelines for improved responses to refugee and humanitarian crises. But preparing for a more comprehensive and effective UN response requires adequate funding, resources, and political support from UN member states.

A comprehensive approach

The almost inexorable growth of forced migration in recent years should alert us once again that piecemeal measures are no substitute for a solid international structure to deal with the entire scope of international migration. The current refugee regime has a number of important gaps in institutional mandates, with the result that entire groups of forced migrants, like internally displaced persons, are neglected and left unprotected and often unassisted. The international response to forced migration can no longer be run on the basis of existing rules and institutions that are outdated and too fragmented in the face of a host of new challenges. Proposals for an internationally harmonized migration policy involving both sending and receiving states as well as international organizations need to be broadened and backed by a visionary approach to interrelated global issues such as security, trade and development, human rights, and migration.

As future refugee movements become the source of even greater political instability and dangerous upheavals, the international community will come to accept the view that policy responses must go beyond conventional border control and humanitarian measures and become part of their national, regional, and international political and security objectives. Short-term, improvised policies and draconian border controls will impede the long-term initiatives needed to deal with these complex and contentious issues. Simply erecting new barriers against the South and the East to deter population movements will not make the problem go away, nor will it ensure a stable political base for international relations. The destabilizing effects of future refugee movements cannot be dealt with successfully at the national level.

In the longer term, effective international management of this problem requires unprecedented cooperation between sending, receiving, and transit countries as well as the refugees and migrants themselves. The countries of origin have a responsibility for their own citizens, especially in preventing the situations which give rise to refugee and migrant flows, and national sovereignty should not be used to shield governments from their responsibilities. In this regard, the governments in the South and the East must reach accommodation with their ethnic and religious groups and refrain from political repression which can lead to disruptive outflows or even mass exodus, threatening national and regional stability. However, a sole emphasis on the responsibility of the countries of refugee origin and on prevention of refugee movements risks overshadowing the responsibilities of all governments towards asylum seekers and refugees. Governments everywhere have the responsibility to refrain from imposing or contributing to refugee-generating conditions. This means that asylum states, particularly those in the North, have international obligations too, including the support of human rights, the provision of asylum, restrictions on arms sales to refugee-producing states, and the provision of financial and political support to promote equitable and sustainable development in countries and regions of refugee origin.

International initiatives must also be comprehensive enough to address the interplay of political, economic, environmental, and security factors which drive most migration movements today. Respect for human rights, more equitable development, and the growth and enlargement of civil society are indispensable foundations for a more effective and orderly international response to forced migration. A failure by both the industrialized and developing states to take action to stem global poverty, violence, persecution, and other refugee-inducing factors will be costly not only in humanitarian terms but also in the security realm. Dealing effectively with refugee and other population movements both at home and abroad is, therefore, in the self-interest of all states and coincides with their search for long-term global strategic stability.

In the contemporary international political context, generating support for new international initiatives may very well be difficult to accomplish. The political, financial, and organizational impediments already mentioned place significant constraints on new political initiatives. Nevertheless, as noted above, there are reasons of state as well as of humanitarian concern to offer protection to refugees and other forced migrants and to seek solutions to these problems. In the realms of human rights and forced displacement, international and regional stability and idealism often coincide. Policy-makers need to build on this coincidence of factors to achieve the political will both to address these problems and to develop the institutional capacity to respond more effectively to the global crisis of forced migration. Greater international cooperation and the development of a sound and effective international regime to encompass all types of forced population movements and of the institutional mechanisms that could help resolve disputes will be the only effective ways for governments both to manage interdependent issues like refugee movements and to ensure long-term global strategic stability.

REFERENCES

Books and articles

Alston, P. (1995), 'The Downside of Post-Cold War Complexity: Comments on Hathaway', *Journal of Refugee Studies*, 8/3: 303–4.

Bagshaw, S. (1998), 'Internally Displaced Persons at the Fifty-Fourth Session of the United Nations Commission on Human Rights, 16 March–24 April 1998', *International Journal of Refugee Law*, 10/3: 548–56.

Boutros-Ghali, B. (1994), *Agenda for Development*, New York: United Nations.

Cohen, R., and Deng, F. (1998a), *The Forsaken People: Case Studies of the Internally Displaced*, Washington, DC.: Brookings Institution Press.

—— —— (1998b), *Masses in Flight: The Global Crisis of Internal Displacement*, Washington, DC: Brookings Institution Press.

Dowty, A., and Loescher, G. (1996), 'Refugee flows as Grounds for International Action', *International Security*, 21/1: 43–71.

—— —— (1999), 'Changing Norms in International Responses to Domestic Disorder', in R. Vayrynen, *Globalization and Global Governance*, Lanham, Md.: Rowman & Littlefield Publishers, 199–222.

Duffield, M. (1994), 'The Political Economy of Internal War: Asset Transfer, Complex Emergencies and International Aid' and other chapters in J. Macrae and A. Zwi (eds.), *War and Hunger: Rethinking International Responses to Complex Emergencies*, London: Zed Books.

Forman, S., and Parhard, R. (1997), *Paying for Essentials: Resources for Humanitarian Assistance*, New York: NYU Center on International Cooperation.

Ghosh, B. (1998), *Huddled Masses and Uncertain Shores: Insights into Irregular Migration*, The Hague: Kluwer International.

Goodwin-Gill, G. S. (1996), 'Refugee Identity and the Fading Prospect of International Protection', University of Nottingham, Human Rights Law Centre, Conference on Refugee Rights and Realities, 30 Nov. 1996.

Hathaway, J. (1995), 'New Directions to Avoid Hard Problems: The Distortion of the Palliative Role of International Protection', *Journal of Refugee Studies*, 8/3: 288–94.

Hampton, J. (ed.) (1998), *Internally Displaced People: A Global Survey*, London: Earthscan.

Hippler, J. (1995), *The Democratisation of Disempowerment: The Problem of Democracy in the Third World*, London: Pluto Press.

Klare, M. (1995), 'The Global Trade in Light Weapons in the International System in the Post-Cold War Era', in J. Boutwell et al. (eds.), *Lethal Commerce: The Global Trade in Small Arms and Light Weapons*, Cambridge, Mass.: American Academy of Arts and Sciences.

Loescher, G. (1993), *Beyond Charity: International Cooperation and the Global Refugee Crisis*, New York: Oxford University Press.

McNamara, D. (1998), 'The Future of Protection and the Responsibility of the State: Statement to the 48th Session of the UNHCR Executive Committee', *International Journal of International Refugee Law*, 10/1–2: 230–5.

Mtango, E. (1989), 'Military and Armed Attacks on Refugee Camps', in G. Loescher and L. Monahan (eds.), *Refugees and International Relations*, Oxford: Oxford University Press, 87–121.

OECD (1994), *Development Cooperation: Report of the Development Assistance Committee 1994*, Paris: OECD.

The Reality of Aid 1996 (1996) *An Independent Review of International Aid*, London: Earthscan.

Ross, M. H. (1993), *The Management of Conflict: Interpretations and Interests in Comparative Perspective*, New Haven: Yale University Press.

Sayigh, Y. (1990), *Confronting the 1990s: Security in the Developing Countries*, Adelphi Paper 251, London: Brassey's for the IISS.

Schmeidl, S. (1998), *The Political Causes of Refugee Migration*, paper presented for the Pew Migration Policy in Global Perspective Project, International Center for Migration, Ethnicity and Citizenship, New School for Social Research.

United Kingdom, House of Commons, International Development Committee, *Kosovo: The Humanitarian Crisis*, 15 May 15 1999.

United Nations (1997), *1997 Report on the World Social Situation*, New York: United Nations.

UNDP (1996), *Human Development Report 1996*, Oxford: Oxford University Press.

UNHCR (1995), *The State of the World's Refugees: In Search of Solutions*, Oxford: Oxford University Press.

—— (1997), *The State of the World's Refugees: A Humanitarian Agenda*, Oxford: Oxford University Press.

—— (1998), *Refugees and Others of Concern to UNHCR: 1997 Statistical Overview*, Geneva: UNHCR.

—— (1999), *Refugees and Others of Concern to UNHCR: 1998 Statistical Overview*, Geneva: UNHCR.

UN Secretary-General's Report to the General Assembly, July 1997 (A/51/950, para. 186).

US Mission to the UN (1995), *Global Humanitarian Emergencies, 1995*, New York.

Walker, P. (1996), Presentation to the Federation of Red Cross and Red Crescent Societies (16 Feb. 16, 1996), 'Challenges for an Operating Agency in the Next Five Years'. Geneva: international conference Geneva and the Challenge of Humanitarian Action of the 1990s.

Weiner, M. (1996), 'Bad Neighbors, Bad Neighborhoods: An Enquiry into the Causes of Refugee Flows', *Intenational Security*, 21/1: 5–42.

Weiss, T. (1999), *Military-Civilian Interventions: Intervening in Humanitarian Crises*, Lanham, Md.: Rowman & Littlefield Publishers.

—— and Gordenker, L. (eds.), (1996), *NGOs, the UN and Global Governance*, Boulder, Colo.: Lynne Rienner Publishers.

Weiss-Fagen, P. (1996), *Peace Making as Rebuilding War-Torn Societies*, War-torn Societies Project, Geneva: UNRISD.

United Nations Documents

S/RES/688 [5 Apr. 1991]
S/RES/757 [30 May 1992]
S/RES/733 [23 Jan. 1993]
S/RES/807 [19 Feb. 1993]
S/RES/813 [26 Mar. 1993]
S/RES/814 [26 Mar. 1993]
S/RES/841 [16 June 1993]
S/RES/929 [22 June, 1994]
S/RES/1080 [15 Nov. 1996]
S/RES/1093 [14 Jan. 1997]
S/RES/1101 [28 Mar. 1997]
S/RES/1160 [31 Mar. 1998]
E/CN/1998/50, 1998.

9

New International Regime for Orderly Movements of People: What will it Look Like?

Bimal Ghosh

It has been argued in Chapter 1 that in order to be politically acceptable and operationally viable, a new multilateral regime for movements of people must be based on the principle of *regulated·openness*. The first section of this concluding chapter spells out the implications of this concept by discerning the general configuration and salient features of the regime. The next section takes up the question as to what exactly individual countries and the world society can gain from the adoption of such a regime.

The chapter concedes that there are perceived constraints to nations opting for the proposed new regime, and examines, on a selective basis, several of the key points raised in the previous chapters. It concludes by arguing that many of these constraints are either unfounded or exaggerated and sets store on consensus-building to achieve the goal. In developing these arguments the chapter draws on the discussions and the general conclusions reached at the two interregional meetings which were held in Geneva in March 1997 and December 1998 as part of the NIROMP project activities.[1]

---

[1] The first informal meeting concerning the NIROMP project was held in Geneva on 25–6 Sept. 1997, with 14 countries, sending or receiving, participating in it. The meeting endorsed the basic project approach and strongly recommended that further action should be taken to achieve the project objectives. The discussion on the various issues and the conclusions reached also served as an initial input into the process of political consensus building to ensure the success of the project. With funding from the Netherlands' overnment, a second interregional meeting was held within the framework of the NIROMP project on 7–8 Dec. 1998 at IOM headquarters in Geneva to examine policy and operational issues related to return and readmission of migrants. The meeting, which brought together 19 government participants drawn from sending, receiving, and transit countries, intergovernmental and non-governmental organizations and independent experts, agreed that the success of return programmes warranted concerted efforts by all three groups of countries. As a result of two days' free and open discussion, the participants made a significant initial step towards defining an agreed set of principles relating to return

The objectives of the regime

Orderly movements, as distinct from free movements of people

Based on the guiding principle of regulated openness, the broad objectives of the regime should be to make movements of people more orderly, manageable, and productive and to provide, for this purpose, a comprehensive, multilateral framework which combines and balances the interests of all the parties involved—the sending, receiving, and transit countries and the migrants themselves. More specifically, the regime should be designed to:

   (i)   enhance the capacity of governments and societies to deal with inter-country movements of people in different forms and under varying circumstances through, *inter alia*, greater predictability and transparency of migration policies and practices;

  (ii)   widen the choice of the individual on whether to migrate or not (help avoid conditions, political, economic, environmental or other, that lead to forced migration) and enhance the confidence of the public, including the potential migrants, in policies and practices governing the international migration system;

 (iii)   avoid negative externalities, tension in inter-state relations, and threats to domestic security as a result of irregular and disruptive movements of people;

  (iv)   enhance efficiency of the global economy through a more rational allocation of labour and skills and freer trade-related temporary movements; and facilitate short-term inter-country exchanges conducive to cultural enrichment of human society and the strengthening of common human values;

  (v)   ensure, on grounds of both human rights and humanitarian considerations, effective protection and assistance, as needed under varying circumstances, to migrants, refugees, and asylum seekers on a more predictable basis; and

  (vi)   facilitate both their return to countries of origin or third countries in conditions of freedom and dignity and their full reintegration in society while promoting cooperation among sending, receiving and transit countries, involving whenever possible migrants' associations in the process.

programmes. They also recommended that NIROMP's return-related activities should be further intensified and expanded, in full cooperation with the international and regional organizations concerned.

The salient features of the regime

With these broad and specific objectives serving as the main frame of reference, it is possible to move to the next stage in modelling the regime and outline its salient features. What, we might ask, should be the main considerations that will determine these features and shape the overall configuration of the regime? These are examined below.

Transparency and predictability as essential features of the new migration regime

Orderliness and manageability are closely interrelated to the predictability of migratory movements. Disorderly and unexpected movements, including, in particular, those that take place in defiance of established rules and systems, are by nature non-predictable and thus more difficult to manage. On the other hand, when a migration system, sustained by a sound information base and robust but flexible rules and practices, is effective enough to anticipate the movements and handle them in a fair, confident, and timely manner, the risk of non-predictability is considerably diminished.

Orderliness and predictability of movements also depend largely on the transparency of rules and practices that sustain the migration system. Ambiguity and lack of transparency in migration policies and regulations may help certain governments or officials in manipulating decisions in particular circumstances but they make it difficult for the state to manage migration in a sound and equitable manner just as they erode the credibility of the system. When potential migrants are not sure about (1) the conditions governing their exit or entry through legal channels; and (2) their legal and social status in the receiving state; they may unknowingly act in an irregular manner or may be induced to do so by interested parties such as unscrupulous traffickers.

Thus, while from the point of view of operational viability the issues of transparency, equity (or non-discrimination), and efficiency are closely intertwined, the importance of state adherence to these principles goes far beyond. This clearly helps in meeting a basic ethical goal of a multilateral regime—protection of the weak—as underscored by Henk Overbeek (Chapter 3 in this volume). At the same time, orderliness and predictability strengthen the commonalty of interests of developed and developing countries—via suitable pay-offs to both groups—and contributes to what James Hollifield calls an essential 'tenet' of multilateralism (Chapter 4).

The new regime does not supplant the existing arrangements

The regime aims at promoting a more coherent and comprehensive framework to manage movements of people, but it does not supplant those existing arrangements that are working well. At the global level there are currently two main, and widely recognized systems (or subsystems) dealing with move- ments of people: the refugee regime (the 1951 UN Convention together with its 1967 Protocol) and the emerging regime for movements related to trade in services (the GATS, 1994). Additionally, there are a litany of international instruments, dealing with specific issues or aspects of international move- ments, notably those concerning labour migration.[2]

The regime aims at placing these various elements within a coherent framework—while complementing, enlarging, and adapting them, as appro- priate, to meet the existing gaps and inadequacies. As further discussed in the last section of this chapter, this should not be perceived as a new form of supra-national arrangement imposed on sovereign states by a (non-existent) external authority.

The regime covers all types of flows, including return migration

A sound and effective global regime must be comprehensive enough to encompass all types of movements, whether permanent or temporary, and whether driven by political, economic, environmental, or other factors (see also Goodwin-Gill, chapter 7; Gil Loescher, chapter 8). There are at least three important reasons for this. First, contemporary movements are increasingly propelled by mixed motivations or composite factors. There is often an inter- play of economic, political, and environmental factors that build up the emigration pressure just as the economic and non-economic motivations of potential migrants frequently go hand in hand. For example, the motivation of economic survival or opportunity-seeking cannot always be separated from the need or urge to escape from an oppressive regime or generalized violence; and *vice versa*.

A second reason, related to the first, is that, from the migration management perspective, too, different types of flows cannot easily be disentangled. Experience shows that lack of a sound and realistic policy for labour migration or family reunification may build up high pressure on entry channels for refugees and asylum seekers or increase irregular movements. Similarly, inade- quacies or dysfunctioning of systems for legal migration or temporary protec- tion can swell the ranks of irregular migrants and encourage trafficking.

A third reason is that there are many grey areas related to population move- ments or groups of internally or externally displaced persons who needed assistance and protection but are inadequately covered under existing inter-

---

[2] These include UN Convention on the Protection of All Migrant Workers and Members of Their Families, adopted on 18 Dec. 1990 and a series of ILO Conventions and Recommendations, including Convention No. 97 concerning migration for employment, 1949 and Convention No. 143 concerning migrant workers, 1975 (see chapter 7).

national institutions and mandates (see Introduction and Chapter 1). As Gil Loescher crisply puts it in his contribution to this volume (Chapter 8), 'the international response to forced migration can no longer be run on the basis of existing rules and institutions that are outdated and too fragmented in the face of a host of new challenges'.

The new regime must therefore ensure full coherence in the management of all types of flows or groups of migrants. Its systemic character should not, however, overshadow the need to take due account of the distinctive features and specific problems of each major group.

This applies also to return movements. Whether the persons concerned are refugees or labour migrants, and irrespective of whether they are in a regular or irregular situation, if the return does not take place under conditions that can ensure their future safety and are conducive to their meaningful and durable reintegration in society, chances are that they will move—or try to move—again, be it through regular or irregular channels.

The breadth of the regime holds another potential advantage. It makes it easier to maintain a better balance in the treatment of the different components of the migration system and thus in the various interests or political/ideological groups they represent. It also facilitates bargaining across issues (see Overbeek, Chapter 3, and Hollifield, Chapter 4). For example, provision for orderly entry of regular immigrant workers to meet real labour needs of employers and traders should make the latter groups more willing to support refugee assistance. It could also be used as a lever to secure their active cooperation in ensuring better social protection and better integration of existing immigrants.

Protection of basic rights as a major concern of the regime

Effective protection of basic rights of migrants is an essential aspect of sound migration management and must be adequately covered under the proposed new regime. Ineffective enforcement of labour standards and government indifference to the exploitation of migrant workers are sure to encourage irregular and disorderly labour immigration (see chapter 1). Examples also abound of how social and economic discrimination or political oppression of migrant groups can lead to disruptive outflows or even a mass exodus of migrants, threatening national and regional stability. To illustrate further, the return of refugees, rejected asylum seekers and irregular migrants becomes unsustainable, and could even act as a source of new tension and conflict (causing renewed disorderly outflows) if they become victims of human rights abuse following return.

The human rights dimension of the regime lends additional ethical, political, and legal legitimacy to the whole arrangement. Indeed it can be argued, as Goodwin-Gill does in Chapter 7, that the essential justification for the new regime lies in the foundations of international human rights law and the obligation it imposes on the state to fulfil its responsibilities within its territory and beyond through inter-state cooperation.

Not only does human rights protection add to the fairness of the system, but in many ways it also enhances its efficiency. For example, as further explained later in this chapter, protection of human rights tends to enhance irregular migrants' voluntariness to return and makes it more cost-effective as well as politically easier to handle.

Thus, the regime must uphold and reiterate the norms and principles already available in existing instruments on human rights of all categories of migrants, including refugees and those in a refugee-like situation, and fill in any major gaps that remain (UNHRC 1999).

The regime as a collaborative endeavour of all nations

Migration, by its very nature affects both sending and receiving countries; there is also an increasing involvement of transit countries. As part of a global process, it is deeply affected by interpenetration of markets and economies, rapid advance of transport and communication systems, and spread of social networks. And, as already noted in Chapter 1, more and more countries are becoming involved in both sending and receiving migrants.

The logical implication of the situation is that if the global regime is to enhance orderliness and manageability of future movements through harmonized action, it must be based on close cooperation of all parties—sending, receiving, and transit countries and their genuine commitment to its underlying principles.

Additionally, it must be so designed from the beginning that it can have the active support of the migrants' associations and migrant-serving voluntary organizations. It cannot be overemphasized that much of the present difficulties in managing migration stem directly from the absence of meaningful cooperation and mutual confidence between the parties directly involved.

Global cooperation is clearly imperative in order to ensure optimal operational efficiency (for example in the case of anti-trafficking measures) of the proposed regime. More importantly, without active support from a maximum number of states its political viability itself could be at stake. In order to secure the participation of the states in the arrangement and avoid subsequent defection, it is essential that individual states be convinced that all other state parties will respect the rules of the game (Hollifield, Chapter 3).

The root causes and the comprehensive scope of the regime

Movements of people are shaped by a complex and dynamic interplay of a wide variety of factors. It follows that if the proposed regime is to achieve its basic objectives, it must be comprehensive enough not only to embrace the whole range of migration policies and practices as discussed above, but must also be correlated to policies in those other areas (such as human and minority rights, citizenship and democracy, demography and labour markets, trade and investment, development aid, and the environment) that influence movements of people. As Gil Loescher puts it (Chapter 8), proposals for an internationally harmonized regime 'involving both sending and receiving states as well as international organizations need to be broadened and backed by a visionary approach to interrelated global issues such as security, trade and development, human rights, and migration'.

This may seem to be an over-ambitious proposal. Clearly, the policy decisions on these important issues cannot be taken based on migration-related considerations alone. What is important, however, is that the regime encourages nations to take the migration aspects or implications fully into account while making decisions in these other areas. Such policy convergence is of critical importance. For example, as already discussed (Chapter 1), as long as the demand for cheap and irregular foreign labour generated by the expansion of the black economy remains, it will make migration management more difficult.

Or, when trade policies of industrial countries seek to prevent the entry of labour-intensive goods with high employment potential into their markets, it makes it harder for developing and transition economy countries to reduce the pressure for emigration driven by unemployment and poverty (Philip Martin et al., Chapter 6).

As part of a proactive approach, the regime should include a set of internationally agreed set of principles and norms that can be taken into account while formulating policies in areas directly related to international migration. The need for such policy convergence in migration management has been receiving growing recognition at the national as well as regional and international level, but action has lagged behind (Chapter 1). The new migration regime should strengthen this policy commitment and spur more dynamic action.[3]

But this obligation must not be one-sided. The migrant-sending countries must also bring their shared concern for migration management to bear upon their policies affecting matters such as macroeconomic fundamentals, employment and income distribution, trade and investment and use of development aid, human rights and the environment. The regime needs to sensitize the migrant-sending countries about their role and responsibility in this connection and encourage them to positively respond to their reciprocal obligations.

The inter-linkage between migration and other policy areas is still another

[3] For a tentative indication of such guidelines in the relevant areas see Ghosh 1995: 402–3

feature of the regime which facilitates consensus building through negotiation involving pay-offs across issues. For example this could be achieved by linking industrial countries' trade concessions and development aid to measures by source countries against irregular migration; or through source countries' cooperation in curbing employment of irregular immigrants in the underground economy in exchange for orderly and legal entry of a number of their workers (Martin et al., Chapter 6).

Three pillars of the new regime: policies, principles, and institutional mechanism

In the light of what has been said above, it is possible to draw the overall design of the regime. The system would be based on a set of common objectives to be shared by all the parties involved. However a genuine commitment to common objectives, though essential, is not enough to ensure operational viability or the success of the regime. It will need to be supported by adequate instruments of action, both normative and institutional.

Thus the new regime must be based on three central pillars: (1) establishment of a set of shared objectives; (2) development of an agreed and internationally harmonized normative framework to ensure coherence of action at national, regional and global levels; and (3) the settting-up of a coordinated institutional arrangement, including a monitoring mechanism. At present, the responsibility for migration issues at the global level is dispersed among several intergovernmental organizations, without a clear focal point. Through the new arrangement, the current inter-agency relationship could be streamlined and coordination further improved. In addition, the regime is to provide a monitoring mechanism to assess the progress made towards the application of the new norms and principles regarding migration.

Gains from the regime

A logical question can now be asked: what exactly do individual nations and the world society as a whole gain from the adoption of such a regime? The present section deals with this question.

Cutting costs and reaping gains

The potential gains from the regime can be significant. These stem from two main sources: (*a*) cutting avoidable costs or losses associated with the inadequacies of the present arrangements; and (*b*) reaping direct benefits from the implementation of the new system.

Based on the previous discussion, the first set of gains can be recapitulated as follows. By enhancing the predictability of the international migration policies and practices and contributing to their harmonization the regime will increase the capacity of states to respond to different migration-related situations, including human emergencies and refugee crises, not only more promptly, but also in a more effective and concerted manner. This will lessen the political costs and administrative strain implicit in improvised action and protracted negotiation over burden-sharing, as is often happening now.

Secondly, the removal of arbitrariness in the management of movements, combined with improved transparency of the system, better protection of human rights, and closer cooperation among sending, receiving, and transit countries, will boost the confidence of the potential migrants and the general public in the whole system. This includes the efficiency and fairness of control and enforcement measures. These developments should help (1) reduce the attempts to move through irregular channels; (2) encourage voluntary return of rejected asylum seekers and irregular migrants; (3) lower the costs of immigration control; and (4) improve strained inter-state relations.

There will also be new gains. For instance, since orderly movements of people will contribute to a better balance between labour-surplus and unmet labour demand, the new arrangement will reduce mismatch and tension in domestic labour markets and enhance global economic growth and prosperity through a more efficient allocation of human resources, both nationally and across countries. Increased temporary mobility related to trade in services and investment should make it easier for countries in different stages of development to better exploit their comparative advantages.

Also, as a combined result of both these processes there should be wider, spillover benefits. As the new regime becomes firmly established, it can be expected to put an end to the growing fear, most notably in industrial countries, that movements of people are getting out of control. Reinforced confidence in the state's capacity to manage migration will encourage policy-makers to address the challenge of migration through proactive and forward-looking policy measures in keeping with the changing needs and conditions, both at home and abroad.

The overall benefits could indeed extend further. A global system of orderly movements, which is cooperatively managed, combining efficiency, equity, and respect for human rights, could be extraordinarily consequential for the future of the liberal world order (Hollifield, Chapter 4).

The potential gains are thus considerable, even when account is taken of the cost that will inevitably be involved in establishing the new regime and implementing it effectively. Can these gains be quantified? To do so in precise financial terms is difficult, but some dispersed indications are nonetheless available.

Curbing the mounting costs

In the early 1990s when asylum seeking in the OECD countries was witnessing a dramatic increase, it was estimated that the governments were spending between $6 and $7 billion to run the asylum system.[4] However, as already discussed in Chapter 1, the rush to asylum seeking was in part a reflection of the inadequacies of the fragmented and unpredictable migration system. By removing these inadequacies and improving the efficiency of migration management, the new regime can help reduce a considerable part of this huge expenditure.

True, more recently, stringent and costly restrictive measures have led to a significant decline in asylum seeking, but the absence of complementary, proactive programmes to address the root causes of the problem seems to have caused a diversion of the flow to irregular channels, including migrant trafficking. Governments have responded to the situation by tightening up control measures and devoting increased budgetary resources for this purpose—though so far only with little or limited overall success (Ghosh 1998*a*).

The costs have been rising sharply. To illustrate, the budget of the US Immigration and Naturalization Service (INS) was increased more than twofold from US $1.5 billion in the 1993 fiscal year to $3.1 billion in the 1997 fiscal year in order to enhance its enforcement capability and strengthen its efforts to combat irregular migration at the borders and abroad (*Migration News,* February 1997). Compared to 1992, the budget has now nearly tripled. Under the 1996 US Illegal Immigration Reform and Immigrant Responsibility Act the size of the border patrol forces along the 2,000-mile frontier with Mexico was to be nearly doubled, with the addition of 10,000 agents a year for five years until 2001 *(Interpreter Releases* 1997; Ghosh 1998*a*, 106).

Likewise, the array of measures that have been taken in various other countries to combat irregular migration, and in particular migrant trafficking, have meant soaring costs for the government and taxpayers. For example, costs related to trafficked migrants into Canada are estimated at $120–400 million per year. Smuggling of illegal drugs with which human trafficking is

---

[4] As Jonas Widgren explains, 'Accurately estimating the costs of the asylum system is difficult, for a number of reasons. Available data indicate that 1989 government spending on processing of asylum applications and care of asylum seekers in Europe and Canada amounted to at least $4.8 billion, with Germany accounting for 34 percent, Sweden for 17 percent and Switzerland for 6 percent. It has not been possible to make detailed estimates of the growth in such expenditures in 1983–1989, but realistic estimates of average costs in each country for processing and assistance would seem to show that total costs for the asylum systems during the period for the 11 countries examined rose from $8 million in 1983 to about $2.4 billion in 1985 and some $2.9 billion in 1987, and are now about $6–7 billion a year.' Widgren 1993: 92.

often interlocked costs anything between $1.4 and $4 billion. These latter figures refer to only the three most populous provinces of the country.[5]

An optimal mix of regulatory and proactive policy measures under the new regime should make it possible to reduce much of these enormous expenses on immigration control, anti-trafficking measures, and related punitive action.

Indirect, but important, economic gains may also be made as migrant trafficking—and the various criminal activities interinked with it—are put to an end or at least seriously curbed. According to an estimate made by the Vienna-based International Centre for Migration Policy development (ICMPD) in 1995 migrant trafficking was yielding an annual income of $5–7 billion. A 1996 US government study estimated that about 50,000 Chinese were smuggled into the US annually—making it a $3.5 billion industry. The estimate has since been revised upwards to 100,000 Chinese migrants. Elsewhere, based on the estimated number of Thai women smuggled each year into Japan, Germany, and Taiwan for prostitution, the University of Bangkok has determined that the business yields approximately US$ 3.5 billion a year (*Migration News,* February 1996).

These and other more recent indications seem to suggest that the total income derived from migrant trafficking worldwide may well be as high as between US$10 billion and $12 billion year. If account is also taken of the multiplier effect of this considerable outlay, the diversion of resources to less productive (and in many cases antisocial) activities, and the consequent draining of the world economy, cannot but cause concern. Only by curbing human trafficking can this wasteful diversion of resources be countered.

Additional benefits, both tangible and non-tangible, may result from reforms in various specific areas of the migration system. Return migration is a case in point. By developing an agreed set of common principles to encourage return of rejected asylum seekers and irregular migrants in conditions of freedom and dignity, the new regime can help save considerable financial and non-financial costs which are currently incurred in connection with return migration. Incorporating protection issues into a fair and transparent legal framework will enhance the acceptance of return by the general population in sending and receiving countries and by the migrants themselves.[6] Voluntariness reduces the political cost of return by avoiding public resistance

---

[5] The figure used to represent both the costs of the process of refugee determination and costs incurred in the care and keeping of the claimant has been estimated to be between $15,000 and $25,000 per year. Using these figures with the estimate of 8,000 to 16,000 persons smuggled into Canada with the assistance of people smugglers yields costs to Canada that range between $120 million and $400 million per year. See *Organized Crime Impact Study* (1997), commissioned by the Solicitor General of Canada.

[6] For additional information in this connection, see: Ghosh 1998b and 1999 and Noll, 1998.

to it in both returning and origin countries, and minimizes possible tension and conflicts between them.

Just as protection of rights and dignity of rejected asylum seekers and irregular migrants encourage voluntary return, so increased voluntariness in return reduces the risks of infringement of human rights. Legal protection of rights and increased voluntariness in return thus go hand in hand, creating a virtuous circle that encourages new returns. When return is linked to both protection of human rights and development assistance to ensure sustainable reintegration in the country of origin, it becomes a more attractive option for returnees and the origin countries. Return is no longer seen in an adversarial context (Ghosh 1999).

Increased voluntariness in return prompted by the new regime may also lead to some direct savings on the financial costs involved in forcible return or expulsion. For example, in Germany the average cost of an escorted expulsion by air was US$840 in 1995, compared with a price tag of $490 for an assisted voluntary return in cooperation with IOM.[7] The average cost of forcible return is even higher in other returning states. In Sweden, for instance, the average cost of forced expulsion per person was US$3,160 in 1996 (Utrikesdepartementet 1997: 96).

Under the IOM-executed Swiss programme for temporary refugees from Bosnia, which includes a post-return assistance component, the total cost of assisted return was no more than the amount spent on social assistance for a 'protected family' of three persons for 10–11 months (IOM 1998). It is of course difficult to come up with a standard cost figure for development-related assistance for return, for much depends on the type, depth, and duration of assistance. But the package is most likely to be larger than the direct cost of *simple* return, even when it is forced and escorted. It is clear however that in this case the dividend too will be higher. This is because of greater durability of return, possible avoidance of recurrent expenditure in connection with actual or attempted re-entries through irregular channels, and increased voluntary returns.

The world economy gains

What about the direct financial gains? For example, how much will the world economy gain from freer and more orderly circulation of labour? Once again, it is difficult to make a precise estimate. This is mainly because of the wide range of variables involved. However, indicative of such gains are the estimates made of the effects of free circulation of labour by Hamilton and Whaley using general equilibrium modelling (Hamilton and Whalley 1984). These

---

[7] Based on oral information from the United Nations, cited in Noll 1998: 14.

showed that the world GDP would be doubled if all barriers to labour migration were removed. Two key assumptions underlying the analysis are that the
worldwide labour supply is fixed and full employment prevails in all regions.
A simple methodology is used to infer the differences in the marginal productivity of labour between countries and across regions. These differences occur
because of barriers to inward mobility of labour in high-wage countries.
When these are removed and labour reallocated, efficiency gains take place in
the global economy. Workers already employed in high-wage countries lose,
but the owners of capital gain. Overall, the size of the gains from liberalized
labour mobility are so striking that it makes immigration control as 'one of
the (and perhaps the) most important policy issue(s) facing the global economy' (ibid. 70).

Likewise other estimates, though of a more limited scope or of a more
specific nature, confirm the positive economic gains that can be derived from
a freer, but rules-based, system of movements of persons, linked to trade in
services.

The General Agreement on Trade in Services (GATS), adopted as part of
the Uruguay round trade accords, recognizes the importance of such movements as a critical factor in the expansion of world trade in services and the
global economy. Even when services are traded mainly through other modes
of delivery (e.g. cross-border delivery through telecommunication technology
or delivery through commercial presence abroad), temporary movements of
persons often serve as an essential ancillary or complementary mode. For
example, trade-related movements may be needed in order to negotiate the
service contract, to complete the delivery or to provide after delivery services
to customers abroad.

Rules-based freer movement of persons can thus contribute to the expansion of trade in services through a more efficient use of available human
resources, including skills and knowledge. This implies a fuller exploitation of
current and potential comparative advantage of different countries. As a
result, all trading nations benefit. Beyond the initial efficiency gains, industrial
countries could benefit from increased investment—as a result of higher
returns to investment and possibly from innovation and higher productivity
growth. As for the labour-abundant developing countries the gains made lead
to an expansion of employment and an improvement in incomes not just in
the services sector, but also in the manufacturing and primary goods sectors
where services are used as important inputs.

Once more it is difficult to make a precise quantitative estimate of these
gains. However, a study made in 1997 gives an indication of the enormous
potential gains for developing countries in particular (Ghosh 1997*a*). Its
rough calculation, based on 1997 figures, shows that by competing in the
world market only for those knowledge and information-intensive services in
which developing countries have a comparative advantage, they can increase

their export income by \$210 billion while creating up to 30 million additional jobs. For the reasons already mentioned, an essential condition for reaping these benefits in full lies in freer movement of persons as service providers. This is in spite of the fact that the telecommunications system may well be the main mode of delivery.

These various estimated gains look impressive, but they should not all be taken for granted. Much depends on how the principles embodied in the regime are implemented. Nor should it be forgotten that just as freer movements of people yield benefits, they also entail costs, and have important effects on income distribution. The findings mentioned above do not take into account these costs or effects.[8] Thomas Straubhaar addresses this important aspect of the matter in Chapter 5 of this volume. While strongly arguing in favour of freer movements of workers on grounds of improved allocational efficiency, he delves into the negative externalities associated with such movements. These negative externalities could, however, be kept to a minimum through internationally agreed regulatory and operational arrangements. The challenge then takes us back to the paradigm of 'regulated openness'—a paradigm that constitutes, as already discussed, the core of the proposed new regime.

Facing the constraints and dilemmas

What kind of a regime? A hard or a soft instrument?

Granting that a comprehensive and multilaterally harmonized policy framework is needed for cooperative management of migration, what form should it take? More specifically, should it be conceived as a hard or as a soft instrument?

The question was already raised, and tentatively discussed, at the NIROMP meeting held in Geneva in September 1997. Some participants were concerned that unless the instrument was designed as a hard one with appropriate provisions for sanctions in cases of non-compliance with its principles, there were potential risks that many states might chose to be 'free riders'; that is, seek to benefit from the arrangement without meeting their own obligations and contributing to the joint effort. This in turn would erode the efficacy of the collective arrangement and ultimately may even threaten its existence. Other participants, however, took a different view as they felt that

---

[8] While the Hamilton and Whalley study does provide an indication of the distributional effects of liberalizing of movement of labour in different groups of countries and on labour and owners of capital, it does not deal with the various negative externalities of such movements.

the political climate was hardly propitious for the adoption of a hard instrument to deal with a complex and sensitive subject like movements of people.

Clearly, it is difficult to come up with a definitive answer to the question: nor is it wise to take a pre-emptive position on the issue. For, whatever may be the merits of the legal and technical arguments in support of either view, much would depend on the consensus-building process and the political impact it makes on policy-makers, the civil society, and the public especially in major migrant-receiving and migrant-sending countries.

It is clear, however, that despite many receiving countries' sharply growing interest in cooperative action for restricting immigration, especially irregular movements, the immediate political prospects for the adoption of a *hard instrument* on a whole range of migration issues at the global level seem limited. Further, the proliferation of international regulatory instruments in recent years has caused a feeling of fatigue among many governments; this makes the prospects worse for a hard instrument. On a technical level, too, it is doubtful whether the comprehensive nature of the arrangement and, in particular, its wide range of promotional or pro-active policy measures, easily lend themselves as subjects for a hard instrument with sanctions for non-compliance. There is also the delicate question of a central authority to enforce its provisions, including those related to sanctions.

These and other considerations suggest that a wiser option might be to envisage the new arrangement as a framework agreement embodying a set of principles—or simply as a solemn declaration of principles. This, however, does not, and indeed must not, exclude complementary action in the form of more specific, even hard, instruments on particular issues or elements covered by the agreement. On the contrary, to enhance the impact of the relevant principles in the general agreement, the latter should be actively encouraged. Anti-trafficking measures (already under negotiation as a subject of a new international instrument, as mentioned below) is a case in point. Another such issue is return and readmission on which the EU and individual EU member states have already signed a series of bilateral agreements. The essential elements of these bilateral agreements can be adapted and harmonized into a specific multilateral instrument.

The same applies to regional action. Consistent with the general principles of the framework agreement, regional/plurilateral instruments, with a focus on the regional dimensions, could be encouraged to spearhead action or reinforce the impact of the global arrangement at the regional level (further discussed below).

Even if the new arrangement takes the form of a solemn declaration of principles, it does not mean that it will not be sustained by a monitoring mechanism. As already noted earlier in this chapter, the establishment of a mechanism for purposes of monitoring and follow-up is an integral part of the proposed new institutional arrangement. The monitoring mechanism may not represent a 'strong central authority' (considered by some analysts as an essential feature of a regime), but it can nonetheless be endowed with sufficient political credibility. The latter can be achieved by drawing on the considerable experience already available within the UN system, including the UN Human Rights Commission, in setting up similar bodies related to international treaties.

Global vis-à-vis regional approach: a false dichotomy

If close inter-state cooperation is central to cooperative management as envisaged in this chapter, how best to achieve this? Would it not be easier, for example, to develop such cooperation, at least in the initial stages, through regional arrangements?

It is tempting to say 'yes', as the regional approach certainly has a number of clear advantages. For instance, confidence building is no doubt an essential first step towards a harmonized policy approach; and it is perhaps equally true that building such confidence is generally less difficult within a relatively small group of contiguous countries than on a global level. This is even more so if the countries concerned have already attained a high degree of economic and social convergence and share a set of common objectives, as is the case in the EU. Arguably, yet another consideration favouring a regional approach is that, since a significant proportion of cross-border movements continues to take place within the same region, the latter provides a vantage point from where to initiate the process of policy harmonization.

Finally, there is an important practical consideration. A number of powerful states in the industrial world seem averse to becoming engaged in what they perceive to be a long-drawn-out process of global negotiation on a sensitive subject like movements of people. It is not that the policy-makers in these states do not recognize the importance of migration as a global issue or the need for a common global framework for cooperative action to address it. Many perhaps do.

They tend to think, however, that the challenge is too complex and too overwhelming to be tackled at the global level. Some of them who are anxious to explore new ways of cooperative management of migration feel more comfortable to do so within a regional context. Others who perceive migration mainly as a 'problem' would like to 'contain' it within the regional confines. As Goodwill-Gill puts it in Chapter 7 of this volume, 'many states have attempted to contain or "regionalize" the movement of persons, that is, to keep those in need of protection or solutions within their regions of origin, beyond the developed world.' This serves almost as an extension or as a mirror image of the policy of containment under traditional statecraft. Despite this difference in perception and approach, both these groups seem to support cooperative management but through regional initiatives such as the Puebla process in the Americas; the Budapest process in Central and Eastern Europe; the Euro-Mediterranean process (see Overbeek, Chapter 4); or the newly launched Bangkok process in Asia.[9]

If several of these arguments are clearly valid, so are the limitations of an exclusively regional approach. Movements of people are no longer just a regional phenomenon; if they ever were. As repeatedly argued in this chapter, contemporary migration is, and must be reckoned with as, a powerful global process that cuts across regions and continents. Economic globalization, including increased flows of trade and investment and spectacular progress in transport and communication, are reinforcing the process just as the global networks of migrant traffickers are sharpening its global dimension.

True, a large proportion of migration still takes place within the same regions, (Straubhaar, Chapter 5, and Overbeek, Chapter 4) but the pattern is neither constant nor uniform.[10] To illustrate, in the case of the United States, the number of admissions of permanent immigrants from Asia accounted for an average of 47.7 per cent of admissions from all regions in 1980–4 and 41.8 per cent in 1990–4. This can be compared with 41.5 per cent and 36.7 per cent, respectively, from the American region—including Canada during the same periods (UN 1998, Table 11.9). Figures for recent years indicate that almost half of the foreign population resident in industrial (Northern and Western) Europe is from outside the European region. The current *annual flows* show a similar trend. For example, in 1997 immigration into the EU from outside Europe accounted for around 41 per cent of the total flow. If Eastern Europe is excluded (from the European segment), the percentage would be as high as 55 (Eurostat 1998).

It is not just that the main source, transit, and destination countries are not always located in the same region: more importantly, in an increasingly globalized world, the direction of the flows is apt to change in response to changes in the surrounding circumstances. For example, tightening of immigration control by destination countries in one region (e.g. Western Europe) is likely to add to pressures for immigration in other regions (e.g. North America) and vice versa (further discussed below).

---

[9] Another variant of this approach is to encourage the development of a common policy approach among the migrant-sending countries in a given region and then to initiate a collective dialogue with the migrant-receiving countries in the same region or across regions. In addition to most of the shortcomings of a pure regional approach as discussed later in the text, this variant suffers from a major weakness, namely, that once the group position is defined and formalized, negotiation tends to become more adversarial and the negotiators in the two camps are often deprived of the flexibility needed to bring the negotiation to a successful conclusion.

[10] Japan in this context is a special case due to several factors past history, geographical location, highly restrictive immigration policy, and strong attachment to social cohesion and cultural homogeneity.

Another constraint on the regional approach stems from the fact that, contrary to the premiss that it is generally easier to build mutual confidence between contiguous countries within the same region (Overbeek, Chapter 4), wide intra-regional disparities often serve as a potential source of suspicion and mistrust among the member countries. The history of North–South dialogue in the 1970s, the emergence of the Group of 77 and its efforts to develop economic and technical cooperation among developing countries (ECDC/TCDC) across regions show that economically less affluent and politically less powerful states are often fearful of the more dominant states and the leverage they enjoy in any regional negotiation.

This is why, in their effort to minimize the real or perceived hegemonic influence of the dominant states within a region, the weaker states generally prefer to negotiate and cooperate with the more powerful states within a multilateral framework. Not surprisingly, recent initiatives related to regional trade and economic cooperation arrangements, including those already established such as NAFTA (Martin et al., Chapter 6), have shown that pronounced intra-regional disparities invariably act as a source of tension and weariness within the groupings, thereby inhibiting progress. It is therefore wrong to assume that reaching mutual understanding between migrant-sending (developing) and migrant-receiving (developed) countries will necessarily be easier in a regional context. 'Democratic multilateralism' which Henk Overbeek (Chapter 4) is looking for is not necessarily safer in a regional setting. In regions of wide internal disparities the opposite may well be true.

This is also true for developing regions marked by significant disparities in levels of income and development. As a recent international conference observed, regional cooperation in southern Africa on the management of international migration 'had its limitations due to enormous income differentials between countries such as the 40-fold gap in incomes between South Africa and Mozambique' (UNFPA 1998).

Related to the above is the question of the extent to which the pressure for emigration can be effectively absorbed within the confines of each region. A regional framework for cooperative management of migration assumes that a matching of push and pull factors can be achieved and a stable migration equilibrium maintained within each major regional grouping. This then would be a tidy geographical arrangement for managing global migration, with each region taking care of the countries belonging to it. In practice, however, this is far from a viable proposition. Movements of people do not stop at the frontiers of their respective regions. Nor is it possible to contain the emigration pressure within limits of a given group of countries.

By stretching our imagination, let us assume that through cooperative efforts the countries in the Americas successfully work out a stable equilibrium between emigration pressures and immigration intakes within the region and that countries in Eastern and Western Europe do the same within the European region. By stretching our imagination further, we may even assume, however unrealistically, that the flows from North Africa can also be accommodated within a Euro-Mediterranean framework. But what about the peripheral countries in sub-Saharan Africa? And how to accommodate the mounting emigration pressure from South Asia? Will an even wider regional framework embracing Australia, New Zealand, and the Gulf States be adequate to cope with it? Will not the migratory movements tend to defy the expanded regional borders? In short, the intra-regional migration asymmetry is often too important to be contained or managed within the limits of each specific region, even when these are defined in a most flexible manner.

Another important shortcoming of the regional approach concerns the potential danger that different regions may apply different norms both for admission and protection of migrants. In such a situation, migration flows are sure to be diverted to the region with the most liberal migration regime or the least effective immigration control. The consequent destabilizing effect can only contribute to tension between regional groupings. As for countries that do not belong to such a grouping, and may be lacking effective immigration control, they could well turn into a vast dumping ground for all kinds of unwanted migrants, and thus a potential source of international instability.

It is these rapidly growing links between countries and markets that tend to circumscribe the efficacy of measures taken at the bilateral or regional level in isolation from the rest of the world. For example, special bilateral or regional arrangements—such as the levy of a tax to neutralize or reduce negative externalities as proposed by Thomas Straubhaar (Chapter 5)—may run into difficulty due to the pressure from third-country free-riders.

The fact that international migration is a global phenomenon and that its effective management calls for a global framework of cooperation is indeed already recognized by the international community, though only as part of a reactive policy in a very specific context—that of migrant trafficking. Nations have realized that, notwithstanding the increasing efforts at the bilateral, subregional, and regional levels to curb migrant trafficking, it is still essential to formulate a global response to the problem.

Indicative of this awareness is the current United Nations initiative to develop a new international convention against organized crime, supplemented by three protocols, including one on illegal transport and trafficking in migrants.[11] Just as this reactive and punitive measure against trafficking in migration has been placed at a global level, so it is necessary to design the proactive measures for better management of migration within a framework

---

[11] By resolution 53/111 of 9 Dec. 1998, the General Assembly established an ad hoc Committee open to all states for the purpose of drafting these instruments, and the states have committed themselves to ensure the completion of the Committee's work by the year 2000.

of global cooperation. The two sets of measures—punitive and proactive—are complementary, and the same basic logic and operational considerations that have led the proposed anti-trafficking instruments to be designed as global initiatives dictate that a global framework also be used for effective overall management of international migration.

What, then, is the conclusion? If, as argued above, a global framework based on a common set of principles is essential for effective cooperative action, by no means does it imply that the regional initiatives are irrelevant or useless. On the contrary, the latter could be valuable building blocks towards the establishment of a new international regime for better management of migration. Provided, however, that a common frame of reference is used to harness regional efforts and thus avoid the risks of confusion or friction between parallel regional initiatives. Regional and subregional consultations are also extremely useful as inputs to the process of developing global norms and principles in cases where they are still lacking; and global efforts can of course draw support and inspiration from *best practices* already established at the regional/subregional levels. This may be combined with an issue-oriented approach—reaching agreement on specific components of the arrangement—as long as the inter-linkages of issues are not forgotten and the comprehensiveness of the regime fully upheld.

In a recent paper Peter Kenen and Barry Eichengreen argue for a similar composite approach in managing trade and monetary issues as part of the world economy in the twenty-first century: 'mere proximity, however, does not always create a commonalty of interests, and the quest for deeper integration may lead to a second solution—namely, functional rather than regional groups. But functional groups, like regional groups, tend to discriminate against outsiders and close off opportunities for cross-issue bargaining. This is a reason for shunning them, or at least ensuring their compatibility with a third potential solution adapting and strengthening the global institutional framework and insisting that both regional and functional negotiations take place within that framework' (Eichengreen and Kenen 1994: 54).

Likewise, the interregional meeting held in 1997 on migration management under the auspices of NIROMP, expressed the view that efforts at the two levels—global and regional—should go hand in hand, and be so designed that they reinforce each other. This would thus combine the advantages of both the 'top-down' and 'bottom-up' approaches (Ghosh 1997*b*). Viewed from this perspective, the oft-debated dichotomy between the global and the regional approach is a false one.

Development-migration nexus: does development increase or reduce migration?

An important assumption underlying the comprehensive approach is that as labour-abundant countries step up the rate of development and make better and wider use of their labour, the pressure for disorderly migration declines, making migration management less difficult. Parallel to domestic economic reform, the new arrangement seeks to create conditions that would help these countries in the process of development through measures such as increased participation in world trade, greater access to foreign investment, and development aid as well as debt relief.

On the other hand, however, it is now part of conventional wisdom that development has a J-curve effect on migration—first more and then less migration. The transition period of high emigration is sometimes called the 'migration hump' (Martin et al., Chapter 6). The 1990 US Commission for the Study of International Migration and Development, for example, strongly argued that while development is the only effective means of reducing pressure for migration, including irregular migration, it takes many years—even generations—for development to achieve the desired effect.

This seeming paradox creates a dilemma for policy-makers. Indeed, the paradigm tends to leave them in political limbo. If the migration hump effect of development is true and inimitable, should not then the governments that are anxious to bring down migration pressure stop all development efforts? More so in a democracy where the average duration of a government is probably less than five years. But this of course is an absurd proposition. It is therefore useful to delve further into the dynamics of interaction between development and migration. In the context of NAFTA, Chapter 6 gives a rich explanation as to why freer trade may not be a substitute for migration from labour-abundant countries as assumed in standard trade theories. Given their less advanced technology and infrastructure, and thus lower factor productivity, migrant-sending countries cannot always benefit from their low-cost labour even for trade in labour-intensive goods. The same reasons—lower efficiency and inferior production function of labour—tend to constrain the inward flow of capital to these countries. It is not that capital is not attracted by low wages of the labour-abundant countries, but the process stops short of closing the wage-gaps between rich and poor countries. Rich countries, on the other hand, may continue to have a comparative advantage even in some of the labour-intensive products and attract capital due to advanced technology, infrastructure, and economies of scale, as well as the positive externalities associated with all of them. This is a simple and necessarily incomplete explanation of why economic liberalization is not an adequate answer to high pressure for labour migration from poor to rich countries. (for further details see Martin et al., Chapter 6).

This however does not imply a diminished importance of development in managing migration. It is true that economic development may initially stimulate some new streams of emigration. The main reasons for this are that development brings changes in social institutions and family relationships, often causes some dislocation in existing industrial and farming activities, and increases spatial mobility. It also tends to create new aspirations. While these may not be immediately matched, development enhances the ability of people, both financially and otherwise, to move across countries. However, as development makes headway on a sustained basis and people become more optimistic about the future, the demand for emigration tends to fall despite the increasing ability to migrate. As this happens the stage is set for what is known as *migration transition.*

The question remains: what time frame is needed for this to take effect? The answer is difficult since the time dimension in the migration transition is not an independent variable. It is simultaneously correlated to (i) the pattern and characteristics of development, and (ii) the types and causes of migratory flows. A desegregated, rather than overarching, view of both migration and development is useful to capture how the time element interacts with them.

As the history of past transatlantic migration shows, in countries of Western and Northern Europe it indeed took a long time—some two generations—for migration transition to take hold. By contrast, countries in East and South-East Asia—such as Singapore, Malaysia, and more recently the Republic of Korea and even Thailand—have brought emigration under control within a relatively short period, in some cases only in ten years. In the Caribbean, migration transition occurred even more quickly in several small economies such as the Bahamas, the Cayman Islands, and the US Virgin Islands following rapid expansion of tourism and offshore banking activities. Much seems to depend on the pattern of development and its impact on employment, income distribution and the *rate* of economic growth.

Also, the effect may not be the same for all types of migrants. A distinction I have made elsewhere between those who move mainly to improve their opportunities (*opportunity-seeking migrants*) and those who are forced to leave due to poverty and extreme economic hardship (*survival migrants*) is useful in this connection.[12] Even a high level of economic growth can coexist with considerable pressure for survival migration if it pays scant attention to employment creation or poverty eradication or aggravates inequality. Conversely, when development is based on low-wage, low-cost export strategies and fails to create high-level and well-paid jobs through technological upgrading of the economy, it is likely to induce opportunity-seeking migrants to look for better jobs and higher incomes abroad. This may have occurred in the Caribbean in the recent past.

When development is broad-based and at the same time geared to dynamic economic growth and better income distribution, generating a new optimism

---

[12] It is recognized that in certain situations the motivations underlying the two types of movement could become meshed together, making the distinction somewhat blurred.

among the potential migrants about the future of the economy, the demand for emigration, whether driven by poverty and unemployment or opportunity seeking, tends to fall quickly. There will still be migration in search of better opportunities, helped by increasing economic integration, as within the European Union. But this will not take the form of massive, irregular movements and it is clearly much easier to manage.

The point about the development-migration nexus can be further clarified by asking another question: what happens if there is no development? There is little doubt that if the economies of labour-abundant countries fail to make progress or, worse still, slide back, the pressure for emigration, driven by poverty and unemployment as well as opportunity-seeking, will sharply increase. As discussed in Chapter 1, extreme economic hardship compels even poor people to move or try to move; and the practice of deferred payments (by signing personal bonds), widely encouraged by migrant traffickers, now makes moving easy. It has also been noted that even if many of these anguished people cannot cross borders, they remain a potential source of political and social instability, both internal and external. An additional disturbing aspect is that in a situation of economic stagnation and despair even the opportunity-seeking, skilled migrants may feel inclined to move through irregular channels, as seems to be happening in Russia.

The discussion may now be summed up. Over time and on balance, economic development tends to reduce emigration pressures in a labour-surplus country. Although in the short term, development may encourage some new streams of migration, if broad-based it also tends to lessen the pressure of potential migration driven by poverty and unemployment. Second, the time period needed for the migration transition to take place is far from constant; it is closely and simultaneously correlated to the pattern and strategy of development and the predominant causes and types of flows. Third, development-induced new streams of migration are mostly related to the search for better opportunities, increasingly linked to economic globalization. These opportunity-seeking migrants find easier social acceptance in the receiving society, and usually do not seek entry through irregular channels. Fourth, in the absence of economic development, the volume of pressure for migration will be overwhelming, the nature of the flows will tend to be disruptive and disorderly at both ends, and irregular migration, especially in the form of trafficking, will be further encouraged.[13]

Thus from the perspective of migration management, the case for development is much stronger than the conventional wisdom might suggest.

---

[13] These last two paragraphs are taken from Appendix 1 in Ghosh 1998*a* which also gives more detailed information on the subject.

Is sovereignty an obstacle to the development of a global migration regime?

Implicit in the concept of national sovereignty is the state's prerogative to control immigration—the authority to decide who may or may not enter its territory. Given this widely accepted doctrine, some scholars and analysts tend to perceive a global regime for migration as an intrusion into state sovereignty and therefore an unrealistic objective to be seriously pursued. Likewise, not infrequently, governments—at least those which (for the reasons mentioned above) are unwilling or fearful to address the challenge of migration at a global level—often find it convenient to invoke state sovereignty as a plea to avoid facing the issue. Paradoxically (or perhaps not, in the light of what has been said above), some of the same governments appear somewhat less hesitant to deal with it at a regional level.

The perception that state sovereignty stands in the way of an international regime for migration is however seriously flawed for two important reasons. First, it stems from a confused vision of the nature of the proposed regime. Second, it ignores the past evolution of the nation state and the conditions needed for its continued survival as the mainstay of the world political and economic system.

As regards the first point, the new regime must not be seen as a supranational construct; nor should it be imagined as a constraint imposed on states by an overarching external authority. Rather, it is envisaged as a mutually convenient arrangement, freely negotiated by independent states, to enhance their common interest. The latter reflecting the sum total of optimal national interests of all the parties involved. An important point to note is that while the framework agreement lays down a set of common norms and principles, individual states retain their respective rights to apply and implement them within their national territories. Thus, for example, it is for each individual state to continue to set the level of immigration and control the flow, although in doing so it is to be guided by the set of agreed principles to which it will have already subscribed as part of the new arrangement. Likewise, national control measures will remain a vital part of and a necessary condition for the new international regime—except that control will become easier. In Mark Miller's words,

national control measures are only a necessary condition for achievement of cooperative management of international migration. The sufficient condition is expanded and enlightened multilateral initiatives . . . there is no shared vision, no model to point the way unless it is that of an international regime. (Chapter 2)

There is little new in such behaviour and policies of nation states—a fact that leads us to the second point mentioned above. Modern states have been accustomed to developing new forms and areas of inter-state cooperation ever since they were born some 200 years ago (Overbeek, Chapter 3). But for such cooperation, shared values, and agreed norms of conduct for peaceful coexistence, the very survival of nation states might have been at stake. These norms provide the basis of inter-state relations and much of the sources of international law in a civilized world society. Clearly, these agreed rules of the game have constantly evolved and their frontiers extended over time in response to changing needs and circumstances and the pressures generated by them.

Increased interdependence of nations or fast-moving globalization of the world economy as we are witnessing today does not imply the end of the nation state or the abdication of its basic functions. Rather, it signals an added role and responsibility of the modern state, as it is challenged to manage events and processes which extend beyond national territorial limits. To meet this challenge the states need to strengthen their mutual cooperation beyond the national frontiers and extend them in new ways and directions to fill in the transnational space. As the Commission on Global Governance observed, 'Globalisation diminishes capacities to deliver at home and enlarges the need to combine efforts abroad' (Commission on Global Governance 1995).

A unique convergence of three types of factors is now challenging states to strengthen their mutual cooperation. First, on a domestic level, state policies and behaviour are now largely shaped by the dominant power groups that have strong links with the global market and thus have a strong interest in stable inter-state relations. Second, states are also under pressure to increase cooperation among themselves in order to operate in the transnational space to: maintain peace and order; enhance economic prosperity through expansion of trade and investment; ensure an efficient global system of transport and communication; fight extra territorial terrorism; protect the environment; manage the 'global commons'; and so on. A third set of transnational factors that are also having a gradual but perceptible impact on state behaviour concerns an evolving sense of common human values and a growing concern for humanity, such as the respect for basic human rights and protection of people in extreme danger or distress.

Such inter-state cooperation for managing migration has now become an imperative need. Increasing interpenetration of national economies and labour markets has made management of migratory movements a matter of direct concern not only for trade and industry groups which rely on imported skills and labour; but also for large numbers of domestic workers who stand to gain or lose from the inflows. Disruptive and disorderly movements are proving to be a threat to internal order and stability. On the other hand, to the extent that orderliness and predictability in movements are an essential condition for the smooth running of the world economy, they could be seen as global public goods.

Admittedly, international migration differs from other forms of exchanges or types of movements such as flows of goods, services, and capital between countries in one very important respect: it involves people, and not inanimate objects. This makes it a more sensitive issue *vis-à-vis* territorial sovereignty, which the nation state seeks to zealously preserve. But this also makes the stakes in the whole game of managing migration particularly high. It is easy to see why, compared to flows involving inanimate objects, movements of people, especially the manner in which they are handled, can trigger political passion and human emotions more easily; and why the latter can shake sending and receiving countries and the international community at large. It is precisely this human aspect that makes the perils of mismanaging migration particularly alarming, highlighting the imperative need for its better management through new forms of global cooperation.

Goodwill-Gill highlights this need from a human rights perspective when he argues in Chapter 6 that 'the sovereignty of the state exists within a community principle; [and that] given the manifestly international dimensions to migratory and refugee movements, a significantly high degree of cooperation among states is now called for.' Thomas Straubhaar and Mark Miller emphasize the same point but from an economic point of view. As Miller puts it, 'globalization and greater economic interdependence have meshed sovereign societies and created greater need for orderly movement of persons between societies for economic purposes. The development of global markets has made a [global] legal immigration framework imperative to economic growth and socio-economic well-being' (Chapter 2). And from a politico-economic perspective, James Hollifield cogently reiterates the argument for inter-state cooperation when he warns that 'any weakening on the part of liberal states in their commitment to support orderly movements of people could threaten the "the new liberal world order" ' (Chapter 4).

To sum up, powerful economic, political and humanitarian factors—often working in combination—have already impelled nation states to accept a set of common norms and principles in specific and narrower areas of movements of people such as trade-related temporary movements (GATS), and flights from political persecution (the UN Convention on the status of refugees). What seems important, however, is to place these instruments within a more comprehensive and balanced framework and fill in the gaps that exist. The proposed international regime seeks to do just that. It must not, however, be seen as an externally imposed constraint, but as a positive act of mutual cooperation among sovereign nations. It should be envisioned as a joint endeavour to promote optimal benefits for each participating state while protecting orderliness in movements as a valuable common global good. Viewed from this angle, the issue of sovereignty can no longer be an argument against the new initiative. The challenge then lies in convincing governments, the civil society, and the people—as the ultimate guardian of sovereign power—of the enormous potential gains to be derived from such inter-state cooperation.

REFERENCES

Commission on Global Governance (1995), *Our Global Neighbourhood: The Report of the Commission on Global Governance,* Oxford: Oxford University Press.

Eichengreen, B., and Kenen, P. (1994), 'Managing the World Economy under the Bretton Woods System: An Over View', in P. Kenen (ed.), *Managing the World Economy,* Washington, DC: Institute for International Economics.

Ghosh, B. (1995), 'Movements of People: The Search for a New International Regime', in *Issues in Global Governance,* London: Kluwer Law International.

—— (1997a), *Gains from Global Linkages: Trade in Services and Movement of Persons,* Houndmills: Macmillan Press.

—— (1997b), *Report on the Informal Meeting, Managing Migration: New International Regime for Orderly Movements of People (NIROMP),* Geneva: IOM (Sept. 1997).

—— (1998a), *Huddled Masses and Uncertain Shores: Insights into Irregular Migration,* London: Kluwer Law International.

—— (1998b), *Informal Report,* Report on the IOM/NIROMP Interregional Meeting on Return and Readmission of Migrants, Geneva: IOM (Dec. 1998).

—— (1999), 'The Promise and Pitfalls of Return Migration', paper presented to the Conference on International Migration, Development and Economic Integration of Migrants, Stockholm (Sept. 1999).

Hamilton, B., and Whalley, J. (1984), 'Efficiency and Distributional Implications of Global Restrictions on Labour Mobility', *Journal of Development Economics,* 1414: 61–75.

Interpreter Releases: Report and Analysis of Immigration and Nationality Law (1997), 74/7 and 11, Washington, DC.

IOM (1998), *IOM-Assisted Return Programmes in Europe and North America,* Geneva: IOM.

Noll, G. (1998), 'Protecting the Dignity and Human Rights of Different Categories of Returnees', paper presented to the IOM/NIROMP Interregional Meeting on Return and Readmission of Migrants (Dec. 1998).

UNFPA (1998), *Executive Summary,* Technical Symposium on International Migration and Development, The Hague, Netherlands (June–July 1998).

UNHRC (1999), Report of the Working Group of Intergovernmental Experts on the Human Rights of Migrants, submitted to the 55th session of the UN Human Rights Commission, Geneva: UNHRC.

United Nations, Convention on the Protection of All Migrant Workers and Members of Their Families, adopted on 18 December 1990.

—— (1998), *World Population Monitoring, 1997,* Population Division, Department of Economic and Social Information and Policy Analysis, New York: United Nations.

US Commission for the Study of International Migration and Cooperative Economic Development (1990), 'Unauthorized Migration: An Economic Development Response', Washington, DC (July 1990).

Utrikesdepartementet (1997), *Verksallighet och kontrol I utlanningsarenden*, SOU 1997:128, Stockholm.

Widgren, J. (1993), 'Movement of Refugees and Asylum Seekers: Recent Trends in a Comparative Perspective', in OECD, *The Changing Course of International Migration*, Paris: OECD, 87–95.

INDEX

Abell, N. A. 175 n.
Achermann, A. 175 n.
Ad Hoc Group on Immigration 200,
    238 n.
Africa 16, 40, 98 n.
    Central 9, 17, 82
    forced migration 195, 205–6
    and GAMP 112, 115
    globalization and sovereignty 50, 56
    North 7, 16, 57, 238
    Southern 9, 51, 65, 237
    sub-Saharan 7, 10, 11, 57, 79, 238
African Charter of Human and People's
    Rights (1981) 166, 170, 171
African Charter on the Rights and Welfare
    of the Child (1990) 173 n.
Aguayo, S. 69
Albania 8 n., 12, 170 n.–171 n., 196 n., 198
Albanians, Kosovar 82, 90, 193
Algeria/Algerians 29–30, 37, 60
Alston, P. 197
American Convention on Human Rights,
    1969 (ACHR69) 166, 167 n., 168 n.,
    169 n., 170–1
American Indians 118, 144, 206
Americas 50, 100–1, 236, 237
    Latin 41, 79, 103, 205–6; Central 7–9,
        56, 65–6, 154, 175, 180, forced
        migration 198, 206; and GAMP
        112, 115; globalization and
        sovereignty 54, 56–7, 65–6; and
        NIROMP 7, 11, 16, 17 n.; South 7,
        41, 59, 65
    North 7, 8, 40, 79, 199, 203
    and GAMP 112, 116, 117
    globalization and sovereignty 51, 54,
        57, 65, 66
    see also United States; Canada
Amsterdam Treaty (1997) 39, 62, 67
Andean Pact (1979) 41
Andean region 206
Andrysek, O. 174 n., 182 n.

Angola 205
Annan, K. 209
APEC (Asia Pacific Economic
    Cooperation) 56, 101
Ardittis, S. 8
Argentina 13
Armenians 30, 193
ASEAN (Association of South-East Asian
    Nations) 65, 110
Asia/Asians 30, 79, 96, 115
    Central 7, 57
    East 7, 11, 54, 79, 115, 241
    financial crisis (1998) 9
    forced migration 203, 206
    and globalization 50, 54, 59
    and NIROMP 100–1
    South 57, 79, 115, 206, 238
    South-East 79, 175, 206; and
        globalization 57, 59, 60, 65; and
        NIROMP 7, 9, 241
Australia 13, 58, 155, 184, 199, 238
Austria 13, 58, 60, 66, 117, 163 n.
Austria-Hungary 30, 64
Azerbaijan 179 n.
Azeris 193

Bach, R. L. 85
Bagshaw, S. 209 n.
Bahamas 241
Baja California 144
Balkan War (1999) 82, 99
Balkans 16, 30, 192, 194, 197–8
Baltics 65
Bangkok process 236
Bangkok University 230
Bangladesh 179 n.
Barcelona 65
Bauböck, R. 86–7, 104
Bauer, T. 117
Belarus 66
Belgium 12–13, 58, 60, 67 n., 141, 201
Bellagio 2